FIRE AND RAIN

FIRE & RAIN

The James Taylor Story

Ian Halperin

MAINSTREAM PUBLISHING

EDINBURGH AND LONDON

First published in the United States of America in 2000 by
Citadel Press, Kensington Publishing Corp.
850 Third Avenue
New York, NY 10022

First published in Great Britain in 2001 by
MAINSTREAM PUBLISHING COMPANY (EDINBURGH) LTD
7 Albany Street
Edinburgh EH1 3UG

ISBN 1 84018 790 5

This edition, 2003

A catalogue record for this book is available from the British Library

Typeset in Perpetua and Design Medium
Printed and bound by Cox & Wyman Ltd

This book is dedicated in memory of three of the most important people in James Taylor's life who recently passed away: his father, Isaac Taylor; his brother, Alex Taylor; and his musical collaborator, Don Grolnick.

CONTENTS

Acknowledgements 9
Foreword by Joel Risberg 11
Author to Reader 13
1. A Big Night in Vegas 15
2. Sweet Baby James 22
3. Rebel Without a Cause 39
4. Knockin' 'Round the Zoo 44
5. Good Ol' Folks in the Village 57
6. Back Home 68
7. The British Invasion 71
8. Heroin and Alcohol 88
9. Back in the USA 94
10. Persistence Pays Off 98
11. Taylor's 'Time' Has Come 112
12. Joni Mitchell, the Woman He Loved Too Much 123
13. 'You've Got a Friend' 134
14. The Birth of a Rock Family 143
15. Enter Carly Simon 151
16. Walking Man Stumbles 168
17. The Geffen Factor 174
18. Carnegie Hall, a Night of Magic 182
19. The Big Match: Columbia Versus Warner 189
20. Two Great Hits: Little Ben and 'Your Smiling Face' 197
21. More Family Feuds 203
22. Sally and Ben Cope With Famous Parents 207
23. Carly Turns to Travolta 215
24. Taylor's Smiling Face 230
25. Taylor Gives Back 238

26. Understanding Nirvana 242
27. JT TV 249
28. Taylor and Simon Reunite 256
29. 1996: A Tragic Year 259
30. Hourglass 264
31. Another Loss, Another Friend 270
James Taylor Discography 273
Index 275

ACKNOWLEDGEMENTS

I would like to acknowledge the many people who made this book possible. I am especially grateful to my editor Hillel Black for his patience and passionate commitment to *Fire and Rain*; Joanne Jones for editing and moral support; my agent, Noah Lukeman, for his advice and for always being there when needed; and Esmond Choueke, the well-known journalist who has followed Taylor's career closely and who provided some great anecdotes and photos.

Special thanks to Jennifer Walker, Todd Shapiro, Michael Feldman, Burt McFarlane, Pete Seeger, Barry Shrier, Fubu, David Nanasi, Stuart Nulman, the Weston family, Martin Smith, Allan Katz, Lieutenant Peter O'Grady, Arlene Bynon, Max Wallace, Stanley Trudeau, Mark Fleming, Jaime Roskies, Nicole McGill, Nancy King, Anthony Guest, Trevor Redding, Bobby White, Barry Weiner, Herschel Mendelson, Lyde Meunier, Timothy Hawkins, Jeremy Yankovitch, Jacquie Charlton, Chaim Zelman, Jean-Pierre Ousset, Peter Desantos, Thelma Cassidy, Robert J. Bornstein, Keystone Agency, Franco Carlucci, the late Kevin Kitchens, the late Carlos Vega, Stephanie Ridell, Orlando Salazar, Dr. Rupert Brennan, Allan Wright, Ross Coleman, Vivienne Gore, Albert Bell, Brian Kapshaw, Bonnie Brown, May Walker, Walter Fryman, Daniel Sanger, Julien Feldman, Lou Beaton, the New York subway system, the Los Angeles taxis, public libraries, the Troubadour Club, the residents of Martha's Vineyard, Kate Markowitz, Lily Davidson, Esther Ballantyne, Wendi Rosenburg, Myron Rothman, Earl J. Leiberman, Paula Shulman, Shlomo Cohen, Andrew Jones, Miles Horowitz, Harvey Littman, Al Taylor, and Hazel Cho.

I would especially like to thank my parents and family for their unwavering support.

I'm also indebted to many sources for background information about

James Taylor and Carly Simon, including *Billboard* magazine, *Time* magazine, Joel Risberg's James Taylor Online, Bellows Archives Information, Sony Music, Timothy White, and Isn't It Nice to Be Home Again – The James Taylor Web site.

FOREWORD

'Fire and Rain' changed American music when it hit radios and turntables around the world. Though I wasn't born until two years later, my own exposure to James Taylor's music was less an introduction than an indoctrination, hearing JT played around the house long before I was even allowed to put the needle down on the *Sweet Baby James* album myself. But for all those who heard it for the first time, they knew something had changed. Acid rock was out, said the reviewers, and soulful balladeering was in.

Singer-songwriters were given credit for the change, and James was crowned as their very young king. Of course it wasn't a one-man music movement, but *Time* magazine thought 22-year-old James's influence was strong enough to merit a cover story about him and his family in 1971 – an era before news magazine covers regularly featured faces from the entertainment world.

The *Time* article – and just about every other piece of writing about JT since – characterised him as a troubled soul, an on-again, off-again drug addict, and the inevitable product of a family of means that expected a little too much of its kids. To some extent, all of it was true. James did find inspiration for much of his life's work in his emotional torment. He did spend years fighting drug addiction and depression. And he was from a well-heeled, musically talented family that could afford to send its progeny to expensive prep schools and even pricier private mental hospitals. Nowadays, though, the James Taylor in his fifties has the benefit of hindsight to moderate his grudge against a press that persistently pigeonholed him – first as the Kurt Cobain of his day, and much later as a sleepy crooner with his most creative years behind him.

'Hey Mister, That's Me Up on the Jukebox' tells the tale of an artist lost among the machinery of big business that threatens to overshadow his creativity. What's become a common refrain today – how an artist can still struggle to find happiness amid overwhelming financial success – had rarely been asked publicly until then. It's a question JT is still addressing in his music and interviews to this day. In 1985 the title track 'That's Why I'm Here' covered similar ground, but with the benefit of hindsight. JT paints a picture of a career and a life in which the good overshadowed the bad and the pleasures of creating music for an audience bring him joy over and over again.

That's the JT we all love today: a musical force who manages to be just as honest and endearing off-stage as he is when performing. Like proud parents, we fans enjoy all his successes almost as if they're our own. Whether it's his phenomenally successful *Hourglass*, his long-awaited Rock and Roll Hall of Fame induction, or even his recent marriage to Kim Smedvig, we're always watching proudly. On behalf of his thousands of fans on the Net and off: thanks for the music JT.

Joel Risberg
Webmaster, James Taylor Online
http://james-taylor.com/

AUTHOR TO READER

An enormous amount of research is necessary for any thorough biography, and this was especially true in the case of *Fire and Rain*. It even took more time to track down sources close to James Taylor: former lovers, classmates, co-workers, friends, neighbours, journalists who have covered his career, groupies, mentors, Taylor's former mechanic, and members of Taylor's family.

More than 150 people interviewed for this book talked openly about Taylor's life without seeking Taylor's approval. I am extremely grateful to several sources who knew Taylor's father, Isaac, and his brother, Alex, and who helped re-create quotes from James's childhood experiences. The hours they spent describing what it was like for Taylor when he was growing up proved invaluable. I would also like to thank the many people on Martha's Vineyard, the place Taylor now calls home, for providing me with endless anecdotes about Taylor and his failed marriage to Carly Simon.

During the course of my research I travelled to New York and California to visit some of the places that were important in Taylor's career, including the legendary Troubadour Club in Los Angeles, the club that gave Taylor so much exposure during the early years.

It is important to say that although several people I interviewed had some negative things to say about Taylor, especially his life during the '70s, the majority of people spoke about him with the kindest words. By most accounts, Taylor is one of the nicest people in the music business and one who has earned the respect of both the public and his colleagues including Sting, Garth Brooks and Pat Metheny. Taylor is one of the few pop icons from the '60s and early '70s who is still able to tour to sold-out venues all over the world, putting him in the same class as Bob Dylan and Paul Simon.

1

A BIG NIGHT IN VEGAS

7 December 1998. The MGM Grand Hotel/Casino in Las Vegas was jam-packed. It looked like a rock 'n' roll circus. Everybody who was somebody in the music industry was there, from Stevie Wonder to Garth Brooks to the Backstreet Boys. They had come to celebrate the 1998 *Billboard* Music Awards, which would shortly be beamed around the world to more than 250 million people. Backstage, James Taylor's spirits were up. At 50, Taylor was as lean as the year he turned twenty, and his clean-shaven face and wire-rimmed glasses lent him a sophisticated and vibrant air. His long mane had thinned, with a huge patch of baldness occupying the middle of his head. He chatted animatedly with folksinger Shawn Colvin, who was thrilled to be able to hang out with a living legend whose music she has admired since she was a teenager. 'It feels great to be here,' Taylor told her. 'If I look back at my career, this is definitely one of the biggest nights for me.'

The '70s troubadour made famous by songs like 'You've Got a Friend', 'Sweet Baby James', and 'Fire and Rain' was about to accept the *Billboard* 1998 Century Award, the publication's highest honour for creative achievement (named for its hundredth anniversary). Ironically, the most influential singer-songwriter of the '70s was accepting the prestigious award in a town renowned for vice, hangovers, sex, drugs, tackiness and Lady Luck. For thirty years, Taylor's life has been largely plagued by personal loss, stormy marriages, and atrocious habits. In recent years Taylor was devastated by the deaths of his father, Isaac; his brother Alex; and his musical collaborator Don Grolnick, as well as by the breakup of his second marriage, to actress Kathryn Walker. Though many ups and downs have accompanied his career over the years, his fans have always stayed loyal to him. They loved him and never lost belief in his musical talent – despite the criticism of his detractors and his never-ending string of personal problems. Even though he hadn't cut a new standard in years, Taylor enjoyed the allegiance of his audience much as the Grateful Dead did with the Deadheads.

'I drove all the way from Vancouver for this,' said Erin Johnson, a Taylor worshiper for more than twenty-five years. 'I've bought every one of his albums and I've seen him in concert more than thirty times. James is a living legend. Nobody deserves this award more than him, especially if you consider everything that he's had to endure over the years.'

Garth Brooks – a last-minute sub for Madonna, who was a no-show – opened the show suspended from pulleys to make a Peter Pan–type flight around an arena filled with screaming teenage girls. Afterwards, Brooks, who would capture six awards that night, including top album of the year by a male artist, praised Taylor backstage. Indeed, Taylor is an all-time favourite of Brooks, who has been such a big fan for so many years that he even named his daughter for him. 'Every performer here tonight owes something to James Taylor,' Brooks said. 'I can't say enough about the man. His music has lived for decades, and he's influenced almost everybody, whether they sing country, folk, or pop. He's a terrific songwriter who is also a first-class human being.'

Shania Twain, dressed to kill in a formfitting silver-sequined gown, was named female artist of the year. Backstage, she also sang Taylor's praises. 'I remember listening to his music when I was a kid. He moved me then and still moves me now. He's written so many beautiful songs. He's a legend.'

Between performances by Celine Dion and Hole, Shawn Colvin took to the stage and introduced the man she said had had a big influence on her career. It was fitting to have Colvin introduce Taylor, because the pair were good friends and performed together regularly. In the past couple of years, Taylor had served as a spiritual guide to Colvin, giving her advice about making music and also about handling the daily rigours that accompany being a pop star. Colvin told the audience that she fell in love with Taylor when she was only 15 and never would have imagined that 25 years later, she'd be sharing a stage with him.

'He's played guitar for me and I've sung backup for him,' Colvin later said backstage. 'The man is a true artist who has done so much for so many people. It was a big honour for me to introduce him to receive his award.'

Taylor stood in the wings. His face was gleaming and his heart beating wildly with excitement as he listened to Colvin's tribute. When he sauntered to centre-stage the audience's roar stopped him cold. The spectators were on their feet cheering, pounding their hands together, and whistling. It was as if the audience had fallen through a time warp. When the ovation subsided, Taylor, dressed casually in a black blazer and low-collared shirt, made a brief acceptance speech. Many of his longtime fans thought that their hero was uncomfortable because he was surrounded by artists who were too young to have known him at the height of his career.

'I felt sorry for him because he looked a bit out of place at the *Billboard* Awards,' said Warren Hughes, who has followed Taylor's career closely for years and made the trip from Minnesota to see Taylor honoured. 'His speech was short and you got the feeling he wanted to get offstage because he was surrounded by rap and R&B artists who really weren't at all that familiar with folk music or his career. But in true James Taylor fashion, he still accepted the award with class, and it was nice to see everybody give him a big ovation.'

In his speech, Taylor thanked his mother, who was at home watching the show; his former longtime manager-producer, Peter Asher; his recently appointed new manager, Gary Borman; and, most of all, his fans. Afterward, he admitted that he was a bit overwhelmed.

'So many thoughts were going through my head before I went onstage to accept the award,' Taylor said. 'It's been a long road, but if I weren't a musician I have no idea what I'd do. Receiving this award and the support from everybody makes me want to keep going for many, many years to come.'

Taylor's longtime road manager, Brian Reed, works diligently out of the Santa Monica offices of Borman Entertainment booking Taylor's tour schedule. 'It's not a difficult sell. He is still in very high demand all over the world. Not many people manage to last in this business as long as he has. Aside from having such great talent, he's one of the nicest guys in the music business. He doesn't put himself higher than anybody else.'

Backstage in the dimly lit press-room, nobody was able to excite reporters as much as Jerry Springer, who was greeted with journalists' chants of 'Jerry, Jerry!' Springer, accompanied by Steve – one of the bouncers on his number-one-rated syndicated talk show – said he was happy for Taylor. 'He's overcome a lot to get this award,' Springer said shortly after fulfilling his official duty as an award presenter. Asked if it meant a lot to be part of the homage to Taylor, the abrasive talk-show host responded that he was not even sure how he got the gig in the first place. 'Why am I here? . . . Did they expect a fight to break out?'

Bruce Gowers, director of the *Billboard* show, said that the award was given to Taylor for the work he created not only in the '70s but also in the '80s and '90s. 'He's an artist who has made great music in several decades,' Gowers said. 'This award is a tribute to all his music.'

Through the years, Taylor has done all he can to divest his songs of their status as anthems. He retools arrangements and usually includes fresh material in his sets. But he must still rely on his old hits. 'I like those songs too,' Taylor said in an interview. 'And they help. The state that I'm in when I go on, I'm very anxious, and I'm very concerned with it going well.'

In his first Internet online chat a few weeks before receiving the *Billboard* award, Taylor was asked to compare the message of his recent work with his past. 'I don't know,' he responded. 'There's not any kind of a conscious thread or anything that holds these things together. They come at random. There are patterns, but I don't think that there is any particular identifiable shift or change . . . Maybe I'm moving more from the strictly personal to the more universal.'

A surprising number of Taylor's songs still get lots of radio airplay. His fans continue to make annual visits to his concerts to hear the charismatic entertainer address most of his songs like intimate friends. Even though in his music Taylor has dealt with the same protest issues that many of his colleagues from the '60s and '70s sang out against, he never did so with the bittersweet voice of Bob Dylan or the angst of Jim Morrison. He always did it with a gentle touch.

'James Taylor is in a class by himself,' said Meg Griffin, a veteran New York DJ who has played Taylor's music for years. 'At the beginning he was gentle and sweet. Then he branched out with the social-conscience thing – the *No Nukes* concert, all the work he's done for rainforest awareness. So he's brought a lot of people in. And he's got a great sense of humour, offbeat, but very funny. He's flawed, but he doesn't try to hide it. He's human.'

One of Taylor's biggest fans is the rock icon Sting, who credits Taylor's music with being a big inspiration to him before he catapulted to pop superstardom with his band, the Police. Many of the songs Sting wrote early in his career were influenced by Taylor's lyrics and his guitar playing. 'James has always reminded me of Abraham Lincoln because of his height and his lugubriousness,' Sting told *New York Times* writer Stephen Holden. 'He's the archetypal southern gentleman and a great storyteller.'

After the *Billboard* awards show, the casino bars were filled with friends, associates, and fans of Taylor who came to pay homage to their hero. In the lobby of the MGM Grand Hotel, Taylor was approached by one of his fans and asked to sign an old photograph of himself. He obliged without hesitation. He asked the fan where she came from. 'Chicago,' the elated fan replied. 'I came here to see you get your award and also to try to learn some basic blackjack strategy. By the way, how's Carly doing?'

'Very well, she's coming along fine,' Taylor said, in reference to his former wife's recent breast cancer surgery.

It wasn't long ago that Taylor and his ex-wife Carly Simon were constantly at each other's throats. Their marriage was fraught with ironies and contradictions. They went through a highly publicised acrimonious divorce and were not on speaking terms for years. Involved in the ugly tangle were friendships of long standing. The vicious free-for-all between Simon and Taylor remained major news for years. The smouldering, sensual and beautiful Simon once publicly denounced Taylor by calling him an 'absentee husband and father who cares just about himself'. It was taboo for many years to bring up Simon's name in front of Taylor. And vice versa. But the air between the two cleared entirely when Taylor rushed to Simon's bedside after she was stricken with breast cancer in April 1998.

Almost to the point of compulsion, Taylor spent days chatting with Simon on the phone and in person. Taylor blamed their disastrous marriage on himself and promised to make it up to Simon if she got better. For hours, she listened to him reminisce about the good times they had had together. Many of Simon's close friends believe she had never known sustained happiness because of her stormy marriage to Taylor; yet they agree that without Taylor's undying support during her cancer battle, she might not be alive today.

'At first Carly was very depressed and not too optimistic about living,' said one friend. 'But it was James's support that really helped her make it through everything. James was busy touring at the time, but he made sure he spent every available opportunity he had supporting Carly. There are not many men in this world who would do that for their ex-wife. It really meant a lot to Carly.'

Taylor stayed close to Carly during her illness. He watched her diet and made sure that she took her prescribed medications. Often during her recovery period, he sent her flowers, books and letters. His relationship with their two children – Sally, 25, and Ben, 22, who like their parents are musicians – improved and became strong again, and he used his contacts to help get them recording contracts of their own. 'Carly was delighted and deeply touched,' a friend of hers said. 'She didn't want to die, because she realised she had so much to live for. It was the people who cared about her that helped get her through this terrible ordeal.'

Did the trouble-plagued singer-songwriter make amends with Simon because he suddenly found peace and tranquillity? After a series of personal losses, including his father, brother, and several musicians to whom he was close, Taylor picked himself up and breathed new vigour and meaning into his life. 'I could have easily self-destructed many times,' Taylor said. 'But I find my peace and spiritual nourishment in music. I've made many mistakes along the way, but I'm able to pour out all the emotion when I'm performing onstage.'

A poignant tribute to Taylor for receiving the *Billboard* Century Award came from *Billboard*'s editor in chief, Timothy White. In an article that featured Taylor on *Billboard*'s cover for receiving the award, White said: 'One of the most gifted and utterly natural musicians of his time, James Taylor is also an artist who represents a timeless link between Stephen Foster, Jimmie Rodgers, Hoagy Carmichael, Pete Seeger, Ewan MacColl and other great troubadour/stylists of modern times.

'Another hundred years from now, James's music will still sound as ageless and intimate as it does today. . . . But more than anything else, generations of listeners know that the heart has no hiding place from the simple, hymnlike truth of Taylor's art. And that's why *Billboard* can think of no artist more deserving of the 1998 Century Award than the peerless James Taylor.'

Halfway around the world, in England, Paul Stanton – who works as a bartender in North London and has closely followed every move of Taylor's career since the singer lived in London in the late '60s – played only Taylor music while patrons of his pub sipped pints of lager. Stanton said Taylor's lasting appeal came about because his songs have a self-consciously retrospective air. 'Even though he's American, it's an honour for us that he received the *Billboard* award because he lived in London and got his first break here.' With Taylor's 'Handyman' playing in the background, Stanton added, 'He's gone through a lot in his life, and you can tell that by the lyrics, which we can all relate to in some way or another. We're only playing James Taylor music tonight in honour of his award. Not many people last that long in music – or for that matter in any other business. I know that when I'm gone, my grandchildren's great-grandchildren will still be listening to James Taylor songs.'

2

SWEET BABY JAMES

Spring was in the air when James Vernon Taylor was born in Boston, Massachusetts, on 12 March 1948, in Boston General Hospital at 5:06 p.m. For those who place some credence in astrology it meant James is a Pisces, a cardinal passive natural sign of twelfth-house ruler Neptune whose key words are *compassionate*, *artistic*, *sympathetic*, *overtalkative*, and *introspective*. Among those sharing this birthday and sign with James are Jack Kerouac (1922), Liza Minnelli (1946) and Darryl Strawberry (1962).

Taylor was born in the year that Boston baseball fans' hopes for a world championship were shattered twice after Lou Boudreau's Cleveland Indians upset the Red Sox at Fenway Park in a sudden-death playoff game, then went on to beat the Boston Braves in six games in the World Series. In the year 1948 Jewish leaders declared the statehood of Israel and fought to maintain their homeland despite stiff Arab resistance. It was also the year that the Russians blocked the western sectors of Berlin, and America's 33rd president, Harry Truman, created a massive airlift to supply Berliners until the Russians backed down. The cold war began a year later, when the Soviet Union detonated its first nuclear bomb, and America and Western Europe formed the North Atlantic Treaty Organization, a military alliance to protect Western nations.

Isaac Taylor, a hardworking physician raised in the South in a Scottish-American family, and his wife, Trudy, had longed for a daughter. Still, they were overjoyed that little James was born healthy. Several of the nurses at the hospital fussed over who would bathe and comb the infant's thin brown hair. Everybody marvelled at how beautiful and pleasant the blue-eyed baby boy was.

Gertrude and Isaac Taylor lived in Milton, an affluent suburb of

Boston. Married in 1946, the couple both came from affluent backgrounds. Trudy, whose maiden name is Woodard, grew up on Rings Island in Salisbury, Massachusetts, just across the bridge from Newburyport (a picturesque town on the Merrimack River). She gave birth to her first child, Alex, in 1947. It was a tough pregnancy for Trudy, who suffered from extreme nausea almost from the day she found out she was pregnant. She was bedridden for weeks before giving birth and told her husband several times that she wasn't sure if she wanted to have any more children. But she quickly changed her mind during Alex's infancy. She loved being a mother and looked forward to filling up the house with some brothers and sisters. She didn't want little Alex to grow up an only child. A year later, Trudy was pregnant again.

Trudy was the daughter of a successful Massachusetts fisherman and boatbuilder. There were many creative and artistic people in her family, and Trudy herself sang in various local choirs when she was a child and teenager. She also loved theatre and dancing. Trudy dreamed of being a ballerina, and used to practise moves for hours in front of her bedroom mirror. She realised her musical ability was much stronger than her dancing, however, and enrolled in the New England Conservatory of Music, where she trained as a lyric soprano.

Trudy's family had eschewed religion, and she didn't attend church. She believed that it was important to have an inner appreciation and respect for life and nature, something she would advocate to her own children. 'Growing up in North Carolina, I missed the boat on most religions,' James Taylor would say years later. 'My dad was basically an atheist or at best an agnostic.'

According to writer Timothy White, Isaac himself had many unpleasant recollections of his childhood. His mother, Theodosia, died two weeks after giving birth to him due to an infection of the uterus. Two months later, Isaac's deeply distressed grandfather contemplated suicide but decided instead to drink himself to death. Isaac recalled years later how continually his side of the family was plagued by battles with booze and drugs. He saw many of his close relatives, who were alcoholics, destroy their lives. His own life was filled with episodes of alcohol abuse and, as a result, his marriage ended disastrously.

James seemed to have inherited many of his forebears' destructive habits. He became a heroin addict and considered suicide several times before he turned 20; he had to be committed on two occasions to a mental hospital. He experimented with drugs for years and was severely depressed during his climb to fame in the early '70s. It seemed the more success Taylor experienced, the more screwed up he would become.

'Unfortunately, I guess it must be in our genes,' Isaac said. 'For over two hundred years the Taylor family has had a history of battles with alcohol and drugs.' Isaac's father, Alexander Taylor II, abandoned his son at an early age because of his own lengthy battles with alcohol and women. Isaac's father's temper and abuse of women were so legendary that fathers warned their daughters to avoid him.

Timothy White has traced the Taylor ancestry back to the Angus coast of Scotland. The family recipe for success, beginning with the original Isaac Taylor, was honesty, hard work and ambition. The Taylors were shrewd businessmen who liked to share the wealth among their family and friends. They owned vast shipping interests in the coastal centre of Montrose, a popular stopover for naval vessels and privateers. The original Isaac Taylor emigrated to America in the 1700s and made a fortune trading with the West Indies while he cultivated a plantation in North Carolina. Anybody who didn't have a job was able to count on Isaac Taylor to give them work. He was disheartened to see people watch life pass them by because they couldn't find anything to do.

A series of increasingly debilitating strokes at the outset of his most productive years didn't slow Isaac Taylor down. By the time he died in 1846, Isaac Taylor had developed one of the region's most profitable plantations, with dozens of slaves and labourers. He treated his slaves like longtime friends, a rarity in America at that time. Isaac left his vast fortune to his wife and six daughters, cutting son Alexander out of his will because Alexander was a heavy drinker and not trustworthy. Isaac did not want Alexander to single-handedly destroy his fortune; in fact, he repeatedly warned his son that he would be left out of his will if he didn't change his ways. Alexander didn't take him seriously until the day Isaac died.

Isaac Taylor worked hard harvesting the earth's treasures. He often boasted that his success flowed from his innovations and the impressive network of contacts he managed to build up. Even near the end of his life Isaac Taylor still haggled over details and examined the minutest portions of the daily operation on the plantation. His life was bound up with his work, his fortune and his family.

The Taylors became more sophisticated after the Civil War. They abandoned the rigorous lifestyle of the plantation and instead chose careers as teachers and doctors. To protect their fortune, they invested their cash in several real estate projects. But the family seemed always to have a dark cloud hanging over them; somebody was always getting into trouble because of alcohol or violence. Isaac used to say, 'If you're a Taylor and you're male, then people should stay clear of you because you can erupt at any time like a volcano.'

Many of the Taylor men were distrusted and disliked because of their erratic behaviour. They had a reputation for being honest but not polite or co-operative.

James's father was raised by his aunt and uncle in comfortable surroundings. Isaac lived in fear of inheriting some of his ancestors' characteristics. His lifelong ambition was to attend medical school and become a doctor. He wanted to help people, and he was interested in medical research.

From his early teens, Isaac was intent on being different from the other men in his family. He did not press his views upon others, and he listened more than he spoke. He rarely alluded to how life affected him. He was funny and affectionate with his friends. He seemed wiser and more charming than anybody else in his family. He listened attentively to his elders and treated everyone with respect.

Called Ike, Isaac studied hard enough to attend Harvard Medical School in the mid-'40s. After graduating, he became a lieutenant commander in the US Navy. He loved art and sports and was a romantic at heart, as well as a brilliant conversationalist who put people at ease. Everybody liked him despite gossip about his drinking and philandering.

Before and after their marriage, Isaac showered Trudy with flowers, chocolates and theatre tickets. Usually he would attach a little note or poem telling Trudy how much he loved and appreciated her. 'I've got to be the luckiest man alive,' he wrote during her second pregnancy. 'I've got everything a man can dream of, a beautiful wife, family, and a great job. And now we have another child on the way. There's nothing that can make a man happier.'

Little James – or Jimmy, as he was called by family and friends – was a quiet baby. He would usually doze in his pram while Trudy shopped and visited with friends. Trudy's friends marvelled at how cute her son was. James's rosebud mouth made little sucking movements as he slept, while his brown lashes curled against his rosy cheeks. When James was four months old, his mother took him and Alex to see a local choir perform Christmas carols. After the performance, Trudy walked on stage and passed James into the waiting arms of the choirmaster, whom she had known from her singing days. As James blinked awake, the choirmaster leaned into the boy's face. 'He looks like his mother,' the choirmaster said. 'Maybe one day he'll sing like his mother and be up on stage performing.'

A sister, Kate, was born barely a year after James, followed by Livingston in 1951 and Hugh in 1952. Isaac decided to move his growing family into a much larger house in Weston, a suburb more upscale than Milton.

James was a chirpy and kind child who smiled mischievously and sometimes displayed a solemn and wistful air. He first showed signs of his musical talent aged two when he sang along with his father on 'Little Red Wagon Painted Blue'. Isaac got a big kick out of it. His son seemed so talented. To capture the occasion for posterity, he turned on an old wire recorder – this was before the days of portable tape recorders – and recorded James singing.

'Right then and there I knew my boy was gifted,' Isaac recalled years later. 'James was able to hold a tune from age two. I wish I'd kept [the tape]. Could you imagine what it would feel like to listen to it now? I really regret not holding on to it.'

James grew up in a time when the two-income family was a rarity. Trudy stayed home caring for the children while Isaac worked long hours at the hospital. Isaac had no respect for a man who didn't work hard and could not support his family.

'He practised what he preached,' said Jeremy Garrett, a medical researcher who knew Isaac. 'Isaac used to say that whatever you wanted to do in life would happen only if you put in a lot of honest, hard work. Otherwise, he said that the chances for succeeding were minimal. He was right. And that was the way he achieved things in his own life. It's also the way he taught his own children.'

Isaac wanted to raise his children in North Carolina, where he had grown up. Very liberal politically, he preferred that his children grow up in a rural, scenic, and unrestrictive setting. North Carolina was more liberal than Boston in those days because its governor, Terry Sanford, was an advocate of freedom of expression and civil rights.

'North Carolina was very appealing because Governor Sanford was implementing change,' recalled Dean Alexander, a big Taylor fan. A former New Yorker, Alexander moved to North Carolina with his wife in 1946 and still lives there today. 'A lot of artists and progressive people moved to North Carolina during this period because there was much less economic and racial tension than there was in most places in America. It was a unique place to be in during this period because you didn't experience the type of coldness and hostility there that you did in places like New York or the Midwest. People were simply people and they minded their own business. James Taylor talked a lot about this in his music when he became big. His music is a very good portrayal of what it was like growing up there. I know people who have moved away, and when they get homesick they just put on an old James Taylor album and feel at home again.'

But Trudy was afraid to leave her friends and family. She had great fear that her children would grow up isolated. She wanted them to enjoy the same privileges she had when she grew up, visiting museums and attending concerts. After much effort, Isaac persuaded her to move to a small town west of Chapel Hill, North Carolina.

In 1950 the Taylors moved into a renovated eleven-room farmhouse in Carrboro. The 28-acre woodland setting was breathtakingly beautiful, with fresh running water and large patches of green landscape. There were hardly any people around, though, and Trudy soon became lonely.

'It was hard to get used to the country and not knowing anybody around,' Trudy said. 'Sometimes I felt as though I was living on the end of the earth. Other times I really appreciated the beautiful scenery. It wasn't an easy transition.'

But she kept busy, pouring her energy into raising her children. Meanwhile, Isaac's career received a boost when he was named dean of the University of North Carolina medical school.

Trudy and Isaac were permissive parents. They encouraged their children to do whatever they wished. The kids usually did everything together – playing hide-and-seek, throwing stones in the pond, chasing birds around the land, or playing pitch and catch. James spent more time alone and was more self-contained than his siblings. These childhood traits remained with him during his adult years.

'James was somewhat of a mystery,' recalled a former neighbour. 'His mind seemed to always be preoccupied. He was a bit strange. He was quiet and didn't cause trouble. But he was tough to figure out.'

Trudy and Isaac taught their children to be respectful of their elders and not to interrupt or argue. James was occasionally picked on by his brothers for not wanting to participate in soccer and football games; his sister once said that she thought he was the black sheep of the family. Sometimes James would try to gain his siblings' acceptance by making them laugh at his pranks. He liked to hide his father's shoes or pretend to be missing by hiding under his bed when his mother called him to the dinner table. But he didn't seek out other kids. Something always seemed to be bothering him. He never spoke about it, but his siblings knew that he was often lonely.

'James was the quiet one of the bunch,' his brother Alex once said. 'He didn't seem at ease and sometimes found it difficult to interact with other people. He was not much of a conversationalist. He was different.'

James was, however, the most dutiful of the children. When Isaac assigned the youngsters chores, James was usually the first to finish.

Everybody who knew James when he was growing up agreed that his future would involve music. He loved learning nursery rhymes and made up words to tunes when he forgot the lyrics. He could listen for hours to Frank Sinatra, Woody Guthrie or the Mozart tunes that his mother played on their phonograph. His father remembered him once imitating Al Jolson by singing into a pen when he was only five years old.

'Music captured his heart and imagination,' Isaac said. 'You knew that one day James would be a musician. He dreamed of playing music all the time. It always came naturally to him and he always seemed happiest when he was around music. He was born with a special talent and he worked hard to develop it.'

Before James started public school, Isaac decided to build a family dream house on Morgan Creek Road in Chapel Hill. The new house, a considerable departure from the rustic setting in Carrboro, was typical of the modern, concrete, sun-filled homes being built there in the fifties. There weren't many people around and Trudy was worried that the children would be isolated. In fact, their only neighbours were Dr. Joseph and Helen Perlmutt, Savannah transplants whose children Louis, David and Martin would come over after school to play with the Taylor kids. The Taylor residence always welcomed visitors. Trudy offered her guests lots of home-cooked food and made visitors feel like they were in their own home.

'It's important to always treat other people the way you treat yourself,' Trudy used to tell her children. 'Everybody in this world is equal, whether rich or poor, black or white. It's important to listen to other people and to show them respect.'

'The Taylor home was always filled with so much love,' said an old friend of the family. 'Kids were always running around, and Trudy usually had something cooking in the kitchen. They were different from most families. They were very open people. Nobody who went to their house didn't have a good time. The Taylors liked to have fun.'

In elementary school James excelled in almost every subject. But he did have major adjustment problems due to the pressure to succeed. 'Maybe you'll be like your old man and become a doctor,' Isaac frequently told him. 'Just keep working hard in school and it will pay off one day.'

When he was only in second grade, James's teacher told his father that he was more withdrawn than the other children. 'His teacher liked him a lot,' his brother Alex recalled in 1978. 'But they thought he was a bit strange 'cause he didn't talk too much. They were worried about him because he didn't always seem to be very happy. And he didn't interact with the other kids enough. James was a precocious child and that might have put the other kids off. He was interested in learning about society and culture while they wanted to play tag at recess. But he always tried to respect everybody and not interfere with what they were doing. And he didn't want them to interfere with what he was up to either.'

The Taylor brood loved to hang out at Morgan Creek, which was a five-minute walk from their new home. In summer they would fish there, cooking their day's catch on an open fire at night. After dinner they would sing traditional campfire songs before rolling out their sleeping bags next to the fire. It was during these sing-alongs that James's siblings found out that their brother had a comical personality.

'James was a great entertainer around the campfire,' said his brother Livingston. 'He loved to sing and entertain and oftentimes composed songs on the spot and made up funny lyrics. He sure knew how to put a smile on people's faces.'

'James and his brothers and sister were always into enjoying the outdoors,' said Nancy Ray, who lived next door to the Taylors in Carrboro and was their baby-sitter. 'They were a great family. Something was always going on in their house and they always seemed to have a lot of fun.'

Ever since he can remember, James says, he loved to read books. He developed a sharp critical sense at an early age. His teachers were impressed with his quick grasp of whatever he read, and with the way he interpreted it. He was usually the most creative kid in his class. One day James came home crying because his schoolmates had made fun of the way he read aloud in class. James was usually one of the first students the teachers asked to read in class because of his advanced facility with words.

'They're just envious of you, James,' his mother explained to him. 'Don't take it too seriously. You have courage to read out in class. The ones who don't do it will always be the first to criticise because they're afraid to do it themselves.'

The Taylors were part of a new, young, white liberal generation that surfaced in Chapel Hill. They were staunch Adlai Stevenson Democrats and strongly supported Medicare and Social Security. Even though they were blessed with all the advantages they were deeply concerned about the plight of those less fortunate. Trudy donated clothes and money to various charities, and encouraged friends who were well off financially to do the same. She was socially aware and active and tried to make sure her children acquired some of her humanitarian traits. When James became famous, he followed in his mother's footsteps. He was always one of the first musicians to lend his name to benefit concerts for social justice; he donated tens of thousands of dollars to causes he supported. Although for most of his early life James seemed to be withdrawn, even devoid of love and compassion, he wanted to help people who were less fortunate than himself. He would continue to do so for much of his life.

Trudy was a staunch human-rights activist who marched against racism and injustice. Martin Luther King Jr was one of her heroes, and the humanitarian ideologies that he preached had a profound influence on her. Trudy believed that education and action went hand in hand and were essential in order to create change and awareness.

'My mother was a committed foot soldier,' James said in an interview years later. 'She picketed the local businesses to get them integrated, like restaurants, local theatre, whatever. And she even occasionally pressed us into service, like getting my sister, Kate, to walk the picket lines with her. She was a very aggressive person, generally speaking, as was my father. They both had that northern bent.'

Trudy and Isaac took their children on regular visits to Boston to expose them to the city's rich artistic and social life. Young James was fascinated with America's most historic city. He loved the nasal New England accent and spent his time visiting historical sites such as Faneuil Hall and the Old State House, where five people, one of them a black man, were killed by the redcoats in the Boston Massacre of 1770.

'James always liked to travel and explore ever since he was a tot,' Trudy Taylor once told a close friend. 'He was always curious about the places he visited and its history. It was easy to tell that he'd do a lot of traveling when he got older.'

In July 1953, the Taylor family took the first of their annual vacations to Martha's Vineyard, Nantucket's bigger sister island off the coast of Massachusetts. Its pristine beauty made the Vineyard a magical place of serenity and eccentricity. The island attracted America's progressive *nouveau riche* millionaires and socialites who came back year after year.

The Taylors bought a huge house in Chilmark, an up-island residential area where the wooded hills roll down to meet the ocean. Their home was surrounded by trees, clay cliffs, miles of hiking trails, and the long stretches of white sand on South Beach. There were sing-alongs at cookouts on the beach, motorboat rides and waterskiing, and plenty of fishing. The children loved their time there, and so did their parents and friends. For Trudy it was a chance to catch up with the family and friends she'd left behind. Martha's Vineyard became a more permanent home for James in his formative years. He loved its peacefulness and its artistic and opulent ambience. It was aloof, distant, and at the same time ingratiatingly cosy. The Vineyard became for him the ultimate place to escape.

'I find it a lot healthier for me to be some place where I can go outside in my bare feet,' Taylor once told a reporter when asked why he decided to live in Martha's Vineyard. 'In ways, it reminds me a little bit of a certain kind of atmosphere that was in the mental hospital I spent time in. It's a little bit protective.'

For years the Taylor children were regulars at the Chilmark Community Center sing-alongs and square dances, where they spent hours singing and dancing – some of the most enjoyable times they had growing up. Occasionally, the Taylor kids were asked to perform plays and lead the animated sing-alongs. 'We have so many great memories from those summers there,' Trudy said. 'It was like out of a fairy tale. The kids would be happy playing at the beach with other kids, and we'd always have friends drop by. When you have a summer cottage, you quickly discover a lot of people who are long-lost friends want to visit you. Our door was always open to everybody.'

Martha's Vineyard provided James with his first exposure to what would become a lifelong hobby, sailing. Whatever his skills as a musician might have been, his greatest interest and most devoted efforts involved rebuilding motorboat engines and learning how to sail. He loved being on the water. Isaac rented a 15-foot-long sloop made of plywood with a canvas deck; it was called the *Carrier*. The Taylors enjoyed the tranquillity of sailing on Martha's Vineyard and absorbing its picturesque surroundings.

Isaac used to sail in the Chilmark town races on Menemsha Pond on Wednesdays and Saturdays. He usually allowed one of his children to join him in the sailboat. James said that Isaac always looked forward to participating in the sailboat race, but sometimes took it a bit too seriously. One time, James remembered, he was cruising around in a tiny three-horsepower motorboat that the family had rented when he spotted his father's sailboat. Isaac was getting ready to enter the race, and asked his son to go back to shore and get him a pack of cigarettes; smoking helped him relax during a race.

James went home, returned with a pack of Parliaments, and tossed them to Isaac from his boat. His aim was a bit off, though, and they fell into the water. Isaac became very upset. James and his sister, Kate (who was in Isaac's boat), began to laugh while their father cursed. James retrieved the cigarettes and put them out on the deck to dry; after about thirty minutes they were dry enough to smoke. Later, Isaac laughed with his children about the incident. He teased James about his aim and told him that he would never become a baseball pitcher.

It was times like this that James relished while he was growing up – times when he lived a carefree life. These early memories would contract sharply to the pain and despair of his later years that put him in a mental hospital.

In 1955 Isaac Taylor left to fulfil two years of military service that he had delayed because of medical school. He became the physician at the McMurdo base in Antarctica. His absence left a huge void in his children's lives. Indeed, Alex and James started to cause trouble because they didn't have a father around to discipline them. Isaac's departure upset the Taylor household.

'This really changed our whole family,' James recalled years later. 'Our father went away and we missed him a lot. It was very difficult on my mother because she had left Boston and now she had to raise us alone. Something always felt missing in my family after our father left. When he came back it was never the same. He was almost like a stranger for a long time.'

Isaac stayed away for two of his children's formative years. He had begun drinking heavily before he departed, and James's brothers and sister felt this was the main reason why he left so abruptly. 'He had problems, big inner problems,' Alex recalled. 'We had an inkling of why he left. It was very hard on our mother and the entire family. We were all concerned, and when he came back, it was hard to accept him back into our lives.'

When Isaac returned, he was not welcomed by the family. Trudy was distant – angry that he had stayed away from home to relentlessly pursue his career. Their marriage deteriorated during the next few years before finally ending in a divorce in 1972.

'He was gone for too long, and when he came back, it was like being with a total stranger,' Alex said. 'There were times when I wish he was there for me and he wasn't so I always had a slight bit of resentment toward him. I also was concerned about how he left my mom to take care of us while he was away. It really put a lot of pressure and stress on her.'

Trudy bought James a cello – his first instrument – when he was ten years old; she wanted him to play an instrument that required dedication and discipline. He learned to play the cello in the school band, and when he brought it home, his siblings loved listening as he made sounds with it. James let his six-year-old brother Livingston play it, but it was too heavy for him to hold. Kate, nine, thought her brother was learning how to play 'a big-sized violin'.

James played just for the fun of doing something together with his family. His brothers and sister were also learning music – banjo, harmonica, tambourine – and they started to have regular jam sessions.

'It sounded like a traffic jam,' Trudy recalled. 'Alex played violin and Kate and Livingston both played piano. There were times when I had to block my ears. But when they'd sing a song together it was beautiful. They all had nice voices and would sing folk songs and hymns. It sounded like a mini choir.'

Trudy lent her vocal talents on many occasions and taught her children some old folk standards. She encouraged her children to explore all musical genres. 'I didn't want them to be limited,' she said. 'So I had them listen to all kinds of music, ranging from jazz to folk to classical. I exposed them to as much as possible and let them ultimately decide which type they wanted to play.'

James quickly discovered that learning the cello was a frustrating and rather difficult pursuit. He didn't want to put in all the hours necessary to becoming an accomplished cellist. He preferred popular to classical music and wanted to sing and play an instrument that he could use to accompany himself.

'I'd rather play guitar than anything else,' James told his parents. 'I want to be able to sing and entertain people. I can't really do that by just playing cello.'

After hearing several local guitarists jam folk and blues, he was determined to become a guitar picker. He liked listening to Hank Williams, Patsy Cline, Ray Charles, Sam Cooke and Jean Redpath. But the person who influenced him most at that time was Woody Guthrie, with his country-folk-style guitar playing.

'I used to listen to the children's record of Woody Guthrie a lot,' Taylor told a reporter. 'I didn't have an amplifier or anything. His strings stand three-quarters of an inch off the fret board and he uses . . . you know, a doubled-over Shell credit card as a pick. It just gets out there. Big cables and his bridge is bulging up like that. The guitar is ah . . . ! And that's fine. I think that's part of the reason he played that way.'

James hinted to his parents for months that he wanted a guitar for Christmas: 'If I ever get one,' he said, 'I'll be the happiest person in the world.'

On Christmas Day 1960 12-year-old James was ecstatic when he woke up to find a nylon-stringed guitar under the family Christmas tree. His parents bought it mail order from Schirmer & Company in New York. In the following months, James taught himself how to play the guitar. A neighbour showed him some chords, and he listened for hours at a time to the radio, trying to copy the sounds he heard. He began making up his own songs only days after getting his guitar, playing one or two chords, then putting melodies and words over them.

Brother Alex mischievously repainted the guitar blue one afternoon when James was at school. 'He painted the strings, too,' James recalls. 'I think he was looking for the expression on my face.' Wherever he went James always carried his guitar strapped over his shoulder. Sometimes he would sit under a tree behind the Taylor house and strum for hours. Other times he could seen strumming and singing on a park bench in Chapel Hill. The first chords he learned were C, D, and G. He improvised for hours over those three chords, and in fact would use them as a base for dozens of his songs in the years ahead.

'It was amazing how dedicated he was,' Isaac Taylor said. 'James was determined, very determined. . . . When he first started playing, it sounded awful. But in the next several weeks and months, it started to sound better. He's always been a quick learner at what he sets his mind out to do.'

At 13, Taylor was in search of a musical mentor and found one in Danny 'Kootch' Kortchmar, a crusty and engaging 15-year-old peace-loving hippie-type teenager who regularly jammed at the local coffeehouses on Martha's Vineyard. To James, meeting Kortchmar seemed an almost incredible piece of good luck. He looked at Kortchmar as a role model, admiring his commitment to singing and playing guitar.

They first met behind the post office, where Taylor caught Kortchmar playing with a new throwing knife. In sharp contrast to James's peaceful and quiet demeanor, Kootch was outgoing and loved being the centre of attention. James did his first professional gig with Kootch, who remained instrumental in Taylor's musical development for years. 'James and I hit it off right away,' Kortchmar said. 'He was very curious about my knife. We wound up buying about four knives each and used to play games throwing them around at things that didn't move. It was innocent fun and nobody got hurt.'

A certain amount of musical competition could be sensed between the two – competition in which James always seemed to emerge a step or two ahead. Throughout their music careers it always seemed that no matter how hard Kortchmar tried to succeed, Taylor, the less talented guitarist of the two, always got the big break that Kortchmar dreamed of.

In 1961 Kortchmar and Taylor started playing music together jamming for hours at Kortchmar's house – sometimes with two guitars, other times with one guitar and one harmonica or percussion player. It was common for the duo to start jamming in the early afternoon and finish in the wee hours of the morning. During breaks, they would eat pizza, smoke cigarettes and drink beer. They loved hanging out together. Both of them had a romantic streak and driving passion for music and art. Kootch taught James new chords and ways to structure a tune; James listened attentively and tried to perfect what he'd learned. On a few occasions, they put on shows in Kortchmar's backyard and would sometimes pass a hat around to earn extra cigarette and beer money. 'Danny really inspired me,' Taylor recalled. 'He was very gifted and taught the chords to a lot of songs. He was like a teacher to me.

We both like similar music, the folksy coffeehouse style. We had a lot of fun playing together.'

Kortchmar taught Taylor the geography of the guitar, showing him chords up and down the guitar's neck, and giving him pointers about figuring out simple fingerings. (The only pointers James had received till then were from his brother Alex and from a blind man in Chapel Hill, who taught him some basic blues and folk.) James never thought it was necessary to take formal lessons because he liked the exercise of figuring out songs by ear. He was very good at it, too; sometimes he was able to lift songs off the radio after hearing them only once or twice.

At age 16, James started to take more notice of the opposite sex. Before he started playing music, he had a tough time attracting girls. The girls at school thought there was something baffling about him; even Taylor himself had trouble figuring out what made him tick. He seemed to have several conflicting personalities. When he was alone in a room with a girl, he was painfully shy, uncomfortable and hesitant. He wanted to talk to girls but he didn't know how.

'I realised right away that girls were attracted to musicians,' he once said. 'That was one of the reasons why I wanted to become a musician.' Whenever Taylor and Kortchmar jammed, there were usually adulatory teenage girls around.

'Danny was popular because he played guitar and was a sweet guy,' said Beth Smith, who met Kortchmar and Taylor when she vacationed with her family one summer on Martha's Vineyard. 'I remember hearing them jam at a folk house and it sounded pretty good. Danny and James were two of the most interesting boys who spent their summers on Martha's Vineyard. They weren't like the other boys, who were into sports and were loud and obnoxious. They had the aura of artists, and that's what made them different than the rest. And they were both good looking.'

By his own admission Taylor was farther ahead sexually than the rest of the boys his age. He had already had sex with a 20-year-old girl – four years his elder – and he usually dated two or three girls at a time. 'The girls liked him a lot,' said Kortchmar. 'James always seemed to have a different girl on the go. He was a genuinely nice and real guy. Once he started playing music he never had a problem getting a date.'

Music was Taylor's ticket to getting laid. And he wasn't afraid to use it. 'Music helped me get the girls,' he recalled. 'It was all innocent fun. It's one of the reasons why people want to become musicians. They want to get the chicks. It's a feeling of being wanted.'

Playing with Kortchmar inspired Taylor to write his first song, 'Roll River Roll', which he spent hours perfecting. He used to invite his siblings to pick up instruments and jam with him. None of the Taylor children were trained musicians; they all played by ear. Kate, Alex and Livingston all took music lessons briefly but were determined to develop on their own. Having grown up in a house where music was almost as important as food, they were able to appreciate it. They were proud of James's talent and often accompanied their brother on piano, violin and percussion while he played guitar and sang. They also sang backup harmonies and sometimes would suggest a lyric or two that James would use in his songs. 'We had a lot of fun,' Alex said. 'We always loved to play music with each other. It was a bit lonely in North Carolina, so we felt the need to express ourselves with music and art. There weren't many people around to talk to.'

Taylor spent more time learning guitar than studying, or doing anything else. His parents grew concerned, and eventually decided it would be better to send their musical son to a stricter school. In 1952 Trudy and Isaac made several inquiries into private schools. 'We really supported James's musical interests when he was young but we also wanted him to get a good education,' Isaac Taylor said. 'We knew he had talent but we thought you could only go so far with music. We wanted our children to have something to fall back on.'

Meanwhile, inspired by the electric sounds of Chuck Berry and Muddy Waters, James saved up forty dollars to buy a second guitar and an amplifier. He spent hours playing his single-pickup Silverstone guitar and trying to emulate the moves made famous by Berry. A couple of years later, Taylor bought a Gibson J-50 for a couple of hundred dollars, which he played in bands until he was twenty-one. At the time not many youngsters his age could afford an authentic Gibson guitar. His friends were thrilled when he let them play it. Taylor ultimately recorded his first three albums with the Gibson before switching to an expensive custom-built guitar. Taylor wanted to make sure whatever guitar he used preserved his distinct acoustic sound.

After his Gibson, James bought custom-made semi-acoustic guitars made by his friend Mark Whitebook, who also designed guitars for jazz legend John McLaughlin. Whitebook designed guitars that resembled the popular Martin guitars, with a cedar top, rosewood body, triangular-shaped neck, and Takamine pickups. Taylor became hooked on Whitebrook's custom-built instrument. Even today, he uses guitars made in a similar style, though he has experimented with dozens of others over the years.

At 15, Taylor and Kortchmar teamed up on harmonica and guitar and won a hootenanny contest in Martha's Vineyard. The boys were sounding better each day, attracting more and more attention. There was a bond between the two that transcended their approach to life. 'We didn't want to do anything but make music,' Kortchmar remembered. 'We were just innocent kids having some fun singing and writing music. We never really thought anything would come of it.'

3

REBEL WITHOUT A CAUSE

In the fall of 1963, James's parents sent him to Milton Academy outside Boston, an all-boys prep school notorious for discipline and a heavy academic workload. Now a teenager, 15-year-old James had a feeling of dread even before he attended his first class at Milton. At first, James had no friends. He was not particularly gregarious, and seemed to prefer his own company. Most of the boys enrolled at Milton came from wealthy East Coast families. James resented being forced to mingle with affluent preppies and became even more withdrawn.

At the very beginning James tried to do his schoolwork, but he became discouraged when he realised how far behind he was in his studies. Soon he was spending most of his time learning chords on his guitar. 'James was bright and could have been a scholar,' Isaac Taylor said. 'But he didn't have the discipline and work ethic that was required. If he would have spent a fraction of the time studying that he did playing guitar he would have been an honours student.'

The other students viewed Taylor as an eccentric and called the tall, lanky, pimple-faced youngster Moose. Taylor took his new nickname as an insult. He began to feel self-conscious and developed feelings of inadequacy and failure.

A Milton classmate of Taylor introduced him to smoking pot, something that he enjoyed immensely and would do almost daily for years to come. Taylor grew attached to readily available drugs and struck up friendships with several local dealers. Marijuana would inevitably alter his personality and intensify several of his character traits – including his laid-back side and recurring paranoia. Taylor's drug habit soon got him into trouble: during lunch hour a classmate caught him lighting up a joint in the bathroom and threatened to report him to the principal's office if he did it again.

'We were definitely concerned about James,' admitted Milton's dean John Torney. 'James was different from the rest of the students. He was definitely a bright young man but he had trouble fitting in with the rest of the crowd. He seemed to be a bit bothered and uncomfortable. And I'm sure he knew about drugs long before anyone else here.'

Taylor did not have much in common with any of the other students. Some were straitlaced, some were straight-A students, and some acted like brats. Taylor didn't fit into any of these categories. He was rebellious and refused to become friendly with his teachers the way some of the other boys did. Instead he escaped into dope. He was also more comfortable being stoned, he said, because it enhanced his creative process. 'I was insecure and I didn't feel like facing the world every day. So I experimented with drugs because it gave me the escape I needed. And I felt that I needed drugs to help me make music. It was my medicine.'

Taylor also needed some privacy to help him come to terms with his insecurities. 'We all knew that James had a lot of emotional problems to deal with,' a Taylor family member said. 'He was always thoughtful and respectful to others but he was uncomfortable being around other people.'

Rather than resolving his paradoxes at Milton, Taylor magnified them. He didn't have many friends. The only person he seemed to confide in was his longtime friend Stan Sheldon. They would take long walks in the countryside, and Taylor would talk about his most intimate feelings. He also told Sheldon on several occasions that he wasn't always comfortable being in this world, and that sometimes he thought about suicide.

'Sometimes I wish that I could just play music and not worry about anything else,' Taylor said. 'People get so caught up in themselves that they eventually lose focus and wind up miserable.'

Most people close to Taylor agree he felt comfortable performing on stage because he was able to make people smile. It also helped him escape his own problems. 'James loved helping make people forget the everyday grind of life with his music,' his sister, Kate, said. 'He had a unique ability to sing a song and get the whole room to relate to it in some way. Singing helped him vent his own frustrations in life. It was a medium that he felt most comfortable expressing his feelings about life.'

Each summer Taylor spent his school break at his family's home in Martha's Vineyard, where he continued to evolve as a musician. He took his guitar to the beach every day and practised there for hours. The music he wrote was a logical outgrowth of his boyhood years in a rural setting. It had a soft, gentle, mellow feel that sounded like a cross between folk and country with a touch of R&B. James did not have a very wide vocal range, but he sang and played guitar with strong sentiment and conviction. Each time he repeated a song, he sang with more confidence and crispness. His music had traces of Woody Guthrie's white folk on the one hand and Muddy Waters's blues on the other. He showed it off to friends and family whenever he could.

'Our jam sessions were some of the happiest times we had in our house,' his brother Hugh said. 'It was a time when we could just all let our hair down and have a ball.'

But when fall came around, Taylor got depressed because he didn't want to go back to Milton. The day before he was supposed to return to Milton in 1964, he begged his mother to let him stay home. He said that he had enough of Milton, and that he preferred to go to school in North Carolina so that he could be closer to his family and friends.

'It's awful there,' Taylor moaned. 'I don't know why I'm wasting my time trying to learn in a place that is not the most stimulating for me.' His mother, however, convinced him to go back. She told him that he would make a monumental mistake if he dropped out. 'You'll get a much better education at Milton and you're halfway finished so you might as well try to finish it off,' Trudy said. 'It'll go by very fast. Your father and I want you to get the best education you can.'

Everybody in the Taylor household knew that James was unhappy, though – that it would only be a matter of time before he did something rebellious. He was like a walking time bomb. 'James was so talented on his guitar and it was obvious that music was what he wanted to do,' according to Effie Hairston, the Taylor family cook and caregiver for over twenty years. 'The only time he seemed unhappy was when he was not with his guitar. Everybody in the family was talented but he seemed to have something a bit extra than the rest.'

The elder Taylors insisted that their offspring be straight-A students, but by now James could no longer live up to their high standards, and the grades of the other youngsters also started to slide. None of the kids was interested in following in the footsteps of their academic father. 'The basic orientation in my family,' Taylor recalled, 'was that simply because you were a Taylor, you could and should be able to accomplish things with high standards.'

A miserable and dark James Taylor began to emerge during his third year at Milton. He spent most of his time in the tiny room he was assigned in the schoolmaster's house. His overall demeanour could now best be described as sullen. He went to his classes unshaven and exhausted. He was extremely depressed and contemplated suicide several times. He was no longer the easy and approachable teen his classmates had grown fond of. He found it difficult to sleep because of recurring, obsessively violent thoughts. Taylor was convinced that suffering was the ineluctable consequence of being human. He wondered if he was manic-depressive: whenever he had periods of elation or wonder, he reasoned, they were usually succeeded by wild mood changes into gloom, self-reproach, and inaction. On one occasion during a chilly November night he went to a nearby river with his guitar in hand and contemplated drowning himself. He drank several bottles of beer and fell asleep before he could carry out his plan. When he woke up the next morning he decided to abandon his attempt to commit suicide.

'I don't know if I really have the guts to ever commit suicide,' he once said. 'But there were many times when I just wanted to put an abrupt end to my life. I had a lot of emotional problems and I found the toughest thing was just managing to stay alive.'

As James Taylor's grades continued to slide, he found it impossible to escape his unhappiness. He was still passing every subject but he had completely lost interest in academic subjects. He stopped doing homework and instead spent all his time practising guitar. His teachers were well aware that his internal struggles were tearing him apart, but he was otherwise a mystery. There were rumours around school that the tall, thin teenage Taylor was experimenting with drugs and alcohol. Milton's obedience rules were very strict, and James would have been expelled immediately if he were caught smoking pot or drinking booze. But his teachers and headmaster were never able to prove their suspicions. Nobody at Milton really knew what Taylor was up to.

At Thanksgiving Taylor, 16, thought again about suicide. He returned home for the holidays and didn't want to go back to Milton. He told Kate that he felt like a complete failure. He broke down in tears several times that weekend. He was tired and bewildered. Confusion and despair seemed to hang over him. He yearned to have meaning and love in his life but was unable to find anybody capable of understanding what he was going through. His existence had become peripatetic and paranoid. He couldn't confide in anybody, because he was afraid to have his trust betrayed. He found life at Milton boring, demanding, and repetitious. The only consolation was that he didn't have any money worries because his well-to-do parents supported him.

Taylor became convinced the way to vanquish his sorrows would be to drop out of Milton and pursue his music career. He left Milton midway through his junior year. When he returned to North Carolina, he finished his junior year at Chapel Hill High School. His mother, however, pleaded with him to return to Milton. 'Think a bit harder about your decision,' she told her son. 'If you don't go back, you'll wind up without an education. Your father and I want you to have something that you can always fall back on.'

4

KNOCKIN' 'ROUND THE ZOO

When Taylor returned to North Carolina in 1964, he seemed determined to escape the drug habit that had become a central part of his life. His brother Alex asked James to join him with a band called the Fabulous Corsairs. Alex was also going through a rebellious period, and had fallen into disfavour with his mother for hanging out with people she deemed undesirable. She was not happy when James joined Alex and his friends, who, by all accounts, liked to party with drugs and alcohol. They had no interest in school; a couple of them wound up in jail when they were caught holding up a local corner store. The tension between Trudy and Alex would rise when Isaac was away on business. He would start fights with his younger siblings and encourage them to engage in disruptive behaviour.

'Alex was a bit messed up,' Trudy Taylor recalled. 'He had a lot of difficulty behaving. He was a tough child to handle because he was the eldest. It didn't help that his father was frequently absent for long periods.'

Alex grew tired of being typecast as a bad boy and used music to release a lot of bad feelings. 'Growing up was very tough, especially as a teenager,' Alex said. 'It was a very confusing and frustrating time. I acted rebellious because I felt alone. I always loved my family a lot but I was never able to express it properly to them.'

James played rhythm guitar in the Fabulous Corsairs and also shared vocal duties with the band's other members. The Fabulous Corsairs belted out startlingly good, authentic rock-'n'-roll cover songs and began to make a name for themselves on the local circuit. Alex was proud to have his younger brother in the band and kept a watchful eye over him to make sure he didn't participate in any of the postconcert partying with the other members.

'We didn't do anything out of the ordinary but it was a lot of fun,' Alex recalled years after the band broke up. 'I tried to make sure James kept out of trouble, because everybody was into a lot of partying then and my mother told me that if James got into any trouble, she'd take him out of the band. My mother knew he was a bit distressed about Milton so I had to keep a close eye on him.

'Rock 'n' roll was the big thing then and everybody was listening to Chuck Berry, Little Richard and Bill Haley. James was just starting out as a musician and I wanted to help him get some experience playing in a band.'

In this outfit Taylor tested the boundaries of his musicianship. He had to play in tempo with the other musicians; he couldn't play with song structures the way he did when he improvised on his accoustic guitar at home.

'James had talent but he didn't know how to play with other musicians,' recalled Zach Wiesner, one of the original members of the Corsairs. 'I remember the first couple of rehearsals, he was totally lost. But he always caught on fast to whatever he touched. We weren't playing anything too complex but we still had to respect things like rhythm and the arrangement of the tune. After a week he fitted right in and also was able to give the group some creative input that definitely improved the way we sounded.'

In the few months Taylor spent back in North Carolina playing in his brother's band, he rejuvenated and regained his morale. In its nascent period the group survived by taking on whatever gigs they could get, and often wound up playing for free. Taylor bought a Fender Mustang guitar to play rhythm for the Corsairs. The group received local attention because they had more charisma and style than the other bands in the area. And they were able to rise to occasions. Soon there was a demand for them playing at frat parties, beer bashes and the dances at high schools and local clubs. The Corsairs gave James his first taste of the rigours of playing in a band. He had never realised, for instance, how arduous loading and unloading the equipment could be.

'I was used to carrying around just a nylon-stringed guitar,' he said. 'When I first started playing in a band, it was a whole new experience. The easiest part is getting up on stage and playing. There's so much other stuff that goes into playing a gig, like lugging around equipment and doing a sound check.'

Taylor's musical tastes, however, differed considerably from those of the other band members. He wanted to cover the blues and folk songs that he heard on the radio. He soon got bored playing straight-ahead rock 'n' roll and decided to take his parents' advice: he packed up his guitar and returned to Milton. He appreciated the experience having played with other musicians, but he needed to return to his own folksy coffeehouse-style music. Also, Taylor was afraid of the trouble his absence from Milton could have caused him, because he had only one more year before graduation. He felt his parents would disown him if he didn't finish school.

Up to this point in his life, Taylor's only means of financial support was from his parents, who were equally generous to each of their children. He was afraid that if he didn't go back to Milton, they might make him get a full-time job. They wanted him to be happy, of course, but they were concerned that he was headed in the wrong direction. He had become known as the family's black sheep.

'James just wanted to play guitar all day,' Isaac Taylor said. 'If he dropped out of school he knew that he'd have to go get a job. If he got a job he wouldn't be able to play guitar. At school he'd bring his guitar and find time during recess and lunch to practise. So he decided to go back to Milton.'

It didn't take long for James to become emotionally distraught again, and his anguish was obvious. The other students were well aware of his troubles and started to tease him and talk behind his back. His teachers were concerned because he kept missing classes. When he did show up, he was usually late. It was the most difficult and unstable time of his life. Many days he would lock himself in his room all day because he didn't want to face the world. The only thing that he wanted to do with his life was to play chords and sing.

In 1965 Taylor, then 17, left Milton for good. Suicidal again, he phoned his sister, Kate, and told her that he needed help. He said that he didn't have the will to live and that he wanted to die. After a long conversation, Kate, 16, convinced him not to take his life and to seek professional help.

James was convinced that he had to take action if he didn't want to end his life. He went to see a psychiatrist and immediately broke down in his office. The psychiatrist suggested that Taylor enter a mental hospital, so he checked himself into the McLean Hospital in Belmont, Massachusetts, one of the state's most expensive hospitals for the mentally ill. Taylor's hero Ray Charles had spent some time there for drug and alcohol abuse. McLean's thirty-six-thousand dollar annual fee, however, was far more expensive than the twenty-seven-hundred-dollar a year tuition at Milton. But money didn't matter to the Taylor family. Isaac was well off and he wanted his son to get the best available treatment. All that was important, Isaac told James, was for him to get better.

Taylor was a bright, idiosyncratic teenager with a sense of humour. But he was losing control of his life and it was no surprise to those close to him that he wound up in a mental institution. He shunned family and friends who were trying to be kind. He would lie in bed for hours wondering if there was any way to end his constant pain and confusion. He needed answers; he felt lost and alone. He had no direction, and his insecurities completely overtook him. Sometimes he would walk along the river and think about drowning himself. Another time he considered swallowing a bottle of sleeping pills. During one of the few occasions on which he went out with a group of friends, he left hurriedly because of stomach cramps. The next day he told a friend that he didn't feel comfortable being around so many people because he was paranoid. His fears came and went. In later years Taylor would openly acknowledge that his instability was not the only reason he checked himself into a mental hospital: he knew that his mental problems would also help him avoid being drafted to fight in Vietnam. He was against the war, and often cried when he watched Vietnam footage broadcast on the news.

'He was an artist and was extremely sensitive about things,' recalled his brother Hugh. 'He had a lot of things to work out in his inner self. He needed to get himself together and McLean was his best alternative at that time.'

Taylor didn't like the bland food and was unimpressed with the hospital's psychiatrists, with whom he had regular consultations. He didn't feel that they were able to relate to what he was going through. Because they were much older than he was, James didn't think that they could properly understand the problems facing America's youth. He talked on and on to his psychiatrists, very quietly, about his life, trying to rationalise it. McLean was nothing like the stereotypical *One Flew Over the Cuckoo's Nest* ward. The patients weren't drugged without their permission and were given considerable freedom. They were allowed to listen to the radio, participate in numerous artistic and sporting activities, and sleep on comfortable beds in large, sunlit rooms.

'It was an expensive hotel,' said Brian Saltzman of New Jersey, who was a patient at McLean in the early '70s. 'You had to be very rich to go there and there were no guarantees that you'd come out cured. Many patients I know needed more help when they got out of there. It wasn't your stereotypical mental institution. It had more of a country club atmosphere.'

Taylor made a friend of Carl, his burly bedside attendant, who listened attentively when James explained why his life had been filled with so much loneliness and depression. Taylor told Carl that his parents' feuding relationship coupled with the fact that he didn't have many friends while growing up were the major reasons why he felt depressed. He added that the only reason he had to live was his desire to play music. 'It keeps me going,' Taylor said. 'If I'd never found music I'm sure I'd be in much worse condition. It's the only release I have.' Taylor rehashed his childhood years in North Carolina, and told Carl how he wallowed in his private misery at Milton. 'I never liked it there,' he said. 'I needed a place that was more artistic. Once I get out of here I'm just going to travel and play music. That's all that I want to do with my life.'

McLean's heavy protective screens on the windows made Taylor feel he had been incarcerated. 'It was very depressing,' Taylor recalled. 'At first it felt like you were almost in prison. But I got used to it after a while. I was used to the beautiful, picturesque rural scenery in North Carolina and Martha's Vineyard and now I felt like I was trapped in a concrete jungle. It made me realise how fortunate I was to grow up where I did. I missed the smell of the fresh air back home.'

Inside the hospital a lot of Taylor's fears resurfaced. The strong antidepressants he was prescribed helped him fall into a peaceful sleep at night, but he couldn't overcome his paranoia. He was afraid that the people around him at McLean wanted to hurt him. Sometimes he had screaming fits when he was sleeping. When he woke up, all that he could think about was how much he had failed his family. He felt like a pariah. He didn't know if he'd ever snap out of his increasingly depressed state of mind. At night, if the medication could not put him to sleep he would resort to masturbation, fantasising about many of the pretty females he had met in his life. If he didn't fall asleep a couple of minutes after his first orgasm he'd come again and again, until he was able to fall asleep.

'James used to talk about how much he missed women,' recalled Doug, who was a patient at McLean the same time as Taylor and now works as an accountant in Tempe, Arizona. 'He used to read a lot and was more detached than the rest of the patients there. I spoke to him several times because I was interested in music and I knew he was a musician. He was an extremely nice guy who appeared to be very level-headed. I asked him why he was there – because he seemed to be more together than the rest of us – and he replied, "If I wasn't here I'd be dead by now."'

Doug, who didn't want his real name to be used for publication, said it was common for males of Taylor's age to check into McLean in order to avoid the draft. 'No matter how screwed up he was, he didn't appear to need to be checked into a mental hospital,' Doug said. 'He was withdrawn, but maybe he needed a social-skills teacher instead of a shrink. He was definitely the type of person who didn't want to go anywhere near the army. There were a few people like that at McLean, myself included. And in hindsight I don't regret using McLean to avoid going into the army.'

During a group discussion among several McLean patients, Doug remembered, Taylor cast a disgusted glance at another patient who said he'd rather be in the army than at McLean. Taylor's rheumy eyes beat rapidly and he seemed annoyed. 'You should have seen James's face,' Doug said. 'It was filled with so much tension. He told the guy that he should kiss the ground and thank his lucky stars that he was able to be in McLean and not have to wake up every day at 5 a.m. to do army exercises.'

Doug continued, 'James was obviously from a more liberal and progressive background than most of the other people in the hospital. He was different from everybody else, and he was very outspoken against conservatism and war. A lot of people talked behind his back and thought he was sympathetic to communism. They made a lot of outrageous remarks about him because he was so different. One patient said he thought James could be a Russian spy, because everything he did seemed to have socialist tendencies. I got a kick out of it all 'cause I knew that it was just a load of bull. James was just a simple, nice guy who was in because he was confused about life. Sure, he was different, but that's what made him so interesting compared to the rest of us. We were all in there 'cause we had serious problems, and some of us posed a danger to society. James was in there, I think, because he just had trouble understanding society and the meaning of his own existence. I never really thought his problems were as serious as most people in there. He seemed to be together. I remember he was always the first guy to volunteer to help out other patients when they needed something. Sometimes he'd even do other people's chores if they weren't up to it.'

Taylor usually called his parents every weekend to assure them that he was all right. He told his mother that the living conditions were good, even though he usually couldn't stand them, because he didn't want to worry her. 'I'm doing fine, Mom,' he would say. 'This is just what I need. I'm learning a lot of things here about myself and life. When I come home, I'll be a different person. This experience has made me realise a lot of things and has given me a different outlook on life.'

Trudy knew James wasn't telling her how he really felt. She appreciated that he didn't want to alarm her but she didn't stop worrying about him until the day he was discharged. She often wondered if things would have turned out differently if Isaac had been around more to guide and discipline the children instead of always being away with his work.

Taylor, then 18, didn't admit to his mother that he was lonely, desperate, and homesick. The only companions he desired were stony silence and his brothers and sisters. He missed his siblings, he missed his mother's cooking, and he especially missed the serene setting of North Carolina. He felt estranged and detached from his family and, deep down, wondered if they would still be there for him when he got out. He missed Alex's mischievous ways and Kate's glowing smile. He also missed being able to act as a big brother to Hugh and Livingston. He would always ask his mother for updates about his siblings lives and usually remembered to call them on special occasions like birthdays and holidays. Despite all of his turmoil, Taylor tried to put his family first. Even though it often seemed that he didn't care about anything or anyone, he had a great love for his family and never blamed them for any of his problems. He often wondered if his hopes to have a close relationship again with his siblings were a fantasy because he had been separated from them for so long. He couldn't help feeling guilty for what he perceived as the bitter failure of his life.

'I'm sorry for all the problems I've caused,' he told his mother over the phone. 'I just find it hard to deal with certain things. I promise that one day I'll make it up to you and the rest of the family.'

James was intent upon doing his time at McLean and then getting back on the road with his suitcase and guitar. He tried to hide what he was really thinking, especially when he talked to his psychiatrists, because he didn't want to stay an extra day there. He knew he had to be careful to say nothing that the staff could use to prolong his stay.

'He played his cards right,' Doug said. 'He did what was expected of him and didn't do anything extra. In a way he outsmarted the staff. He didn't really belong in there, and usually if you don't after you've been in there for a while you start to feel like you do. But he was way too smart. He just played the game and came in and out looking like the exact same person. It was almost as if he treated his experience there as a holiday from real society. I think because he was an artist, he used his experience there to help him more for artistic inspiration than emotional inspiration.'

After a couple of months, Taylor became more accustomed to life at McLean and started to come out his shell. During his spare time he wrote long letters and poems, as well as devouring the English literature and psychology books he was assigned to read by his teachers. McLean offered a high school program, from which Taylor graduated during his nine-month stay there. For the first time in years, Taylor didn't mind going to school.

'McLean was much better for me than Milton,' Taylor said recently. 'I didn't have lots of time on my hands like I did at Milton. My days were full and I kept busy. That's what I needed in my life. Otherwise I would have too much time to think too much. And sometimes too much thinking isn't too good for you.'

Talking to the other patients at McLean turned out to be Taylor's best therapy. He realised that he was not the only teenager in America who was lethargic and cynical. In the '60s, divorce, inner-city rot and economic instability contributed to the proliferation of teenage suicides. It was common for teens to have a sense of hopelessness and isolation, even in loving families, that drove them to take their own lives. Their families told them that they were just going through a phase – that they would soon grow out of it.

'We were America's youth and we felt misunderstood,' Doug said. 'And our parents didn't make it easy for us by simply telling us that we're just going through a phase. Today, 30 years later, the same thing is happening in our society. That's why youths rebel. But today it's a bit more out of control, 'cause there's more access to guns and hard drugs. If you look at James Taylor's case, he was an upper-class kid who was not comfortable being alive at that time. That's why he went to

McLean. And that's why I went too. It wasn't a phase, because you can be miserable as a child or a grumpy old man. James Taylor was a beautiful, peaceful guy who was extremely sensitive to some of the bullshit that is unfortunately ever-present in our society.

'When we had discussion groups I remember that James listened to every word being said. He wanted to hear the experiences of other teenagers. And when he heard them he realised that his situation was not by any stretch the worst. People his age had worse problems, mental problems. Everybody at McLean knew that there was nothing really wrong with James. He was a very smart and likable guy. He was also a genius. You could tell just by talking to him. I knew that when he got out of McLean, he would go on to do great things.'

Doug went on, 'In there he was definitely one of the brightest. But he shared similar problems and insecurities that other teens faced at that time. He told me once, about six months after he entered McLean, that he felt more comfortable because he met people who were similar to him. I think his problem, before he came to McLean, was that he was at a school with boys he couldn't relate to and had nothing in common with.'

During his last month at McLean, in May 1966, Taylor no longer appeared beset by his emotional problems. He was preparing to resume a normal lifestyle. He was anxious to leave McLean and dreamed about playing music for a living. He told his psychiatrist that he felt great and was excited to get on with his life. His psychiatrist was convinced that James was ready to re-enter the real world. He said that life would be good for him now, but warned him to expect recurring bouts of depression or turmoil. 'I understand and appreciate your wisdom,' Taylor said. 'But now I think I'll be able to deal with things as they come without getting extremely depressed. I'm ready to get back out there and start life over.'

During his time at McLean, Taylor leaned heavily on his sister, Kate, for moral support. He spent hours on the phone talking to Kate about his ordeal and the psychiatric help he was getting. He told her that at McLean he felt he was becoming detached from the real world; he was anxious to get out and get on with his life. 'By staying cooped up in here I'm not doing anything to advance my music career. I feel like I'm starting to stagnate. I just want to get out of here and get a fresh start. I feel like I've been through so much.'

Ironically, a year later Kate would also check herself in to McLean after experiencing a disturbing emotional time at the Cambridge School of Weston, Massachusetts. 'It was tough for our family because we all wound up being a bit fucked up,' Alex said. 'Our mother tried to hold the family together but it was hard because all of the kids were getting into trouble.'

Kate honed her musical skills at McLean when she became active in its music therapy program. She started a group with other patients, calling it Sister Kate's Soul Stew Kitchen. Another Taylor, Livingston, checked himself into McLean shortly after James left. Livingston was lonely at a Quaker school in Westtown, Pennsylvania, and, with his mother's urging, decided to enter McLean. The Taylor children couldn't escape the terrible emotional problems that seemed to be hereditary in their family. All had erratic personalities, and in searching for meaning in their lives became more messed up with pain and confusion. And all turned for temporary relief to drugs and alcohol.

'It wasn't out of the ordinary for families to send two or three of their children to McLean,' Doug said. 'McLean was expensive, so the only way you could send your kids there is if you had the bucks. My younger sister also went to McLean, because she became very depressed at a school in Boston. I knew a few people at McLean who had brothers and sisters who had also been there. Looking back, I'm not so sure it was a good decision, because it's pretty élitist. You only get to mingle with rich, white kids. There were no blacks there. Today, I wouldn't let my kids go to a place like that, because I want them to be with kids from all kinds of different backgrounds. If a kid has emotional problems today there are much better alternatives, like guidance counsellors and social workers. In those days we didn't have a lot of choices. There were very few options.'

A former McLean nurse, who cared for Taylor during the eight years she worked there during the late '60s and early '70s didn't think that McLean was the best choice for him. 'So many times I've seen kids like him come to hospitals like ours and wind up more confused by the time they get discharged. Like many of the other patients at McLean and other expensive private psychiatric hospitals in the country, James became distraught with life at an early age and was convinced that being committed to a mental institution was his only alternative. Let me tell you, in most cases, young kids like James make the wrong decision. They shouldn't even contemplate a move like this until they are at least 25. A lot of these hospitals are only interested in gouging them as much as possible, because they come from very rich families. And the kids are left the burden of carrying on their shoulders for the rest of their lives the fact that they were once in a mental institution. Many of them never get over it. It's always lurking in the back of their minds. I've seen so many of them commit suicide or wind up deeply emotionally scarred for the rest of their lives.

'I can't talk specifically about James, because it's against my professional ethics. But I will say that the times I treated him I wondered to myself why he was even in there. He was so bright, articulate and friendly. Sure, like so many other young teenagers, he had some problems, but I'm sure that they could have been worked out. It all stems back to the family. Lots of rich families like to take the easy way out and ship their kids off. They don't put in the time needed to help their children. I know if he was my kid, there was no way I would have considered sending him off to a psychiatric institution, even if he was suicidal. The best way to handle these things is for the family to rally behind the kid and to bend over backward to deal with it. A messed-up kid can never get the same attention and comfort at a mental hospital that he can get in his own home. But it all depends on how committed the family is to dealing with the problem.'

A shocking *CBS 60 Minutes II* report in 1999 echoed this nurse's words, unearthing a disturbing mountain of evidence of patient deaths and injuries, along with falsification of records, at hundreds of the United States' psychiatric hospitals. The report singled out the hospitals belonging to Charter Behavioural Health Systems, America's largest chain of for-profit psychiatric hospitals. Veteran reporter Ed Bradley opened the report with a horror story of a 16-year-old boy who was committed to a Charter hospital in Greensboro, North Carolina, about a twenty-minute drive from where Taylor grew up. The boy was asphyxiated by a towel wrapped around his face while he was under 'therapeutic restraint', his wrists and ankles strapped and tied down to the hospital bed. He was the third patient in four months to die while he was 'under restraint' at that hospital.

The CBS report also detailed the common practice of hiring unqualified workers – who regularly handled patients without medical supervision – and the use of unjustified force. Contacted by phone to respond, a Charter employee said, 'We've been instructed not to comment about the report.' After being pressured for more than a minute, the employee admitted, 'We've all been told that anybody who comments will lose their job. I advise you to talk to someone else.' She then banged down the phone.

Dr Dennis O'Leary, president of the Joint Commission on Accreditation of Health Care Organizations, which is entrusted with accrediting psychiatric and other institutions, told Bradley that he was unaware of how prevalent such incidents of abuse are. June Gibbs-Brown, the inspector general of the federal Department of Health and Human Services, took action against several Charter hospitals after viewing Bradley's report.

On 20 April 1999, the night before the *60 Minutes* report aired, Bradley appeared on *Larry King Live* and said that America had had a long history of abuse of young people in its private psychiatric hospitals. He added that these hospitals are more interested in turning huge profits than patient care. Bradley's investigation resulted in expressions of concern and second-guessing among the families of anyone who had ever been committed to a private psychiatric hospital.

'When I heard about the *60 Minutes* piece, the first person who came to mind was James Taylor,' said author Esmond Choueke, who over the years has written about and photographed Taylor for several newspapers and magazines. 'I've always wondered how he ever wound up in there. It didn't seem right because in public he always appeared to be so together. I feel bad for him because a lot of what was said in the *60 Minutes* report must hit home with him. He fits the typical description of the confused rich kid who winds up in there. I'm sure that he must be doing a lot of second-guessing after seeing the report.'

Having finished his high school diploma at Mclean and with only days to go before his discharge, Taylor's thoughts became disjointed. He didn't know what to expect when he got out. He wondered how his family and friends would treat him in North Carolina and if it was even worth going back there. He made an impulsive move only three days before he was scheduled to be discharged: he packed up his belongings and threw them into the back of his friend Dave Barry's station wagon. He crashed at Barry's apartment and decided that he would stay in Boston.

'I don't feel comfortable going back home,' Taylor told Barry. 'There's nothing to go back to. I need to find my own way and the only way to do it is to start a life free of family pressure. I just want to find a job to support me until I can make money performing music. Life doesn't have to be so complicated. I want to keep it simple.'

After a two-day job search, James found work at the Bort Carlton Handbags leather bindery in South Boston. A week later, he decided to quit. He realised that thanks to his family's wealth and his parents' self-absorption, he was almost totally oblivious to the workings of the real world; he could not function there, much less hold a job. He didn't want to return to school, but he still had hopes of making something of himself. He decided to leave Boston and pursue his music career in New York, a city more conducive to the arts.

5

GOOD OL' FOLKS IN THE VILLAGE

When he arrived in New York midway through 1966, 18-year-old James Taylor spent his days endlessly walking through Greenwich Village. He loved observing the freaks, hippies, bums and camera-toting tourists who paraded through the streets. He also enjoyed going into some of the funky secondhand clothing and record stores and browsing for hours. Most of all he was fascinated by the Village's bohemian atmosphere.

The Village reverberated with the sounds of folk music and jazz. Poets and artists inundated the Beat scene. Taylor worshipped many of the Village's legendary Beat poets; he could hardly believe that he was now living next to them. He would hang out in basement coffee shops just to hear the rambling conversations of the people sitting nearby. He felt like a kid in a candy store.

During his first few weeks in the Village, Taylor experienced a sense of rebirth. He wanted to be in the same place where his hero Bob Dylan had received his big break, and from the day he arrived he felt like he was following in Dylan's footsteps. The '60s had already seen the emergence of a brand-new pop music due to the enormous success of the Beatles and Dylan. It seemed that almost every teenager wanted to pick up a guitar, leave his family, and hit the road in search of fame and fortune. A new breed of musicians had been born, and hungry record executives couldn't wait to discover the next budding star. The competition was keen but it didn't deter Taylor. He'd come to New York to start his career, and the only thing that could stop him was himself.

Back home in North Carolina, James's parents worried about their son. They were concerned about the drugs and crime in Greenwich Village; they didn't think it was the right place for James to live, because of all the things he had been through during the past few years. 'They supported his decision but they were not too happy,' said a close family friend. 'They would have preferred it if James had been going to college instead of roaming the seedy streets of New York. Trudy was afraid that it would be easy for James to get involved with undesirable characters there. She didn't want her son to go through another tough time. He had already been through so much. One bad experience could put him back in a psychiatric hospital. He was still very emotionally fragile.'

Taylor said that before he arrived, he knew about the systematic abuse of striving musicians in New York. 'Musicians have a tough time making a living there and you often have to work for peanuts,' he noted. 'But New York was the place to be and if you got the right break you had a good chance to do very well.'

Taylor rented a room on Columbus Avenue and Eighty-Fourth Street in Manhattan and joined his longtime musical buddy Danny 'Kootch' Kortchmar, who had been living in the Village playing guitar in a band called the King Bees. After a couple of the band's members had a huge fallout, the King Bees broke up. Kootch decided to form a new band, and he wanted James to be the frontman. Taylor got very excited at the prospect of singing lead vocals; the two spent hours huddling in a café working out the logistics and details. Kootch was so happy Taylor had joined him that he even proposed to name the group after him.

'Let's call it Stringbean [one of Taylor's nicknames] or the James Taylor Group,' Kootch said, as Taylor listened attentively. 'We'll get some local gigs and start recording our music. Then if things go well we'll buy a van and hit the road.'

Kootch and Taylor finally settled on calling the band the Flying Machine. They recruited Vineyard alumni Joel O'Brien on drums and Zach Wiesner on bass. Taylor and Wiesner moved in together to a tiny room with little sunlight at the dilapidated Albert Hotel on University Place and Eleventh Street. This was one of the seedier hotels in the Village, frequented regularly by junkies and prostitutes. A fire a year earlier had charred a good part of it, but its owners refused to close the hotel and rented rooms on the floors that were not gutted.

One of the prostitutes who hung out at the Albert called herself Flo. Between tricks, she used to bum cigarettes from Taylor. Flo was a teenage runaway from Buffalo who came to New York wanting to be a model but wound up turning tricks after failing to find work and falling into the Village's drug subculture. She was stabbed to death in 1973 by a former boyfriend.

'There were lots of weird people constantly hanging out at the Albert,' said Bradlee Dixon, who once worked late shifts at the Albert. 'We had an eclectic mix of clients, from hookers to Mafia types to artists. It was wild and we just pretended not to notice what was really going down in the hotel. I vaguely remember Mr Taylor, but after he became famous I recognised him when I saw him on TV. He was always polite, and I remember that he dressed like a hippie. I also remember him because Flo was a regular client of ours and I saw them on a couple of occasions smoking outside of the hotel. I always remained good friends with Flo and we used to go out occasionally for drinks. When she died, I thought to myself that the only time she seemed happy was when she hung out with artist types like Mr Taylor. I remember that she thought he was a really nice kid and she admired him immensely.'

At Kootch's insistence, the Flying Machine rehearsed relentlessly in the basement of the Albert. The music was distorted because they didn't have a proper sound system; still, after only a few weeks the band began to play in a polished fashion. The combination of talent, circumstance and American dream inspired Taylor and his band mates to get gigs in the Village. They developed a repertoire of folk-rock songs, took their lumps and then looked for patrons, managers, and record companies to support and promote them. They were ready for their first gig. Kootch and Taylor combed the Village's cafés and nightclubs trying to convince club owners to hire them. They got a gig as the regular band at the Night Owl Café on West Third Street off MacDougal because the club owner thought their youthful good looks would attract a fashionable crowd. 'The gig's yours as long as you and your friends don't play too loud and do damage to the place,' the owner told Kootch. 'I want you boys to play good to bring in the people. As long as there's people you have the job.'

The entertainment lasted until the early hours of the morning at the Night Owl. A deep haze of cigarette smoke usually curled around the room while the club's patrons listened to the music. The Night Owl's clientele was an eclectic mix of hippies, actors, models and even some mafioso types who held business meetings in the back of the room.

The Flying Machine usually played four sets a night and earned 15 dollars for their work. Between sets, guest musicians would jump onstage and get a chance to play a couple of songs. The band's gig at the Night

Owl lasted for almost nine months. During this time a lot of problems erupted among the four musicians. And it didn't help that the owner of the club did everything he could to make life miserable for the boys.

'It was an opium-den-type atmosphere,' recalled Julie Berger, who lived in the Village for six years during the '60s and saw Taylor perform with the Flying Machine. 'But the management didn't treat the musicians well because they were only interested in making a lot of money and paying the musicians next to nothing. They [the Flying Machine] were definitely the best group who played there, at least when I went there. You could easily tell that they were not from New York because they were more laid-back than the other groups. James was the one the girls liked the most because he was tall and handsome and had a peaceful and natural aura about him. He seemed shy onstage but it was easy to tell that he was the most talented. He had a very distinctive voice. I remember one of my girlfriends told me during one show how much she drooled over James and that she'd do anything to sleep with him. A week later she told me that she cornered him after the show, kissed him on the lips, and wound up in his apartment a couple of hours later having sex all night with him.'

At the end of the evening's gig, Taylor and his tired band would stumble over to an all-night coffee shop and hold a nightly postmortem of their performance. 'We've got to play tighter,' Kootch often told the boys. 'If we don't we'll be replaced by another band. And we're too stiff onstage. Let's have a bit more fun. If we look like we're having fun, then everybody in the place will also have fun.'

Taylor did the bulk of the songwriting for the Flying Machine. The most famous song he wrote during this period, 'Knockin' 'Round the Zoo', was about the time he spent in a mental hospital. Taylor said he wrote it to try to help him come to terms with his nine-month stay at McLean. He also wanted to deliver a direct message to his friends and family about the tough time he was going through. In the last verse, he expressed how much he felt that society was ostracising him. In later years, 'Knockin' 'Round the Zoo' would become a popular conversation piece among Taylor's fans. 'It really described what he was going through at that time in his life,' said Peter Baxter, a loyal Taylor fan from Illinois. 'So many great artists have songs that are autobiographical. If I had to choose one for Taylor, especially early in his career, it would definitely be this one. He really expressed what he was going through at that time.'

In the song's catchy chorus, Taylor describes a regular day at McLean lightheartedly. His reference to 'counting up the spoons' notes the way the hospital's staff accounted for every eating utensil after meals in order to ensure that none of the patients carried a potential weapon.

'Rainy Day Man' and 'Night Owl' were also written when Taylor was with the Flying Machine. These three songs became well known long after the band broke up when Taylor recorded them on a major label.

Taylor and Wiesner wrote 'Rainy Day Man' in the apartment of one of his girlfriends, who lived on Fourth Street. Years later when the song got more attention most people suggested that the 'Rainy Day Man' was a heroin dealer – something that Taylor denies to this day, even though he was using heroin at the time.

'That would be a reasonable interpretation of it,' Taylor told *Billboard* magazine. 'And certainly, at the time I was dabbling. But I didn't really have that in mind. The lyric is pretty much self-explanatory; it just says it will do you no good to try to cheer up someone in this state. What they need to do is to go down, all the way down, to the bottom.'

These songs were typical of Taylor's songwriting for years to come. In his lyrics, he liked to emphasise that the events of his personal life heavily influenced his art. Indeed, his gift for bringing to life and communicating his experiences with love, hate and social injustice found expression over his entire career. Taylor has been one of the few artists of the last 30 years to consistently use flawless imagery. He forged his reputation by creating imagery that never wavered in expressing his true inner feelings.

The Flying Machine got its break after a producer for a local label heard the band play and offered members a record deal. Chip Taylor (no relation) had produced several records and also gained a good reputation as a songwriter with 'Wild Thing' and 'Angel of the Morning'. He thought the group's sound needed polishing, but he was impressed by the boys' charisma and enthusiasm. He signed them to a deal with Jubilee Records. No guarantees were made and the boys were a bit wary, but they didn't have anything else lined up – so they decided to take a chance. If nothing came of it, they reasoned, at least they would have a record to show off.

In September 1966, on a shoestring budget, the group recorded 'Night Owl' as a single, with 'Brighten Your Night With My Day' on the flip side. They had more than enough material to produce an entire album but couldn't raise enough money to do it. The session went smoothly, despite the usual fooling around and ritual alcohol, drugs and late-night partying that accompanied so many musicians to the studio. Each of the band's members, however, knew right away that his performance was mediocre at best, and that their chance of attracting major-record-label interest was slim.

'We really didn't know what we were doing during this time,' Taylor said. 'It was all innocent fun. Those were the days when you did music for the love of it and never really worried about the business aspect of it. Sure, we were broke, but it didn't matter. All that mattered was making music and having fun.'

Even this early in his career, Taylor had established a pattern in his recording sessions that he would continue throughout the years with only minor variations. He composed many of his lyrics and melodies during the sessions, rather than spending a vast amount of time touching up guitar and vocal tracks (as most major artists did). He firmly believed in capturing the moment and the feeling of playing live.

The atmosphere in the Flying Machine was poisoned by the lack of success the single achieved, and a couple of the band's members grew impatient of their hand-to-mouth existence. Zach Wiesner, the group's bass player, was homesick and left the band after only three months. 'I needed a change,' Wiesner said. 'It was hard being in a band and making enough to survive. Everybody was strung out in those days and I felt like I was going nowhere.'

Also, the band was deeply concerned about Taylor's drug habits, which started to intensify. Taylor was a free spirit. One minute he would be practising his guitar and the next he would lie unconscious on the floor, not caring who saw him. It is hard to exaggerate the calamitous consequences Taylor's disposition produced. Even Wiesner, his staunchest defender, was not thrilled by Taylor's behaviour. Before he quit the group he expressed his concerns to James. 'It was hard because there were so many drugs around,' Wiesner said. 'There were occasions when I told James to try to control himself before he ruined his life. We were young and naive and were living right in the heart of all the action of New York. I was worried because things were getting out of hand and that's why I decided to leave the band. I didn't leave angry or bitter. I cared a lot about Kootch and James and to this day I still consider them to be good friends.'

The failure of the band's first recording and Wiesner's departure resulted in Taylor going through another period of abject depression. Again he felt alone and suicidal. He once told Kootch that he didn't expect to live more than another couple of months.

Everyone, except Taylor, felt he was talented. No matter what accolades his friends and family paid to his musical ability, he knew that there were many people who could play guitar and sing better than he could. But Taylor had no ambition to pursue anything else in life, so he persisted. And when things got too heavy, he had his booze and drugs to turn to for relief.

Now 19, he spent his days hanging out and thinking about the meaning of life in the Minetta Tavern Restaurant at the corner of Minetta Lane and MacDougal. The place was legendary for being frequented by celebrities, artists, and progressive types who drank there during the day before heading to a jazz or folk club in the evening.

'It was a cool place to be,' Taylor remembered. 'Kootch and I would plan our set for that night before heading over to the Night Owl. Occasionally you'd see well-known people in there. It was a good place to hang out in because of the relaxing atmosphere. Everybody in there felt at home.'

He missed the more natural, rural setting of North Carolina but stayed in New York for a year and a half out of loyalty to Kootch, who had a lot riding on this music project. Taylor didn't want to abandon his longtime buddy.

Taylor, to this day, has always stayed loyal to his friends, often helping them when they needed him. He even stays in touch with some of his ex-girlfriends, many of whom he felt he betrayed. 'James was always supportive of the people who were good to him,' his mother said. 'No matter how many problems he had, he'd never put them on other people. He's never been close to a lot of people, but the ones that he is good friends with he treats like a friend for life.'

By the time 1967 rolled around, James was in a bind. He had become dependent on heroin and was spending every penny he had buying it. His life was again in disarray. Not only was he stoned out of his mind during the day, but the other members of his band had grown weary of his being late for rehearsals and showing up drunk and high at gigs.

Repeatedly told by everybody around him to control his drinking and drug intake, Taylor still lived in denial and seemed intent on ruining himself. He couldn't stop. During the day he would hang out with seedy characters, including dope dealers, junkies and strippers. If they needed a place to crash, a benevolent Taylor would give them the keys to his room. When he got up in the morning he started his day by shooting up. His weight slipped from 160 to 145 pounds and he was as white as a ghost. He couldn't leave the drugs alone. He was becoming very temperamental and would often sit for hours alone, staring. His band mates knew that it was only a matter of time before his addictions tore the group apart.

Taylor had also started rehearsing songs on his own and devoting more energy to his own material. He was not motivated or inspired to contribute anything to the band. Often, he would sit alone in Washington Square Park in the Village with his guitar and compose songs. He liked to mingle with several of the junkies who hung around the square, smoking pot with them to help stimulate his creative juices. Sometimes he would stay late into the night, falling asleep stoned with his guitar by his side. He would wake up in a slumped position and saunter home in the early hours of the damp, dark morning. Then he fell into bed and woke up at four or five in the afternoon. Taylor's mood swings were a sore point for everybody. His band mates stopped hanging out with him and so did several of the close friends he had made in the Village. He was no longer pleasant to be around because it was impossible to forecast what state of mind he would be in.

'He was a young kid who was messed up,' said Joe Walker, a New York musician who hung out with Taylor several times. 'He had all the talent in the world but he was overcome with his insecurities. I really felt bad for him because I thought he was such a nice guy who shouldn't have been involved with a lot of the people he was hanging out with. It was obvious that he was heavily into drugs and that they were taking a toll on him because every time I saw him he seemed to have become more bummed out.'

'His mood changed after about six months in New York, and he started to self-destruct,' Kortchmar said. 'I was concerned about him because he was hanging out with some shady characters. But there was nothing I could do because James has always been his own person and he'll do what he's got to do. He's always been one to live and learn.'

Taylor's parents had no idea that their son was in dire straits. He was much sicker than they could have imagined. In their weekly telephone conversations, James tried to sound upbeat and stressed how well things were going. 'We'll soon have a record deal,' he told his father. 'Things are great and we're making good money doing shows. After we get a record deal, we'll do a tour and then I'll come home and spend some time with the family.'

Taylor's involvement with two notorious Village dopeheads was the start of what would result in two torrid decades of consuming herculean quantities of pills, heroin and booze. They dealt drugs in the Village and, when desperate for cash, would resort to robbing people. They were typical New York street hustlers. Both were well known to the police and had spent considerable time in prison before turning 20. They found a sympathetic friend in Taylor and asked him if they could move in with him after a warrant had been issued for their arrest. Without hesitation, Taylor allowed them to stay with him. He thought they were genuinely nice; he also felt they'd be able to help feed his drug habit. Bobby and Smack enjoyed hearing Taylor sing and play guitar, and that was another reason why he let them move in; even though he was shy, he needed people around to flatter and reassure him.

The two undesirables also made sure that he was always supplied with drugs. Traces of alcohol and drugs could be found everywhere – used needles under the bed and in the bathroom, pot stashed in the pockets of shirts hanging in the closet. Empty flasks littered the bedroom floor, along with the previous night's round of empty beer bottles.

The three friends injected heroin during the day and drank and smoked dope late at night when Taylor came back from his gigs. James was sinking deeper into a mentally unstable state. He was reaching the point of desperation and would verbally lash out at anyone who dared to criticise him.

As time passed Taylor tired of living in a dump. He had suddenly gone from a boy in an affluent family to living like a desperate pauper. Many times he had thought about what would happen if he died. Maybe if his life ended he would be at peace and relieved of his misery. Taylor often said he was not afraid to die but deep down he wasn't sure. In North Carolina he often felt he loved life and looked forward to each new day. Now, he didn't want to face the world, which seemed to him to be cruel and evil.

'Why are so many people poor and less fortunate?' he often asked his friends. 'Why are so many people greedy and evil?' He found it difficult to accept reality, and his only way out was to fool himself with drugs.

He reached the point where he did drugs all day in his room and emerged only when he had to. He constantly felt sick to his stomach and experienced several mental blackouts. He could barely remember what he'd done the previous day. There were very few times in New York when Taylor wasn't totally out of it. He barely took care of himself.

His father remembered getting a phone call in March 1967, when 19-year-old Taylor finally faced the moment of truth. James and Isaac had had their differences in recent years, and their relationship often seemed strained when they were in the same room. James's contempt for his father had grown since the older man had returned home from the Antartica only to avoid his family, leaving Trudy to care for their children. James always remained polite but distant when he was with his father. As a boy he'd often asked his father for advice and for help in things like fishing, sailing and rebuilding motorboat engines. Now his father had become no more than an acquaintance. James tried to avoid asking him for any favours because in many ways he felt his father had betrayed him. So when Isaac got the phone call, it was the perfect opportunity for redemption.

'I could sense that James was desperate,' Isaac Taylor said. 'I told him to stay put and that I'd go right away to New York and take him back home. I asked him for his address and at first he was reluctant to give it to me. He said, "Dad, don't worry about a thing. I'll be fine." But I knew that he was in trouble and I wanted to help my son. Many times in my life I felt bad because I wasn't around a lot for my children when they were growing up. But this time I made sure that I was there for James. He really needed me.'

Isaac Taylor rented a station wagon and drove from Chapel Hill to New York, stopping only for gas, to pick up his disoriented son. During the ride, Isaac broke down in tears several times because he couldn't help feeling responsible for his son's personal woes. He wondered if his children could have avoided their problems if he'd been around for them more often – if he'd been a better father. When he reached New York, Isaac gathered up all of his son's belongings and drove James home. During the ride back to North Carolina James thanked his father profusely for coming for him, and promised to make it up to him.

'Don't worry,' Isaac said. 'Things happen and that's what family is for. You'll go home and clear your mind and everything will work out. And we're always behind you a hundred percent. No matter what happens.'

Taylor said one last goodbye before he left. He told Kootch that he had decided to leave New York. Kootch had always been the first to come to Taylor's defence, but now he realised that his friend was in dire need of help. 'Go home and clean yourself up,' Kootch said. 'When you get yourself together we'll start another band. It's time for both of us to move on right now. If we don't, we're going to both wind up on skid row.'

The Flying Machine was finally grounded. The band's last two gigs were played at a United Jewish Appeal fashion show and at a club called the Joker's Wild in Freeport, Bahamas. Both were a disaster; the boys appeared tired of playing together. Then everybody went their own way. All that was left were the recordings and the many memorable gigs together. 'I became a better musician in New York,' Taylor said. 'But I got too caught up in drugs. I definitely got a quick lesson in life there. I hung out with all kinds of strange characters and really got caught up in the Village life. There were times when I thought that I'd never get out of there alive.'

6

BACK HOME

James Taylor returned to his parents' home for a six-month period of self-imposed detoxification and rest. Both Isaac and Trudy tried to convince him to enrol in college. Taylor, however, still only had visions of becoming a musician. His brothers and sister had improved as instrumentalists, and they spent time jamming together during his return. It was good for James to be surrounded again by the familiar faces of friends and family. He was temporarily able to erase from his mind the problems that had made his life miserable during the past few years.

Taylor went on the annual summer excursion with his family to Martha's Vineyard and did all the outdoor activities, like camping and swimming, that he'd missed during his stay in New York. His drug habits improved during this time; even though he smoked a lot of pot and enjoyed having a couple of drinks, he did stop using heroin.

Labour Day weekend brought the family together for one last time. Energised by the familiar faces and landscape around him, Taylor enjoyed every moment he spent back in North Carolina. But he didn't feel fulfilled. He was certain that soon he would return to a life of music.

Before long, Taylor made an announcement that would change his life forever: he told his family he was moving to England. On impulse, he'd purchased a plane ticket to London. His parents were stunned. They pleaded with him to reconsider because they were afraid that he might mess himself up the way he had in New York. 'Maybe it's too soon for you to move again,' his father told him. 'You just got back from New York and you need time to recuperate from your experience there. And besides, London is too far. If something happens there, you'll be at the other end of the world.'

Taylor missed the freedom he enjoyed in New York. At his parents' home he felt like he was being watched 24 hours a day because of their concerns about his drug habits. When he was on his own he did whatever he pleased, whenever he wanted. He was free to roam and felt unfettered and alive. He still felt the painful scars of failing in New York and was determined to become a success in England. 'Sometimes you have to go somewhere else to get noticed and get the recognition you deserve,' Taylor often said. 'Very few people make it in their hometown.'

Taylor's family continued to plead with him until the day he left. It was hard not to notice how thin and pale he already looked. They wondered what would happen to him if he went away again and returned to drugs. His parents threatened to cut him off financially, and his siblings warned him he was making a big mistake. 'Don't go,' Kate said. 'After everything you've been through, how can you be leaving so soon again? Stay for the sake of Mom and Dad. They're worried sick about you.'

The one ally James found was his rebellious brother Alex, who encouraged him to pursue his lifelong dream and kept him from feeling utterly alone. 'If you stay here you'll never make it,' Alex told James. 'Nobody gets a record deal in North Carolina. You have to go to the big city. England's the place. All the big bands are coming out of there now. Don't listen to what everybody tells you. Use your own judgement. If music is what you want to do, then don't let anybody stop you. You only live once.'

Taylor knew that his decision had broken his parents' heart. Most of his disputes with them were about the people he chose to hang out with and the direction in which he was heading. They tried to be sympathetic to his drug problems and hoped that he would eventually grow out of them. 'Every kid was experimenting with drugs back then,' Isaac said. 'We knew our son had a problem and the only thing to do was to help him and not condemn him.'

Taylor did not worry about his decision. No facts or arguments could have changed his mind to go abroad. It was time to move on, time for him to pursue his dream of becoming a well-known musician. He convinced himself that he had nothing to lose – no firm commitments at home, no school, no job. The last thing he wanted to do was to settle down.

Before he left, James met privately with his mother. Taylor's respect for Trudy never wavered, as it sometimes did for his father. He'd always admired her ability to lead the family while Isaac was away and he held her in the highest regard for her lifelong commitment to human rights and freedom of speech. Her liberal values were to be keys to Taylor's character and attitude later on as a grown man.

Taylor tried to calm his mother's fears. He noticed that Trudy, still with a fine-looking graceful figure, appeared tired and pale. She seemed genuinely distraught. 'I just want you to be happy,' she told him. 'I think it's great that you have dreams but I'm worried about your condition. You've been through so much.'

A hushed silence came over them for a couple of minutes. Then Taylor tried to reassure his worried mother. He kissed her forehead and took her hand and squeezed it. He promised that he would only be gone for a short time.

'You and Dad said that you always wanted us to pursue our dreams,' he said. 'Well, I love being at home here but I have unfinished business to do. Music is my life and I have to live it now. I'm sorry for all the pain I've caused you and Dad, but I'll make it up to you and the entire family one day. Right now I just want to live the life of an artist and express myself. And to do that I need inspiration, which I hope to find in London.'

Isaac told James to call him immediately if anything went wrong abroad. This meant a lot to James, because it reassured him of his parents' love and support. All of Taylor's siblings have always agreed that no matter what trouble they got themselves into, their parents' support was there for them.

'You must support your children no matter how severe the problem is,' Isaac used to say. 'Every family goes through its ups and downs, but parents have a responsibility and duty to be there for their kids when they are needed the most. If you can't fall back on your parents, then you can't fall back on anybody in life. It's that simple.'

'The Taylors went through a lot of hard times,' recalled one family friend. 'But their commitment to each other remained strong. I felt bad for Trudy. She was such a wonderful woman. She had to put up with so much crap from her children and her husband. If not for her, things would have become so much worse. She's a very strong person. Somehow she was able to deal with all the problems and keep the family relatively intact.'

7

THE BRITISH INVASION

London had long since emerged from the gloom of postwar austerity. The rock 'n' roll era had just got under way. On the Tuesday Taylor arrived in March 1968, it was damp and chilly and the streets were filled with immigrants from Spain, the Middle East, India and Africa. Taylor could hardly believe how multi-ethnic the city was. He had envisioned a London filled with white men in business suits and bowler hats. Although he was jet-lagged, he couldn't sleep because he was so in awe of the city and the London scene. In the following days, he would walk for miles in the West End and marvel at his new surroundings. He enjoyed hearing people talk with an English accent, and he got a kick out of the red double-decker buses. When he had nothing to do he often rode on the top level of a double decker, usually stoned, for hours to get a view of the streets of London. He loved the variety and vibrancy that filled the historic city.

The first thing that caught Taylor's attention was the legendary fogs. The second was the many black people with English accents. 'After being in New York for so long it was weird to hear a black person talk with a distinguished English accent instead of talking the street language that a lot of blacks use in New York,' Taylor said. 'From the first day I arrived there, I felt very inspired.'

After a stop for a coffee at a trendy café in the Bayswater area during that long first day, Taylor strolled up and down Oxford Street and eventually wound up in a pub in Covent Garden. He knew that this was the city renowned for giving many great writers and artists their first break. Taylor immediately felt more at home in London than he had in New York; he found the English city was more laid-back, and he also felt somewhat more important and special because he had a different accent than the majority of people. When he went to a local shop or asked someone for directions they usually noticed his American accent and asked him where he'd come from. 'I always loved travelling,' Taylor once said. 'And when I lived in London it was interesting the way people would always treat me so nice because they noticed my accent and they were curious what I was doing there.'

Taylor had gone to London to find himself, both spiritually and artistically. It meant a lot to him that one of his heroes, Jimi Hendrix, had already achieved stardom in London; England was also the home of the Beatles and the Rolling Stones. Hendrix, like Taylor, had spent considerable time in New York before Chas Chandler discovered him playing in the Village's Café Wha and convinced him he would get greater recognition and acclaim playing in England. Hendrix quickly gave England the biggest dose of black music it had ever seen and within weeks of his arrival became England's biggest guitar sensation, even overtaking British rock gods Eric Clapton and Pete Townshend. Taylor wondered if he could achieve just a fraction of Hendrix's success with his folky pop style.

Taylor rented a room in a flat in London's artsy Notting Hill Gate district, the same area where Hendrix lived. Notting Hill Gate was full of inexpensive restaurants, antiques shops along Portobello Road and lots of alternative-looking flower-power hippies and musicians. The skinny, long-haired Taylor, wearing a blue-jean jacket and toting a backpack, fitted right in.

'Notting Hill was always the place in London where the progressive artist types hung out,' said Colin Crowe, a London musician who has lived in the area for more than thirty-five years. 'And it's always been one of the best places to get the best drugs in London. There's lots of dealers there. A lot of London's well-known musicians have come here for years to get their drugs. During the '60s, Portobello Road was where all the action was. I remember seeing guys like Van Morrison play on the street there before they became well known. John Lennon and Mick Jagger were regularly spotted there. It was so vibrant, more vibrant than even New York or Paris. Everybody was into peace and love. The artists here were treated with respect and they were able to make money.

'I think James Taylor got a lot of his creative influence in Notting Hill, because it showed up in his music in years to come. He was a subdued combination of Van Morrison, Paul McCartney, and a mellower John Lennon. I have a few musician friends who hung out with him, and by all accounts he was a very likeable guy. He was eager to learn and develop his career. When he heard another musician play a cool riff, he'd ask the musician to show it to him. He was very curious and open to learning new things. That's one of the big reasons why he was able to get a record deal and do so well. He wasn't pretentious and he didn't put himself above anybody else.'

Taylor's rise to stardom began in London. His late-night jam sessions in pubs and cafés along Portobello Road are legendary. He also played guitar on the street occasionally to pick up some extra spending money. The lanky party boy could often be seen drinking beer at the local pub at a table full of musicians and beautiful women. Sometimes his critics sputtered and fumed, because they thought Taylor had ulterior motives.

'He used to come into the Portobello Road Café with his guitar and play a few tunes,' recalled Jack Hawkins, who had an antique jewellery stall on Portobello Road during the '60s and '70s. 'I remember him well because he was so tall and a bit goofy looking. He used to play outside on the street quite a bit, too. But it looked more to me that he was playing to get the women's attention. Whenever a beautiful girl passed, he'd give her the eye and try to impress her with his guitar.'

The free-floating Taylor found much more success with women in London than he had at home. Even though he was usually shy because of his thinness and tremendously long arms and legs, he didn't hesitate to converse and feed the routine pickup lines to women. Indeed, he often chatted up women in the middle of one of his sets and went back to their apartments when he finished work. 'I wanted to emote and really get as much attention and satisfaction and gratification as I could,' Taylor said in a *Rolling Stone* magazine interview. 'I wanted to perform. I wanted to write songs and I wanted to get a lot of chicks.'

Taylor was on a roll and he wouldn't let any of his hang-ups disturb the success and fun he was enjoying. There were so many women around that he developed a strategy of moving immediately to another woman if one he hit on resisted him. By the end of the night, he'd usually found someone to go home with.

Most of the musicians Taylor knew in London also had day jobs. The cost of living was high, and it was almost impossible to eke out enough money by playing music unless you had a record deal. Taylor didn't have working papers and most club owners were afraid to hire him because he would be working illegally. Also, the competition was stiff; most artists had booking agents who usually got first call on new gigs, making it more difficult for guys like James to get hired.

Taylor had experienced a long drought in his sex life because of the time he spent at Milton and McLean. He wanted to make up for lost time. Even though things had not gone the way he planned, he was staying out all night hanging out with girls and partying. He gave up trying to get gigs and decided to make a demo to pitch to record labels. He knew that if it was half decent, he had a good chance of getting signed. Record companies were desperate for new talent, because hungry music fans were always seeking something new.

'The late '60s was a time when record labels were signing almost anybody who walked through the door with a guitar in his hands,' said Robert Katz, a former executive with Mercury Polydor Records. 'Records were selling as fast as we put them in the stores. When we signed somebody, sometimes we put him in studio the same day and stuck a microphone in front of him right away and recorded an album within a few days. It was the wildest time ever in music. We'd pluck unknowns off the street and make them into stars within a matter of weeks. Most of them wound up having short careers and very few of them are making records today.

'When James Taylor came to London it was a gimme that he'd get signed. He was different from most of the other artists; he was willing to pay the price for fame. He liked to work hard. Sure, he was a bit messed up, but so was everybody else, including myself, at that time. I used to keep a bag of cocaine, some weed and at least two bottles of Scotch in my desk at all times. And I restocked it at least twice a week. The thing about Taylor was that he was erudite and it was easy for him to appeal to the same people who were into Bob Dylan or Pete Seeger. And whoever signed him was right because 30 years later he's still at the top and is one of the most respected musicians of all time.'

Taylor looked in the classified sections of several local newspapers for deals on recording; he wound up paying eight pounds to record his music in a rundown two-track studio in London's Soho district. He recorded all his songs live to tape and used up all of the 45 minutes of recording time he had paid for. He was interested in making a solo album and wanted to use this demo to get signed. He contacted his old pal Danny Kortchmar, who was in London working as a guitar session player, and asked him for help. Kootch had made lots of contacts in the music business since arriving in London the previous year. He told James that he would introduce him to the right people.

'Jimmy, this town isn't as difficult as New York was,' Kootch said.

'There's lots of opportunity here. Ever since I came here I've been working nonstop. You can do well here. Labels are signing people left and right. You've just got to work hard and try to get your foot through the door.'

Ambition was gnawing at Taylor. He wanted to become famous like Dylan and Jagger and win the respect and recognition they had. He dreamed about going to fancy parties with women draped around each arm.

'James used to say how much he wanted to be recognised wherever he went,' said Robert Moore, a London musician who met Taylor in 1968. 'He wanted to be the centre of attention, and music was his only way to achieve it. Sure, he was talented, but he seemed intent on pursuing music not so much for artistic reasons as for social reasons. He was a bit of an outcast and he wanted to be accepted by society.

'But he had this intense will to succeed that I had never seen in anybody else. He was going to succeed no matter what he had to do to achieve his goal. He deserves all the credit and respect in the world, because even though he wanted to be famous through music, he wasn't like a lot of other people who go into music for the fame and money and have as much talent as I do in my index finger. James was for real, he could write music, carry a tune and was a nasty guitar player. Throughout the years he's worked harder and harder to improve. Not many musicians last as long as he has.'

Kootch still believed that his good friend had the talent and charisma to become a recording star. The Beatles were actively pursuing new projects and talent for their highly successful Apple Corps and its associated enterprise, the Apple Records label. Apple Records had taken off after the release of its first single, the anthem-like Beatles rock ballad 'Hey Jude'. Fed up with the backroom politics that went along with working for a major label, the Beatles were looking to sign new artists to their label. They wanted to make millions of dollars selling records but also to promote artists, including dancers, painters and filmmakers.

'We want to see if we can get artistic freedom within a business structure . . . and sell,' John Lennon said. 'Without charging three times our cost.'

It happened that one of Kootch's good friends was involved in the project. Peter Asher was a bright, 24-year-old rock musician with the band Peter and Gordon; he'd been hired by Paul McCartney to serve as Apple's chief talent director. Kootch knew Asher because his band the King Bees had once toured with Peter and Gordon. Kootch figured that if he knew one guy who could finally get Taylor's career off the ground, it was Asher, who had become well known in British music circles and had the connections to get the right people to listen to Taylor's music.

McCartney had been impressed with Asher's profound knowledge of the London scene; he seemed to know everything about all the up-and-coming bands. The fact that McCartney was going out with Asher's sister Jane didn't hurt Asher's chances of getting hired, either. During their relationship McCartney bent over backward for Jane and her family. Jane was the woman everybody thought McCartney would marry before he met Linda.

In the beginning Asher's inexperience resulted in several boneheaded moves, such as hiring inexperienced musicians and arrangers. But he caught on quickly and in a short time had become one of the most powerful figures in the music business.

'Apple was a funny old place,' said musical arranger Richard Hewson. 'It was very haphazard. Nobody really knew what anybody else was doing! Peter didn't know anything about arrangers. All he knew was he knew me, and that I'd been to the Guild Hall and studied classical music. And he thought, "Okay, so Paul wants some orchestra on this. Richard probably knows how to write classical orchestra arrangements, let's try him." That's how I got the job, 'cause they didn't know anybody else. That was lucky for me. If they'd looked around, they could probably have found a real arranger.'

McCartney and the rest of the Beatles genuinely wanted other artists to enjoy success similar to his own. 'After all that the Beatles have been through, we want to help other artists avoid getting screwed by greedy music executives,' McCartney said of Apple. 'Almost anybody who walks through our door with some talent will get a shot. As long as they're not cocky and as long as they're committed to making good music. . . . There's really no limits to what we're trying to do. We're open for suggestions.'

Taylor and Asher hit it off from the moment Kootch introduced them. They talked at length about Taylor's experience in New York, and how he'd wound up in London. Asher was impressed with Taylor's determination to be a musician and the gruelling time he had already spent trying to achieve his goal. Asher knew that Taylor came from an affluent family and could have easily lived in a world of luxury and self-indulgence instead of pursuring the life of a struggling artist.

Taylor repeatedly told Asher how much it meant to him to get a chance to sign with Apple Records. He promised not to let Asher down. 'All that I need is some backing and promotion,' James said, 'the rest will take care of itself. I'm willing to work very hard to make this project a success. This is my dream and I don't want to blow it.'

The task facing Asher was immense, but he felt optimistic because of Taylor's positive attitude. A compulsive achiever, Asher wanted to work with somebody to whom he wouldn't have to explain how to get things done. Taylor was now enough of a veteran to realise that recording an album was a lot of hard work and required self-motivation and discipline. If Asher came through for him there was no way Taylor would fail him, unless he had another big emotional relapse.

'London's a safer version of New York,' Asher told him. 'Most likely we'll sign you because you deserve a chance to record your music. It's good.'

Asher was impressed with Taylor's demo and told the singer he'd recommend to McCartney that Apple sign him to record a full-length album. Asher thought Taylor's music was inspirational. He was impressed by the smoothness of Taylor's voice and the rapid fluidity of his phrasing. He also thought that Taylor was more original than many of the other unknown artists from whom he had received demos. He understood that James was somewhat of a damaged young man because of his past. But he wasn't deterred. He had a knack for turning people's careers and lives around.

'He's got something special,' Asher told Kootch. 'His sound is fresh and unique. I'm making no promises, but I think it's worth taking a shot. I think that people in London will embrace his style and music with open arms.'

When Asher signed new artists, he was always very concerned about their look and presentation. Originality went a long way with him. He thought people would be interested in Taylor's quirkiness and that his soft American accent would bemuse the British people.

'James has a good look,' Asher told Kootch. 'His look is very distinct and a lot of kids today can relate to the way he looks and dresses. The word hippie is written all over him. I'm not a gambling man, but if I was I'd bet that James will be a big star one day soon.'

Taylor told Asher that he wanted to produce an album without the many effects and overdubs that had become the trend for many popular recording artists. Taylor wanted to capture a live feel. Asher saw Taylor's primary strength as being able to express his true feelings, and thought the music world was ripe for another giant folk star on the heels of Bob Dylan, who for years produced such influential folk rock.

'James had been through so much by the time he was 20 that he had so much to express in his music,' Asher said. 'Other young artists of his age whom I worked with sang about how good or bad life was but really had no idea what they were singing about. James was already singing with the conviction of a singer much older than himself. Everything that he had already been through was evident in his songwriting.'

Asher was impressed the way Taylor seemed able to borrow from the style of traditional folk songs and compose passionate and eloquent lyrics about hope and hardship mixed with timely rhythms to create a unique sound.

Within a week of their meeting, Asher played Taylor's demo for McCartney – who loved it. McCartney's own approach to songwriting had always been to construct strong melodies covered with meaningful, catchy lyrics. He told Asher to sign Taylor right away and to start working on an album. He also asked Asher to make sure Taylor didn't sign with anybody else even though Apple was rumoured to be financially strapped.

'Apple was signing so many unknowns at the time that they went way over budget and were in deep trouble,' said Mary Blackwell, a former London-based record executive who knew several people who worked for Apple. 'When Peter Asher signed James Taylor the label was on the verge of going under, and I don't think Taylor was too aware of that. He didn't care because all that he seemed to be interested in was getting his name on a label to get his career going. So many people's career went out the window because of Apple's desperate financial situation. I think Taylor was one of the first artists they signed, so his career was a bit safer. But his album would have been much bigger if Apple had had its act together.

'Taylor signed with them when the Beatles knew that it was only a matter of time before they'd break up. They were feuding like cats and dogs. I once went to a big party in London's West End that was thrown by Mick Jagger, and I had the opportunity to meet and talk to John Lennon. John showed up alone at the party and I wound up speaking to him for more than an hour. He told me how much he despised what was going on with the Beatles and Apple. I couldn't believe it because he went on and on about how pissed off he was. He said he felt bad for all the artists Apple signed because they were being misled and were not receiving what had been promised to them. John said that it had all turned into a nightmare and the Beatles couldn't even stand working with each other anymore.'

In fact, Apple was on the verge of closing its doors. After the official launching of Apple Records with the August release of 'Hey Jude' – the blockbuster ballad that topped the US charts for weeks, and that McCartney said he wrote for Lennon's son Julian – the Beatles spent millions producing unknown artists. Their accountants warned them that their expenditures had gone way over budget. If they didn't close Apple's doors, they were told, the four Beatles could put their own fortunes in jeopardy. This caused a lot of tension among John, Paul, George and Ringo and hastened their breakup a couple of years later.

'It was a very crazy time in our careers,' John Lennon said. 'Everything was happening so fast that we barely had a chance to catch our breath. We knew right away that there would be lots of problems when we formed Apple, because there was already so much tension among us. But we lived in denial and did it anyway. "Hey Jude" was a success, but from then on everything went into a big downhill slide. And the atmosphere was very unpleasant to be around. I avoided going there as much as possible because I knew that if I went I'd only argue with the other lads.'

Getting a recording contract was the crowning achievement of a singer's career. Taylor thought that he would instantly become a celebrity once he signed with Apple. Asher told him that the Beatles' celebrity would only add to Taylor's forthcoming fame.

'Apple's the best choice for you. You'll get a lot of publicity because the Beatles own the label,' Asher told him. 'Any singer would give his right arm for an opportunity like this. Let's try to take full advantage of the situation.'

Taylor needed musicians to play on his album so he placed an ad in the two biggest British music magazines, *Melody Maker* and *New Musical Express*. He convinced the old drummer of the Flying Machine, Joel O'Brien, to come to London and record with him. To this day Taylor credits O'Brien as one of a handful of people who helped him evolve into a better musician. In only a few days he put together a band and they started recording an album at Trident Studios.

The Beatles were in the midst of completing their *White Album* at Trident at the same time Taylor was in the studio; he had to work his recording time around the Beatles' schedule. He even got to sit in on several of the Beatles' recording sessions, and became friendly with McCartney and George Harrison. McCartney appreciated Taylor's enthusiasm and enjoyed swapping stories about New York with him. Taylor loved hearing about his hero's experiences in the United States when the Beatles first conquered audiences there a few years earlier. For a while Taylor was so close to the Beatles that he almost felt like their fifth member. They treated him with respect and even helped him out on his album by sitting in on sessions, recording some backup vocals and making suggestions about recording techniques that were instrumental in the creation of a great album.

'We were trying to help young artists get with their careers,' John Lennon said. 'People like Taylor showed up at our door and if they had talent we would give them a chance to step into the studio and record. It was a very hectic time. When word spread that the Beatles were searching for talent, we were overwhelmed with offers from all kinds of managers, artists and industry people. It was impossible for us to consider all the offers. It was very time consuming.'

A relative newcomer to the corporate side of the music industry, Asher was determined to pull every lever and collect every IOU he had already earned to make sure Taylor's debut was a success. He tried to persuade all the journalists he knew to review Taylor's album. He also went personally to the major radio stations and played Taylor's music for DJs, hoping to get some airplay.

'In those days, managers and A&R people in the music business walked right into the station with a record and tried to get the DJ to play it right away,' said Brian Whitmore, a former London BBC radio program director. 'Sometimes the DJ would play the song, and if the people listening liked it, the lines would light up with requests right away. Peter Asher was one of those guys who was young and tenacious and he'd do everything possible to try to get airplay for his artists. He was brilliant because he went about it in a more subtle way than everybody else and it worked. You knew right away when you met him that he would be a key player in the music business, because he was smart and he knew how to deal with people better than most other people in the business. He was the type of guy who met you once and when you bumped into him again a few months later, he'd call you by your first name.'

Taylor became the first foreign artist to get a contract with Apple. Never in his wildest dreams had he thought he would become an artist on Paul McCartney's label. When he left America, he just wanted to earn enough playing gigs to support his travels in Europe. At best he felt he might get a deal with a small label and record an album in a dingy studio in some unglamorous neighbourhood. But now he was working for Paul McCartney, who had been his hero for years.

'It was a very high scene,' Taylor later recalled in a *Rolling Stone* interview. 'It was as though, finally, here are some people who have a company and at the same time they're sympathetic to the artist's point of view. They're not just stock owners or chairmen of the boards. They're actually musicians and artists and it sort of had that feeling to it. It was a very exciting company to work for, but I guess there was really no one there who was looking out for the budget, and an awful lot of money went out, and they just about went broke and had to slow it down.'

McCartney was Taylor's favourite Beatle. James respected John Lennon's gritty voice and his determination and passion to focus his music on politics, religion and the self. But he preferred McCartney's sunny and bright demeanour to Lennon, who was fierce, hard and angst-ridden. He also thought McCartney was the most talented Beatle. If there was one musician whose career Taylor wanted to emulate, it was McCartney – who, like Taylor, was the creator of lilting ballads and soothing love songs.

'Things were a bit rough for James when he first got to London, because there wasn't a lot of work for him,' Kortchmar said. 'But things changed for him after he met Peter Asher. All of a sudden he was working for the world's best-known musician, Paul McCartney. James couldn't believe it. It was like totally living in a dream.'

Asher had already gained a reputation in the music industry for setting high goals. He lived, worked and loved according to his own set of rules and belonged to nobody but himself. He rarely speculated on his impulses and motives, and his personality was hard to gauge. He was affable and easy to get along with, but he could go from support to icy sarcasm in a flash. Taylor thought Asher was cast from a different mould than the archetypal record executive. And he was right. As the business – and the money that came with it – grew, Asher did not try to restrict his artists. He encouraged them to let it all hang out.

'Even though Peter was working for McCartney, he was still in total control of his own destiny,' Taylor once said. 'I knew from the first time that we met that he was the right person to steer my career. He had this determination in his eye that I had never seen in anybody before.'

Asher never wasted time. He arranged immediately for Taylor to enter a London studio to rerecord his material. Asher produced the record and used his musical knowledge to make the changes he thought were necessary to help Taylor become a star. A couple of months later, in November 1968, Taylor's debut album, *James Taylor*, was released in Britain. The album received a number of good reviews but commercially it turned out to be a flop. Most critics agree that if Apple had been on more solid financial ground, Taylor's album would have received much more attention than it did.

Several musicians and members of the production team who worked on Taylor's debut album blamed the album's lack of success on Taylor, who appeared stoned out of his mind at many of the recording sessions.

'He was very nice,' recalled Richard Hewson, who created several string arrangements on the album. 'He was an easygoing guy, but he was really out of it at the time. Quite weird, actually. He went to a mental home shortly after that.'

Hewson added that Taylor's album was destined for failure from the start because of Apple's financial troubles. 'After they released *Those Were the Days* [Mary Hopkin] it was all downhill,' said Hewson. 'Apple signed some good talent but they weren't able to do much with it because they had money problems.'

James Taylor was a twelve-song album that most critics, in hindsight, agree was a disaster only because Apple Records did not spend enough money promoting it. With crisp harmonies and tight guitar playing, it was a more sophisticated pop album than almost anything else out on the market. It featured several of Taylor's tunes from his day with the Flying Machine, including 'Night Owl' and 'Knockin' 'Round the Zoo'.

A new song that would later become one of his anthem numbers, 'Carolina in My Mind', received much critical acclaim. In it, James expressed how homesick he was for the rural surroundings in which he grew up. McCartney liked the song and wound up playing bass on it. McCartney felt that Taylor's original version of 'Carolina in My Mind' was weak and decided to produce the final version himself. 'This song has a lot of potential,' McCartney told Taylor. 'It's very catchy. It is reminiscent of the old Beatles style. If we work hard on its arrangement, it might become a hit.'

Taylor says that he remembers writing 'Carolina in My Mind' in three different places. Part of it he wrote at Asher's flat on Marylebone High Street where Asher lived with his first wife. He composed other parts a few days later when he spent five days vacationing on Formentera, an island close to Ibiza. Taylor wrote the rest of the tune with a stunning girl he met there named Karen. James and Karen took the boat over to Ibiza for the day and missed the last boat back. So they decided to spend the evening nestled in a café that wasn't open. Taylor finished his song on a scrap piece of paper that he had picked up off the floor.

Taylor used to spend many nights during his travels in Europe charming women with his music and poetry. Women fell for it right away, and gave themselves up to him after falling under his artistic spell. Some of these affairs were no doubt platonic, even though his success rate at seducing women was very high. Taylor was about to become a star and women couldn't help themselves. Some of those whom he picked up in Europe got in touch with him years later when he was famous, some just to say hello, others to hit him up for money.

'Carolina in My Mind' was structured tightly with Taylor's sparkle-tone guitar style and his bright, calm voice over it. His description of his home was vivid and breathtaking. Even though he was now accustomed to the soot and traffic in the big city, he longed for the serenity and beauty of Carolina. His opening verse set the tone. 'The first time I heard it I had so many memory flashbacks,' said Edward Palmer, who lived in North Carolina for 20 years before moving to California. 'Still to this day I get nostalgic whenever I hear it on the radio. It's a song that makes anybody who grew up in North Carolina homesick. In a way, it's become an anthem song for people who left the state.'

Another successful track was 'Brighten Your Night With My Day', which dealt with Taylor's deep loneliness about love and life. 'It's a song that truly expressed what I was feeling back then,' he recalled. 'I wrote this song at a time when I was doing a lot of soul searching. I was trying to find out who I really was.'

The way Taylor crafted a song was brilliant. His poetry was dark, sometimes even morbid, but it was powerful. And he conveyed it in a much brighter fashion than did some of his contemporaries, like Bob Dylan and John Lennon. Although it was easy to tell that he was a man in deep distress if you paid attention to the lyrics, it was still good music to listen to. He never sounded angry in his songs and didn't resort to power chords and lots of distortion, which were becoming popular at that time.

Taylor's music was an extension of his peaceful and mellow personality. 'I just love singing and making people feel good,' he once said. 'And if they can get something out of the message I'm conveying, then I feel like I've really done my job. I don't think you have to sound angry and aggressive to get your message across in music. If you tell people things in a gentle way, then they're more likely to listen to you.'

Taylor's album had the key ingredients to engage and turn into fans those unfamiliar with his music and haunting lyrics. Reviewers wondered who was the young man behind this fresh, smouldering, mature voice that Apple Records was promoting. Some thought Taylor would be England's answer to Bob Dylan, a comparison Taylor found flattering but undeserved.

'Dylan is in a class of his own,' Taylor told a reporter. 'Everybody's got to have their own voice. I'm just trying to be me. I don't think it's fair at this point in my career to compare me to any of the greats. I'm just starting out and I have a lot of work to do.'

Taylor's album sparked a debate among some music critics. Most of the reviews he received were good, but a few were mixed. Many reviewers agreed that *James Taylor* was grippingly expressive and that the music represented a reality listeners could actually grasp. Some, however, argued that it engendered hostility and had little fervour behind it. Despite all the hype about his album, the British did not embrace Taylor the way they did musicians from their own country.

'It was a great album and it should have shot up the charts right away,' said Martin Smith, a longtime leading London music journalist. 'Maybe the fact that he was an American didn't improve his chances to get airplay. English people have always preferred to support their own artists first. Another problem was that the Beatles were feuding and were on the verge of breaking up when the album came out and they didn't want to inject any more money into Apple. Paul McCartney loved the album and he really believed that it was going to put Taylor on the musical map. But things just didn't work out. I'm sure Taylor would be the first one to admit today that no matter how good an album is, it will go nowhere unless there's a good marketing plan in place.

'If you really take a good listen to this album, I think that it was way ahead of its time. Most material coming out at this time all sounded the same. But Taylor's album sounded different; it had a remarkably fresh and sophisticated sound. I think his lyrics added a lot to it. To this day that album is still my favourite James Taylor album.'

Smith said that Taylor could have been a great marketing tool if he had the right promotional support. 'The British would have eaten him because he seemed to be so nice and he was an interesting-looking guy,' Smith said. 'At the time the only American to really break the British charts was Hendrix, and a lot of British people resented him because he was black. There were still a lot of racist attitudes haunting Britain then. They would have loved to support a white guy whose music many of them could have easily related to.'

Smith said that his favourite tracks on Taylor's album were 'Don't Talk Now' and 'Circle 'Round the Sun', because they struck a chord with society's youth. 'He was singing about the struggles and insecurities of being young in the '60s,' Smith said from his home in Streatham, a South London suburb. 'It seemed everybody else at that time was going the heavy electric route after Dylan abandoned his acoustic guitar. But James Taylor seemed to be able to bring back some sort of passion and reality to songwriting. If anything, his album was real and he became the voice for thousands of kids his age who were confused about life.'

At first, Taylor didn't care that his album wasn't selling. The fact that he'd got a deal was a far-reaching accomplishment for him. He had achieved his goal of being perceived as a somebody. He had no real sense yet of what the music business was really about. He didn't realise how important record sales were in a career. Taylor loved the thrill of live performance and became restless when he realised there were no touring plans to help support his album. He thought that once the album appeared, he would be overwhelmed with offers to perform gigs. It didn't happen. He was becoming more and more confused and told Asher that if things didn't shape up quickly he would leave London to pursue his career back home.

Asher knew that Taylor's career in England was doomed when Apple brought in legendary music impresario Allen Klein to try to rescue the company from bankruptcy. Klein, the pudgy, flamboyant manager of the Rolling Stones, had a reputation for being sleazy and ripping off his clients. He had tried unsuccessfully to wrest the Beatles away from Brian Epstein a few years back. Now was the perfect opportunity for him to prove himself. At the time, the Stones were embroiled in several contract disputes with Klein. Mick Jagger tried in vain to convince the Beatles not to do business with him. He told them that Klein was crooked – that in the two and a half years since he'd taken over as the Stones' manager the group had earned at least seventeen million dollars, but all of its members were still flat broke.

The only member of the Beatles to vote against Klein taking over was Paul McCartney. As soon as Klein's appointment was official, Asher started to sever ties with Apple.

'It was all a mess at Apple and Asher was very aware of the downside of having Klein in charge,' Martin Smith said. 'It was the final nail in the coffin. And in the end, everybody who was against Klein's hiring was right. Apple quickly went deeper into ruins once he was hired.'

But Taylor was still enthusiastic about his career, because magazines reviewed his album and his name was becoming known in music circles. He loved being recognised when he showed up at cafés and clubs. He pretended to be nonchalant about his newfound notoriety, yet he relished the moment whenever a woman recognised him or approached him to compliment him on his talent.

Several of his female admirers developed close friendships with him, some resulting in one-night stands. 'I remember he used to drink at a pub I went to in Notting Hill Gate,' said Alice Ridgely. 'Everybody knew he was a musician, and he used to tell people that he had an album coming out. He was definitely very popular with the ladies because he was good looking and had a certain charm. His body was attractive and it was common to see him meet a gorgeous girl in the pub and leave with her at the end of the night.'

Ridgely said many females clung to Taylor and began to idolise him. 'It seemed to flatter him but it got to the point where it was getting to be embarrassing,' Ridgely continued, 'For god's sake, the boy was only a musician and he couldn't have been a day over 21. There were other musicians who used to drink in the pub, but Taylor got a lot of the attention. He was quiet and women seemed to be intrigued with his mystique.'

The more success Taylor enjoyed with women, the more his emotional problems resurfaced. Every time he found a woman he liked he thought she was the answer to his problems. But it turned out to be the exact opposite. When he discovered that he wasn't compatible with her he would move on to the next, and the next. He had a romantic vision of meeting somebody who would share his interests; they would travel the world and sail off into the sunset together. He often told Kootch that he really wanted to stop dating so many women and find the right person so that he could settle down.

Taylor basked in glory for weeks before realising he had achieved fame without fortune. What's more, Apple was about to dissolve and he would soon be left again without a recording contract. The bloom was finally off the rose. James was homesick and told Kootch that he wanted to go back to the States. Before he left, however, he fell back into his old drug habits and was soon on the verge of another emotional breakdown. He was also burning out after too many drugs, too many women and too many late-night parties. He went on a bender and into a tailspin. He had never been more confused.

8

HEROIN AND ALCOHOL

Peter Asher couldn't believe that Taylor's record sales were so low. He'd thought for sure he had a hit album on his hands. Asher had never before met an artist who could inject freshness, subtlety, nuance, tension, tenderness and simplicity into his music the way James Taylor was able to do. He thought the man was a visionary. Yes, some of Taylor's lyrics were stern and eerie; still he had never heard anybody express them with such poignance.

Despite lack of sales for James Taylor, Asher remained eager and determined to make him a star. Usually in the music business, if an artist fails with his or her first album, the manager hesitates to do another album and searches instead for a new artist. But Asher strongly believed that Taylor was a victim of Apple's woes, and that if he shopped for a deal in the United States, things would change radically.

'Go home and we'll try to work out something in the States for you,' Asher told him. 'Your music is strong and we'll have a better shot selling it in the United States because of the strong folk scene there. England's different because they're more into heavier pop. They just aren't ready for your music now.'

Taylor called his parents and explained to them what was happening. His father urged him to return to North Carolina and enrol in college. 'Now's the time to get yourself together and have an education to fall back on. Travelling is a great education but eventually you've got to settle down and do something with your life. You can still do music, but you'll be able to learn something else that you'll be able to do for a living.'

Taylor understood his parents' concerns but was still adamant about pursuing his dream of playing music. 'Music is the one thing in my life that fulfills me,' he told them. 'I have no idea what I'd do if I didn't play music. But I'll come home soon and think about what I'm doing. I feel a bit confused again. But don't worry, I'm all right.'

In fact, Taylor was not all right. He was doing hard drugs again and felt suicidal. He didn't know how to handle what was going on with his career. He had heard a lot of promises in recent months but everything had seemed to crumble. He had deep trust in Peter Asher and Kootch but he didn't believe in many of the other people he met in the music business. He quickly realised that it was a cut-throat business – that people only wanted to be around you if you were hot.

'It was very difficult for James because when his album came out a lot of people clamoured to be around him, and he wasn't really used to this treatment,' Martin Smith said. 'After it became evident that his album was not going to soar up the charts, I think he became depressed because people were not flocking around him anymore. That's typical in the music business. He must have felt terrible because it was his first big music contract and the label he signed with was having problems, and not many people were buying his album. I've seen so many artists over the years simply fade into obscurity after incidents like that. I really admire him for eventually managing to bounce back.'

Before Taylor bounced back, however, he went through another bout of personal trauma that came close to destroying him. His return to drugs was not attributable only to his emotional problems. He was concerned about the plight of the world and felt there was little hope. In 1968, two people Taylor greatly respected, Martin Luther King Jr, and Bobby Kennedy, were assassinated, and race riots erupted after violent clashes between police and demonstrators outside the Democratic convention in Chicago. America's youth was starting to sway from its once-pacifist peace-and-love agenda.

Although he wanted to return home, Taylor did not feel patriotic toward his country. He also still spent sleepless nights worrying about the draft and Vietnam. He couldn't help but feel a world apart from and sorry for the thousands of soldiers who were risking their lives. He wondered if there was any chance that he could still be drafted when he returned to the States, even though he had already been rejected as mentally unfit.

England was supposed to be a respite and a fresh start for Taylor. His stint in New York was enough to give him a sample of a musician's life. There he had felt enervated by the frenetic pace of life; in England, however, he seemed to be more at home. He loved riding the Tube and strolling around the streets, popping in and out of cool secondhand bookstores and bohemian-style cafés. Sometimes he sat in Trafalgar Square for hours, feeding the pigeons and striking up conversations with interesting-looking people. The conversations usually had the same theme, art. Taylor enjoyed talking to people about not only music but also poetry, painting and writing. He liked to exchange notes with other artists. Doing so often inspired him to go back to his flat and write songs.

This was a far cry from the introverted, insecure teenager who'd almost self-destructed in New York only a year before. James had indeed made a lot of progress and seemed to be coming into his own – until he returned to drugs. Occasionally, he wouldn't hesitate to take out some heroin and dangle it before his rapt friends when he visited them. Many times he spent all night getting high with his musician and artsy companions.

He bought dope from dealers at private parties and in the bathrooms of trendy clubs. Afterward, he returned to his flat and spent the rest of the night getting high. 'That's how I spent most of my time in London,' Taylor admitted. 'I was always looking for a party and a fix. It was like my medicine.'

He usually got high the same way. He would come home, put on some music – generally Dylan or the Beatles – and smoke a cigarette. Then with a match he heated up teaspoons holding the precious grains of heroin mixed with a couple of drops of water. After waiting for the crystals to dissolve, he delicately placed the tip of his syringe into the solution and sucked up every drop.

Taylor then took off his belt and wrapped it around his upper arm, taking one end of the belt in his teeth to pull it tight so he could make the veins in his arm stand out. With the needle pointing upward, he tapped the syringe a few times and pushed out any little bits of air. Now he was ready for the ecstasy he hoped would come. He tapped the veins in the crook of his arm until he was able to find one that looked promising. Still holding the belt in his teeth, he used his free hand to delicately pierce the vein with the tip of the needle. To make sure that the needle was securely in the vein, and that he wouldn't waste a drop of heroin, he 'flagged' the needle by pulling up on the plunger until he verified that his blood was being sucked up into the syringe. Now he knew he had found his mark. With grim determination he slowly squeezed the plunger, forcing the contents of the syringe into his veins.

If he was lucky and hadn't been ripped off by the dealer, he would find his release and ecstasy just seconds later. After a hit wore off, Taylor usually sank into a deep depression, and he'd take another hit to soothe himself. Once he'd started it was difficult for him to stop. It was a roller-coaster ride and invariably he couldn't keep up the pace.

Taylor knew about all the horror stories linked with heroin use; many of his own friends and acquaintances had been seriously damaged, physically and mentally, by their addictions. Worse, many had died from overdoses or drug-related suicides. But James seemed willing to take the risk in order to gain new insights into his own creative processes. Many of his poetic, dark songs have their basis in the heroin-induced creativity during that period of his life.

Sometimes as he looked about his eleven-by-nine-foot London room, strewn with the remnants of partying and junkie guests who had crashed on the floor, he thought about how depressing his living conditions had become since leaving his affluent rural home in North Carolina. Yet he knew the only way to become an artist was to live life among young people who were struggling to evolve, just as he was. Often his friends would demand he help them find a hit. And just as often there was none to be found. His friends and sometimes he himself would lie shivering under the blankets and pillows in the throes of a heroin fit.

At age 20, Taylor was a physical and mental wreck, and he didn't think he would live long. He knew that heroin could easily kill him. He was looking thin, unkempt and pale. It was common for him to go a couple of days without a meal; his nourishment was drugs. What he did eat was usually fast food, like fish-and-chips from the restaurant a few doors away from his flat or cold submarines. Sometimes he wore the same pair of jeans for more than a month without washing them. He had no farther to fall. He had lost control.

Some drugs he couldn't absorb without losing control. One was acid, which gave Taylor the opportunity to escape into a world he called 'psychedelic paradise'. He could sit in his room and listen to rock music for hours in a deeply hallucinogenic state of mind. A heavy acid trip, he has often said, often inspired him to behave in a very unorthodox way.

'A long time ago in London when I was 19 or 20 I took an acid trip with a friend,' Taylor recalled in a 1981 *Rolling Stone* interview. 'There was a candle burning in the middle of the table and we were peaking. It melted down into the dish it was sitting in and made a great pool of wax. And as it did, I took some matchsticks and made a little cabin out of them. Pretty soon the wax was vaporising inside the cabin and giving off a nice light.

'I went out the window at this point, and I swung from one fire escape to another on these buildings. I used to get crazy on this drug. Then I walked along a ledge, stories and stories up, and jumped into a tree in a park along Baker Street. I climbed out of the tree, hopped into my car, a Cortina GT, and blasted around the West End, doing about eighty, just screaming. It was a golden time and I was right in the pocket.

'When I came back to the apartment, I came up the fire escape and in through the window. I found that everyone was kind of spooked and dragged. This plate of matches had become a nova and blown up. The plate was in shards; there was a hole in the table and a big hole in the ceiling. I later thought of that as being pretty irresponsible.'

Everyone, including Peter Asher, Kootch and his family, was worried about James. They finally extracted a promise that he would seek help. They also discussed how he should take time off to decide what he wanted to do with his life. No matter what they said, however, Taylor knew that nothing could stop him from playing music. Still, he kept repeating the same pattern: whenever he encountered hardships he stumbled, and each time it became more difficult to get back up. He spent every cent he had on heroin. His siblings attributed his emotional paralysis and addiction to the fact that he had been away from the family for so long.

'He started to distance himself from us,' Alex said. 'The fact that he wasn't close by to fall back on us whenever he needed support messed him up. When he was traveling he didn't have someone who he could open up to about what he was going through. He became very lonely.'

Alex had for several years been well aware that his brother was using heroin, because he once found paraphernalia in the bathroom. 'I was shocked the first time I found out because James always seemed to be the quiet type,' Alex said. 'He was always my little brother and I was protective of him. Even when he started playing music I looked out for him, showed him how to play guitar, and told him a bit about the ropes of being in a band. I told him not to do it, but I guess he never took me seriously because he knew I was doing a lot of drugs myself at that time.'

Taylor got a big scare when it was reported in the press that several people in London had recently died after injecting themselves with contaminated heroin. He stopped shooting up for a few days, but found it difficult to withstand the pain of withdrawal. The sweating, shakes and nausea grew so excruciating that Taylor felt he was about to die. His only alternative was to shoot up again. He grew very careful about whom he bought heroin from, but he couldn't resist it. Heroin was again part of his daily curriculum.

It was many painful months before he decided to seek help again. He desperately wanted to find balance and sanity in his life, to stop being whacked out on heroin all the time. He considered turning to several religions, including Buddhism. But after experiencing the charge of heroin again, he decided he would have to check himself back into a mental hospital. He was determined not to waste his life.

'I spent a lot of time with a negative faith,' Taylor said of this dark period in his life. 'The world had a nasty surprise around each corner.'

Even though most people thought he was brilliant because of how well versed he was in a variety of subjects, he needed to come to terms with his childhood and his family, which had cast a confusing shadow over his life. He didn't feel anger and resentment as much as disappointment.

'I'm searching for who I am,' he told Kootch. 'And until I find out I won't be able to have peace within my inner self.'

Asher knew by now that the only chance Taylor had for success would be in America. Rumours were swirling in British music circles about Taylor's drug habits, which put a big dent into Asher's plans to market Taylor as a mellower version of Bob Dylan. Asher had hoped the singer would be a kind of flip side of Dylan – clean, gentle and without a bad-boy image. He wanted Taylor to appeal to a new wave of people. This might have been a mistake, because during the late '60s the more trouble musicians got themselves into, the more records they sold.

'His manager could have easily exploited his drug problems and sold a lot of records,' said journalist Martin Smith. 'Look at people like John Lennon, Janis Joplin and Jimi Hendrix. They all had drug problems and their handlers made no attempt to hide it from the public. People were intrigued with their problems and went out to buy their music because they were curious and a lot of them were also doing heavy drugs in the '60s. They were able to relate better to these artists because they felt like they had something in common with them.'

9

BACK IN THE USA

James Taylor, then 20, returned to the United States in October 1968, after being in Europe for more than a year. In December he re-entered a mental rehabilitation clinic at his family's behest. This time he checked into Austin Riggs, a hospital in Stockbridge, Massachusetts. Taylor again spent most of his free time during his five months there reading books and writing poetry. He was given counselling for his heroin addiction and was determined to leave so that he could resume his music career. He knew that if he abandoned music to live with his parents and lead a more normal lifestyle, there was no way he would find happiness or fulfilment. He loved his family, but relations among them were not easy. Another man with Taylor's background might have aimed for a life of big houses and expensive cars. But Taylor was different. He really wanted to live the life of a struggling artist and often forgot that he was from a well-to-do family. Some of his friends say that he didn't know how to handle his family's wealth and lived in denial for years because he didn't want to be judged as a spoiled rich kid. He tried not to take money from his parents; he was determined to make it on his own.

'He had partied his brains out in London and we were all concerned because he had already been through so much in his young life,' his father said. 'James needed our support and I knew that when he got out the only thing he wanted to do was play music. I always wanted him to get a proper education but I had to accept his choice and support him. Music meant everything to him, and he was extremely sensitive when he felt that people weren't supporting him. He had the character that a lot of artists have – very sensitive, temperamental and extremely emotionally fragile.'

The album *James Taylor* appeared in the United States in February 1969. The first single, 'Carolina in My Mind' ('Taking It In' was on the flip side), received minimal attention. A couple of months later another single, 'Something Wrong', was released. American music critics gave his debut a cold reception. Some critics didn't know what to make of his laid-back, smooth approach. Others had difficulty categorising his music. Most agreed, however, that Taylor's music demonstrated a fine synchronisation of diversified moods.

'It was interesting because I hadn't heard anything really like it before,' said New York music critic Peter Allen. 'Was it pop or was it folk? It was a bit hard to tell at first where he was coming from. He was also a bit of an enigma, because I wanted to know why was this folksinger from North Carolina coming out with an album in England before America. It almost made no sense. When I first heard it, I knew that he'd become big if he stuck around for a few albums. Even though it wasn't as rough and in your face as the stuff put out by other big artists at the time, it was very deep and real. I knew that his music wouldn't die quickly, like a lot of other albums did. Hey, this guy was speaking for millions of Americans who had similar problems and situations to him.'

America's tradition of spirituals and folk music is sacred to many. Taylor had big shoes to fill by trying to break into this legendary scene. It wasn't easy for him to get recognition, because of the high standards created by predecessors including Woody Guthrie, Pete Seeger and Bob Dylan. And the big debate among critics was whether Taylor was folk, rock, or pop. Taylor has never liked to place labels on his music; he strongly feels that he's simply a musician trying to express himself. But his critics disagreed and often debated the authenticity of his music style.

Many other folk artists had the same dilemma. When Dylan went electric, he said he was trying to progress and improve his sound – but the folk world felt betrayed and ostracised him for a long time. The same thing happened to Paul Simon and Joni Mitchell. To the day he died, Elvis Presley maintained that everything he ever sang was inspired by the great singers and guitar pickers of the South, who were firmly planted in the folk tradition. Despite all the glitz and glamour that went along with being known as the King of Rock 'n' Roll, one of the things that pleased Presley most – even at the height of his fame – was picking up an acoustic guitar and singing the traditional folk songs that were so popular when he was growing up.

Rudy Orisek, a former ethnomusicologist and TV producer who ran the Gate of Horn club in Chicago in the '60s, was a folk-music lover.

'Folk music is the music of the people, and that covers every known nationality,' he said. 'It's everyday experiences that people talk about in song.'

Ellen Magnet is a founding member of the Sunday Folk in the Park club, which began in London, England in the mid-'60s. Magnet, who is familiar with Taylor's music and has seen him perform live several times, said that the parameters of folk music are unlimited.

'In folk music you can't really define what's genuine and what's fake,' she continued. 'There's no way anybody can say that James Taylor's roots are not deeply linked to the folk movement. The same can be said for Bob Dylan and Paul Simon. What these extraordinary artists are doing is simply taking the traditional folk style and stretching its boundaries in a modern vein. By no means does that mean they should be condemned by the music critics or supporters of folk music.

'Look at Joni Mitchell. She's gone from being a traditionalist folksinger to experimenting with jazz and modern rhythms. But if you listen closely to her music, there's always some mixture of folk that is still there. Lots of artists start out just by playing an acoustic guitar and eventually branch out. But I really do think that it's impossible for somebody who grew up and started out as a folk artist to devoid themselves totally of the music that inspired them.

'As long as the artists are honest and accurately reflecting their true feelings and inspiration, then they'll always have their place among the folk crowd. It's flattering when somebody like Paul Simon or Van Morrison branches out into other musical genres, because everybody knows where they got their start. Folk is the type of music that many musicians use as a stepping-stone, and the true folk artists always remember their roots.'

Phyllis Barney, who was active in the folk scene as executive director of the nonprofit Folk Alliance in Washington, said that there is no exact definition of folk music. 'Once you hang a definition on it, someone is left out who should rightly be included. If you try to make it only acoustic, you leave out anything played on electrical instruments, and that's not right. If you try to make it only music X number of years old, then any song of that age is folk music, and that's not quite what was meant; plus you eliminate the very fine body of work of contemporary singer-songwriters, who are the current members of the travelling musician tradition.

'Fundamentally, once you put a box around such a living art form, you cut off its ties to the rest of the culture. Those ties are what keep it relevant, keep it growing and living.'

Even today Taylor refuses to define the type of music he's making. But he never denies that folk songs were his chief inspiration when he first started playing.

'People can debate all they want whether or not James Taylor is a folk musician,' Magnet said. 'But whenever he talks about his roots, he never leaves out the fact that he once played popular folk songs on the street on an acoustic guitar. And if you hear him in concert today, there's no way you can say that he's departed from his original influences. All that has been added are some electric instruments and drums. But does that mean we must say that he's not a folk musician anymore?'

Perhaps this lingering debate was best put to rest by Jerry Garcia, the late leader of the Grateful Dead. At the height of the Dead's popularity in the late '70s, Garcia was asked by a reporter if he would ever return to playing the simple folk music that had inspired him when he was young.

'I never stopped playing it,' Garcia retorted. 'The only difference now is that I can plug in my guitar so that more people can hear what I have to say.'

10

PERSISTENCE PAYS OFF

Peter Asher relocated to Los Angeles after Apple closed its doors. He was confident that he would be able to re-release Taylor's album in the United States and make a lot of money. He was still convinced the singer would become a huge attraction in America's burgeoning folk scene. Asher told everybody he knew that he represented an artist who would be able to meld folk, rock and blues. 'He mixes them all into one unique style,' Asher said. 'Nobody I've ever heard has been able to do it as well and as convincingly as James. He's going to be a huge sensation.'

Asher convinced Taylor to let him become his producer and manager – to handle every facet of his career. He promised to help James get a new recording deal and that a North American tour would shortly follow.

'It won't be difficult to get you a deal in the United States with a big label because you already have one critically acclaimed album to your credit,' Asher told him. 'People are going to be very impressed that you got a deal with Apple when you were in London. I'm going to try to get you signed with one of the major labels so you'll get enough money to record an album and to back it up with a tour.'

Whenever Asher played Taylor's music, those who heard it were immediately taken by his appeal to America's new hippie generation of social consciousness and awareness. Record producers capitalised on America's prevalent liberal attitudes in the late '60s by bringing several antiwar minstrels to prominence and fame. Bob Dylan's success opened the door for whole new crop of troubadours, including Taylor, Jackson Browne and Joni Mitchell.

In America Taylor was just another wannabe pop star, but with Asher's guidance he managed to avoid many of the obstacles that aspiring musicians face. Asher contacted all the major-label record executives and tried to convince them to sign Taylor. And he wasn't willing to let Taylor sign any contract that didn't guarantee him some stability.

'It's not going to be a one-shot deal,' Asher told the bigwigs at the major labels. 'James Taylor is an artist who has a very promising career ahead of him and is going to be around for years to come. We want to work with a label that is going to get behind him one hundred percent for both his live shows and his albums. We won't settle for anything less.'

Part of Asher's negotiating leverage rested on the power of the glowing reviews Taylor received in London. The executives knew that if Taylor was able to win over Britain's music critics, it would be easy for him to do the same in America. The only major question was whether he would be able to sell more records this time. Would his artistic outlook and drive be enough to win over the American public?

Asher was not happy with the advance money the record labels suggested; he thought Taylor was worth much more than the five to ten thousand dollars that the serious bidders were offering. And he wasn't ready to take any offers without a firm commitment that Taylor's career would be given top priority by the label with which he signed.

'We're not in it just for the money,' Asher told the serious bidders. 'We want to make sure that James will not record one album and then just fall by the wayside. Whomever we work with better be prepared to stand by James through thick and thin for years to come.'

Another major problem was the state of Taylor's health. Earlier in the summer of 1969 he had been in a near-fatal motorcycle accident that placed his career in jeopardy. Taylor spent the summer trying to pull himself together at his family's home on Martha's Vineyard, but wound up doing excessive drugs and partying with several of his old buddies. Initially, he tried to ignore his need for drugs, but the realisation soon hit that it was too difficult to withstand the symptoms of withdrawal. When he was sober he felt like someone removed from oxygen support. He would tremble and become severely depressed.

The motorcyle accident had occurred when Taylor's bike crashed on a dirt road a couple of miles from his family's home. He barely escaped being strangled to death when his clothing got caught up in the bike's wheels. After being rushed to the hospital, Taylor spent the next several months with casts on both his arms and legs. He couldn't play his guitar or even read a book. He had come within an eyelash of losing his life.

Taylor was more disappointed that he wouldn't be able to play at Woodstock. Before his accident, there was talk that he might get an opening spot at the legendary hippie fest. He desperately looked forward to meeting and mingling with Jimi Hendrix, Joan Baez and Crosby, Stills & Nash.

'I would have loved to be a part of Woodstock,' Taylor said. 'But the motorcycle accident slowed everything down. I couldn't even hold a guitar. When I'm not able to play music it's almost like I've stopped breathing.'

The accident ensured that Taylor would never play guitar with the same ease. A few years later he hurt his left hand again by cutting it accidentally with a butcher's knife during a family vacation in the British Virgin Islands.

The movement of both of Taylor's hands slowed considerably after the accidents. He still has trouble playing songs that have complicated chord fingering and rhythms.

Taylor found it difficult to play guitar once his casts were removed. The strength in his arms had deteriorated immensely; he was barely able to play more than a couple of chords in succession.

'At first I wondered if I'd ever be able to play again,' Taylor said. 'It was like learning how to ride a bike again.'

Taylor's nightmarish motorcycle accident did not deter Asher from still pursuing a record deal. The singer had bounced back from one crisis after another in the past, and Asher did not doubt that he was capable of doing it again. Once a deal was in place, Asher was confident that James would have the incentive to make a miraculous recovery.

By the end of 1969 Taylor finally signed a multi-record deal with Warner Bros and moved to Los Angeles to join his pal Asher. Warner wanted Taylor to go into the studio right away to record a new album. Less than two weeks out of casts on both his hands, Taylor composed a new batch of material. Asher hired several musicians to back him up.

Some music critics thought Asher's head was in the clouds. They figured Taylor's career had no chance of going anywhere, citing both his rocky personal past and the way things had turned out when he previously recorded an album for Apple.

'There was no way anybody ever imagined that James Taylor would break out on Warner,' said Brian Goldman, a former pop critic who freelanced in the '60s and '70s for several American music magazines and daily newspapers. 'He had all the talent in the world, but people were sceptical because his first album did so poorly. There was no reason to believe that Peter Asher would be able to get Taylor's career going in the United States after it flopped in England. And the question everybody had was that if the album was good, was Taylor going to be able to play live to support it? He seemed shy and his stage presence wasn't all that good.

'But he was definitely in the right place at the right time. Record labels were signing more people back then and were giving out generous advances. People became stars overnight. Many of them didn't last longer than a cup of coffee. Only a few of them went on to have long careers. Taylor was one of them.'

For both Asher and Taylor, it was a make-or-break situation. Both knew that it would be extremely difficult for a major label to give them another chance if the new album flopped. Asher made sure that he gave it his best shot. He got Kootch to play guitar and hired the multitalented Carole King, who played piano and was highly sought after for her composing and arranging skills. King had become one of the hottest names on the West Coast music scene. She had achieved spectacular success as a songwriter and also had a reputation as a brilliant arranger.

Asher also started to keep a close eye on Taylor to make sure he didn't go AWOL or give way to his drug addictions.

'We've got to make sure there are no screw-ups,' Asher repeatedly told Taylor during the recording stages of the album. 'This is your big chance. If you screw it up there's no tomorrow.'

Taylor was itching to do some live performing, so he convinced Asher to book some gigs between recording sessions. It was the height of the golden folk-flavoured singer-songwriter era, and Taylor thought it was appropriate to perform live to gain a bit of a following.

'I love all the recording but I prefer performing live,' he told Asher. 'When I play live I feel closer to the people and it's much more personal and intimate. I need to perform live, because it gives me inspiration and drive to write new songs and to be more creative. No matter how much I record, it's nowhere near the same feeling I get when I play in front of people. Just provide me with a stage and I'll gladly play my guitar and sing. It's always been my dream to entertain people with my music and make them smile. That's really all I've ever wanted to do.'

Asher wanted Taylor to debut at the famed Troubadour Club on

Santa Monica Boulevard, long regarded as the most influential club in America for showcasing talent. The Troubadour, which seated three hundred people, was usually filled with record label executives and prospective agents whenever a new artist appeared. Over the years Neil Young, Linda Ronstadt, Jackson Browne and Joni Mitchell all performed there before becoming famous. Perhaps the biggest night ever at the Troubadour occurred when Elton John made his US debut. Fans lined up for more than four blocks to see him.

Asher convinced the Troubadour's owner, Doug Weston, to book Taylor on a Tuesday night, when the club showcased some of the country's hottest new talent. Taylor was ecstatic when he found out he'd gotten a gig at the Troubadour – the same stage that helped launch the careers of many of his idols, including the Byrds, Peter, Paul, and Mary and Buffalo Springfield.

'The Troubadour was one of the most unique and respected places to play,' Jim Croce, the late folksinger, once said. 'There would be Cadillacs and Porsches parked outside and inside it was one big wild party. People would be doing drugs and trying to get picked up while young talent was being unveiled on its stage. There was no club that was more influential during the '60s and '70s for promoting new talent than the Troubadour. If you were lucky enough to get a gig there then you had a shot at getting discovered and getting signed to a recording contract.'

Taylor was well received at the Troubadour, many of the club's patrons walked away with favourable impressions of the tall, charismatic singer. They were impressed with his voice and guitar playing, but also concerned about his shy stage presence. Taylor seemed uncomfortable because it had been a while since he had performed live. He was halfway through his set before he felt secure enough to talk to the audience and move around the stage. But by the end of the 75-minute set, not many people walked away without believing that Taylor would soon become a star.

'He had everything, looks, presence and one of the sweetest voices I ever heard,' said Chad Hilburn, an LA musician who used to hang out at the Troubadour and was at Taylor's first concert there. 'He seemed a bit reserved because he was probably nervous, but there was no question about his talent or songwriting. His music was so melodic and graceful. It had a certain kind of spirituality and powerful effect. It definitely had some magical moments. I think everybody in the club that night knew that they were watching somebody who would soon become well known.'

Taylor's performance had improved since he had appeared in New York and London. His technique was finely polished and he sang with much more interpretive assertiveness and authority. He was able to play a song with conviction, something that had eluded him a few years back. He seemed passionate about his music, and his persuasive singing and guitar work were enough to bring a measure of pure, vigorous entertainment to the evening.

Asher knew that he had a potential gold mine in Taylor and expedited the recording of his new album. Based on the favourable reaction Taylor received at the Troubadour, Asher did not want to waste any time.

Recorded on a budget of only eight thousand dollars – a pittance compared to today's million dollar underwritings – Taylor's second solo album, *Sweet Baby James*, was released in March 1970. The timing was great. Within days of its release, it was receiving heavy-rotation airplay by radio stations across the country. Finally, Taylor's career was launched. Nobody in their wildest dreams, including Asher and Taylor, expected the album to get so much attention. Interview requests poured in from every major media outlet. Taylor's critics were silenced; the only question remaining was how the man would cope with his dizzying ascent to stardom. Many close to him wondered what would happen if he couldn't handle the attention and sank back into an emotional abyss.

Sweet Baby James was a very carefully orchestrated attempt to give listeners a taste of the old troubadour folk style. It was an efficient mix of eleven songs of soft folk and pop that would become one of the year's top albums. Indeed, it rose to number three on the pop charts and sold almost three million copies.

Critics embraced *Sweet Baby James* with glowing reviews.

In an article in *Cash Box* magazine, music writer Norm Steinberg described Taylor as 'just a tall, lanky guy with a big rich-sounding guitar'. Steinberg predicted that Taylor was on the verge of becoming a huge star.

'James's work lives on a nontactile level. His songs don't give you anything to touch. They do more. They allow you to visualise and even experience his thought process, his feelings.' Steinberg thought that just by looking carefully at Taylor's album cover, you could tell what he was all about.

'Your first impression is probably, "Yeah, that's *Sweet Baby James* all right",' Steinberg said. 'But there's much more to the cover once you begin to concentrate on his face, especially the eyes. A young artist who studied the *Sweet Baby James* jacket photos said that James had to be a star because he had what she described as 'superstar cheekbones'. But the artist was more interested in the fact that there was a great deal of tension apparent in James's face.'

The album's first single, 'Sweet Baby James' ('Suite for 20G' was on the B side), was released in April. It got a warm reception and brought the album to the attention of the American public. Asher felt that the next single would be the big test, however, because it was the catchiest song on the album. If Asher's premonition was right, Taylor would become one of the most successful music stars.

Perhaps Taylor's best song ever is 'Fire and Rain', the hit song on the album that also became one of the best-known songs in pop-music history. Taylor wrote 'Fire and Rain' as a tribute to a fellow patient who had committed suicide while he was in a mental hospital. It deals with the despair of suicide and the hopelessness of mental illness. It was also intended to deliver a strong message to America's bewildered youth. Millions of confused and depressed teenagers listened to 'Fire and Rain' over and over, trying relate it to their own situations. People memorised every word to help them come to better terms with their own plights. Even today, 30 years later, everyone sings along when 'Fire and Rain' is played on the radio. The chorus is one of the most familiar of all time.

'It's the type of song that everybody knows the words to and can sing along to,' said music critic Paul Jacobs. "Fire and Rain" is a song that belongs in the same category as such classics as "Let It Be", "Wonderful Tonight", and "Light My Fire". Very few songs in rock's history come close to this Taylor classic. It's a song that will live forever and will be played by future generations of music lovers.'

'Fire and Rain' hit number one on the pop charts soon after it was released in August 1970. Taylor, 22, had his first number one hit and quickly became the world's best-known mellow songsmith. He was astonished to learn that so many other people were on his wavelength.

The lyrics had come straight from his heart. To critics it was astonishing that Taylor tossed off 'Fire and Rain' in a single draft. He wrote it as a letter to a friend in which he poured out his soul. This format was to become a *modus operandi* for many more of his songs over the years, and found it the best way to reach out to his fans. When it came to the melody, Taylor allowed the basic, earthy tunes within his mind to be expressed in the simplest fashion. That was how he played it and that was the way it pierced the hearts and minds of fans everywhere.

Taylor would later say, 'I had no music training and I had no idea if people would even like the melodies I invented. In fact I really only knew the most basic group of a handful of guitar chords. I often worried that I was no match for all the great solo guitar players and the great jazz and R&B players. But I just tried to be true to what I was doing. I was just happy and surprised to find that people liked the music that I was able to play. Man, I was so happy.'

'Fire and Rain' caused considerable debate among Taylor's critics and followers. It sounded different from every other song at that time and some critics didn't know what to label it – rock or folk. By today's standards it would definitely be labeled folk, but back then a lot of people considered it rock because of its distinct moving beat and chord structure.

To this day, many of Taylor's fans still argue about what Taylor actually intended to say in 'Fire and Rain'. Fans on his online Internet newsgroup have posted their own theories about Suzanne, whom Taylor refers to in the song's opening verse. The lingering question is whether Suzanne was romantically involved with him or was just a friend. 'His fans are pretty split on the matter,' said Steven Tobin, a pop-music historian. 'Maybe Taylor wanted it to be open to interpretation.'

Some fans say that Suzanne was Taylor's ex-girlfriend who was flying to join him while he was in the studio recording his album. The story goes that Suzanne's plane crashed during her flight and Taylor wrote 'Fire and Rain' as a tribute to her. Another common theory is that Taylor wrote the song after he almost overdosed on heroin one night in New York and was saved by a neighbour named Suzanne.

Joel Risberg, who created the James Taylor Online Web site in 1994, says that a lot of different theories have been posted. Risberg is a longtime Taylor fan who started the popular Web site more than five years ago when he was studying at Florida State Univeristy. 'I decided to make a fan page about Taylor because I grew up listening to Taylor with my family and I had several of his albums on vinyl,' said Risberg, who works out of his home in Los Angeles full time designing Web pages and doing computer-related work.

James Taylor Online gets between fifteen hundred and two thousand visitors a day from all over the world. One of its most popular features is an open forum that Risberg set up to allow both fans and critics to voice their opinions. People post their reviews of Taylor's music and also comment on various aspects and moments in his career. Taylor regularly visits the site to read the postings. Among the forum's theories on the real inspiration behind 'Fire and Rain' are these:

Jonathan Abramowitz wrote: 'The real story behind "Fire and Rain" as I understand it, is that some friends of James were going to surprise James by bringing his girlfriend, Suzanne, to one of his concerts – unbeknownst to James. According to the story, Suzanne's plane crashed ("sweet dreams and flying machines in pieces on the ground") on her way to see the concert and Suzanne dies ("Suzanne the plans they made put an end to you").'

William Palmer posted: 'Something I heard about this line goes like this: JT had a girlfriend that he was really focusing on. Some friends decided that she was a bad influence on him, and convinced her to go away for a while. They bought her a plane ticket, she got on the plane, and en route, it crashed and she was killed in the accident. She was the "sweet dream" and the plane was the "flying machine."'

Another popular online site for Taylor fans is the James Taylor BBS Bulletin Board. Here's what Taylor fan Jenna B. wrote about the controversy: 'Suzanne was a girl James had a crush on for a long time and decided to write her a song to express his true feelings to her and to let her know who he really is. After she heard the song she was deeply touched but it was too late because she was already engaged to another guy. If she would have heard the song sooner she would have probably married JT on the spot. Suzanne couldn't believe how romantic JT was because he wrote the song to tell her about how he felt. Suzanne never had a chance to thank JT in person because he became famous and was always travelling around the world playing concerts and was almost impossible to get in contact with.'

It is hardly surprising that most of these theories conflict; Taylor himself has given different explanations in interviews and to friends over the years. He has never denied any of the numerous stories bandied about, and he admitted to friends that he likes to keep the song's motivation an enigma. 'It's very personal to me and I want people to draw their own conclusions,' he once told Danny Kortchmar. 'Sometimes it's better to let people interpret their own meaning instead of telling them what it's about.'

In a 1971 *Rolling Stone* interview, however, Taylor revealed his true feeling and inspirations behind 'Fire and Rain.'

'The first verse was a reaction to a friend of mine killing herself . . . the second verse of it is about my kicking junk just before I left England,' he told the magazine. 'And the third verse is about my going into a hospital in western Massachusetts. It's just a hard-time song, a blues without having the blues form.'

Privately, however, Taylor has admitted to friends that Suzanne was a girl he met when he was in the Austin Riggs mental hospital. They became close friends because they shared many interests and goals. Suzanne, like Taylor, had several emotional problems and was often deeply depressed and strung out. She didn't like being in a mental hospital and once told Taylor that she would rather die than be confined to Austin Riggs. Suzanne was one of the few people whom James trusted at Austin Riggs; he wasn't afraid to pour out his heart and soul to her. He was deeply saddened when he found out Suzanne committed suicide several months after he left the hospital. At first, Taylor didn't find out about Suzanne's death for several weeks, because his friends were afraid that if they told him he might do a lot of drugs or something drastic to escape the reality of his friend's death. So they waited until he was finished recording to break the news to him. When Taylor recorded 'Fire and Rain' he felt it was appropriate to dedicate it to his trouble-plagued friend, whose spirit and memory would be indelibly in his mind for the rest of his life.

'Fire and Rain', Taylor said, also dealt with two other bad times in his life. The song's second verse was about his severe bout with drugs when he was in New York. Its last verse describes his departure from New York to escape his drug and personal problems, which resulted in the breakup of his group the Flying Machine.

'After I listened to it I couldn't believe how much he had been through in his young life,' said Harry Tanner, who worked promoting new artists in the '70s. 'Nobody in that time made an album that was so revealing and autobiographical. I still play it on my car stereo whenever life gets me down. It makes me realise that my problems are nothing compared to the problems that other people have.'

'Fire and Rain' became so popular that it served as the chief catalyst and inspiration for many young musicians' careers. Even today it possesses oracular power.

'So many people started playing guitar and singing after James released “Fire and Rain”, said longtime Taylor fan Warren Hughes, who has been to dozens of Taylor concerts over the years and has gone backstage several times to meet his hero. ‘I remember after the song came out I went downtown and bought a guitar that looked like the one James played. I brought a picture of James to the music store and asked the owner to find me a guitar that looked like the one he was playing. The unique style James had at that time was unparalleled and it inspired so many people’s lives. Since then I’ve learned at least thirty of his songs on the guitar and I have bought every record or CD that he’s put out. People I know who start learning guitar today usually pick “Fire and Rain” as one of their first songs to learn. It’s definitely an all-time pop classic.’

It seems that almost everybody who grew up in the early ’70s or was in the music business back then has a story to tell about how ‘Fire and Rain’ influenced his or her life. One of the most interesting stories comes from the King of Rock ‘n’ Roll himself, Elvis Presley. According to several people who were close to Presley, several weeks before he died on 16 August 1977, Elvis listened repeatedly to the *Sweet Baby James* album. He found that Taylor’s lyrics mirrored a lot of things going on in his own life. It was one of his favourite albums of all time.

‘Elvis always respected a lot of his fellow artists,’ Minnie Presley, Presley’s maternal grandmother once said. ‘But one of the artists that he really likes is that young kid named James Taylor. He can relate to it because of all the things he’s been through in his own life.’

The deep depression Elvis felt during the last few weeks of his life was relieved when he played ‘Fire and Rain’ on the stereo in his limo or late at night in his bedroom. ‘If I was the character in any song, it would be “Fire and Rain”,’ he once told his ex-manager Colonel Tom Parker. ‘This song relates to what I’ve been through in my life. When I listen to it I cry, my whole life comes before me, and I go into a very deep emotional state of mind.’

Elvis liked Taylor’s music so much that he would often croon ‘Fire and Rain’ or ‘You’ve Got a Friend’ to his daughter, Lisa Marie, when he sang her to sleep at night. He also taught Lisa Marie the words to a few of Taylor’s songs, which occasionally brought tears to her eyes.

‘One of Lisa Marie’s favourite moments with her father was when he’d play guitar and sing for her,’ said Robert Kelly, who knew Elvis and once worked as a consultant for Colonel Tom Parker. ‘Colonel Tom used to rave about the way Elvis sang to his daughter. Apparently it was one of the only times Elvis appeared to be happy in the final days of his life. Elvis played a wide range of tunes for Lisa Marie, including the Beatles and Frank Sinatra. But he had a special affinity for James Taylor and often said how much he admired Taylor's songwriting. Taylor was young at the time, but Elvis thought his writing was very mature. In fact, I remember Colonel Tom once told me that he thought Taylor was going to be just as big or bigger than Bob Dylan. He just wasn't sure if Taylor had the charisma onstage of an Elvis or a Dylan that would make people want to see him play live.'

According to Kelly, Colonel Tom often said that Elvis rarely paid compliments to other artists the way he did to Taylor. 'Elvis respected people like Sinatra, the Beatles and Olivia Newton-John, who was another promising up-and-coming singer,' Colonel Tom said. 'But very few excited him the way Taylor did the first time he heard "Fire and Rain". There were many nights when Elvis entertained women at Graceland to candlelit dinners and would have a James Taylor tune playing in the background to help set the mood for the evening.'

In the years ahead, Taylor rarely varied the songwriting style on his breakthrough album. His fans craved for more songs in the 'Fire and Rain' vein. Taylor realised that he would be able to use the formula of *Sweet Baby James* over and over. Listening to his albums is like listening to the story of his life. He told everyone the things that were important to him through his songs. He's often said that nobody has to write a biography of him; all they have to do is listen to his records, and 'they'll know all about me and what's been important in my life'.

The album's title song, 'Sweet Baby James', is considered by many one of the best pop ballads of all time. Taylor had purportedly written the song as a response to those who supported him but were concerned about his chaotic existence. 'Sweet Baby James' explored the meaning of morality and behaviour and grappled with questions about love and loneliness. It was almost a diary of Taylor's life. 'Sweet Baby James' clearly showed an artist whose sensitivities ran deep and whose dreams seemed achingly within reach. The song's chorus was a strong request to his friends to just let him be himself.

Taylor viewed his lyrics as nothing more than capturing a moment. 'I don't like to philosophise and analyse my lyrics too much,' he has often said. 'In some of the songs I've written, people have come up with their own conclusions about what I meant to convey. Man, some of the stuff that's been said about my writing amazes me. I'm just trying to express my own experiences with words and music. A lot of times people have misinterpreted what I'm saying, but that's the beauty of writing. People deserve to have the freedom and right to draw their own interpretations of what you've written.'

'Country Road' was another *Sweet Baby James* song to crack America's Top Forty list. Music fans loved its eclectic mix of folk, pop, gospel and blues. Taylor also received attention for his references to Jesus in both this song and 'Fire and Rain'. Indeed, he has made reference to Jesus in several of his lyrics throughout his career prompting many interpretations. Nobody expected 'Country Road' to hit the charts because it wasn't as catchy as some of his other tunes. But critics called it one of the most poetic and profound tunes on the album.

Some of his fans thought Taylor wanted to find religion to help conquer all the turmoil and emotional instability he had experienced. Others had a different take. 'When I first saw him I thought that he was trying to look like Jesus,' said Oswald Bailey of Toronto, Canada, a devout Taylor fan ever since the release of *Sweet Baby James*. 'He had long hair, a thin body and he went around barefoot quite a bit. Honest to god, I think he thought he was Jesus Christ.'

Taylor is aware of his fans' comparisons but says that they are not always true. 'When you achieve success people always try to draw between the lines,' Taylor said. 'I like success almost as much as I dislike it.'

The success of *Sweet Baby James* was Taylor's biggest personal triumph to date. He knew that he had arrived. For years he had wanted to be a music star, believing it the only way to escape his turbulent emotional problems. This dream gave him the reason to go on living. During all the days he was strung out and was desperately trying to find meaning in his life, he'd never abandoned his dream of becoming a famous musician. Now that he had finally turned his dream into reality everybody, including himself, wondered how much it would change his life. Only a short time before, he was in a state of utter despair. The fact that he was now living in the glitz and glamour of Los Angeles worried his friends and family. Getting drugs, alcohol and women there would be as easy as ordering pizza.

'We were all so proud of him because he had worked so hard and had to go through so many obstacles to get his career going,' said his mother. 'His brothers and sister were so proud when they used to hear his songs being played on the radio. Everybody was ecstatic. But we were also very concerned because we knew that the music circles in LA were filled with a lot of things like drugs that could have had a bad effect on him.'

While he may have appeared dauntless, Taylor did fear he would overdose in his room alone, and that nobody would find his body for days or weeks. He was afraid that his family would not know what happened to him; that his mother would be worried sick. He envisaged this happening in the prime of his career; he would be remembered merely as another rock star who took his life when he achieved fame and fortune.

Taylor quickly became a favourite interview subject with the media. Journalists were interested in finding out more about his stay in a mental institution and his battles with drugs and alcohol. Publicly, Taylor rarely responds to questions about his history of drug abuse or his fear of death. In interviews, he has always preferred to talk about his music career and does not go beyond a superficial response when asked about his personal problems. Even to friends he has always been extremely careful about what he says. He only opens up when the subject interests him. After *Sweet Baby James* catapulted him to fame and fortune, Taylor collaborated with his manager Peter Asher on how to deal with the media.

'Be honest but don't give them more than they ask for,' Asher repeatedly told him. 'Just be yourself and don't be shy to tell them what's on your mind. But don't give them too many details about your personal life, because they could use it against you. Remember, we want to promote your music, so it's your music that you should be talking about.'

11

TAYLOR'S 'TIME' HAS COME

It seemed everybody was jumping on the 22-year-old James Taylor's bandwagon. He was inundated with offers to perform and quickly became the hottest draw on American college campuses. Perhaps his most memorable live show that year, 1970, took place at Harvard on 24 April. Taylor performed for more than an hour and received a standing ovation for his simple, easygoing singing and guitar strumming. People were deeply touched by the sincerity and compassion that infused Taylor's music, and the way he exhibited such expressive control of the resonance and tone of his voice. More than a mere vehicle for words, his voice had character and imagination and touched people's hearts. Taylor's singing often gave his fans goosebumps because of its authentic and delicate feel. The shy boy from North Carolina finally felt at home onstage and could deliver in his unique way music that came from the heart.

The Harvard concert was recorded and is considered to be a collector's item among Taylor's fans. Not many copies were made; a good one can fetch as much as two hundred dollars. The quality of the recording is poor and filled with distortion, but it is vintage Taylor.

'It's a great piece of rock memorabilia,' said entertainment author Esmond Choueke. 'You can't be a true die-hard Taylor fan unless you have it.'

By the time *Sweet Baby James* went platinum in October 1970, he had become one of the world's most sought-after performers. Asher needed to hire additional staff to help him handle the requests for appearances and interviews. James Taylor had turned into a major enterprise, bringing in millions of dollars in revenue – a feat previously accomplished by only a handful of solo artists, including Elvis, Jimi Hendrix and Bob Dylan.

Curiously, Taylor did not seem fazed by the attention he was receiving. He enjoyed being a star and the benefits that came along with it. He confided to his friends that the money made him feel uncomfortable. His own life epitomised the independent spirit that so frequently imbued his music. Because he didn't fit the stereotypes about folk music, Taylor was often misunderstood. Some people labelled him a sellout. 'Some of the folk diehards didn't accept his commercial style,' Esmond Choueke said. 'They were wrong. Taylor was anything but that. His style was different and it took the purists time to accept it. So what! He did as much as anybody else to help advance and promote folk music.'

Like other great artists, Taylor concerned himself with an inner reality. His music was the first alternative to the idiom of classic '60s folk music. Taylor is quick to admit that he was also in the music business for the adulation and prestige. He loved making music, loved seeing people smile when he played. Taylor often said that he got a kick out of hearing one of his songs on the radio while driving. He felt good that people were paying attention to him. He loved the fact that he was living the dream of thousands of aspiring guitar players, who also wanted to cut records, become famous, attract lots of women and live the high life.

'James knew for a long time that he was going to make it big,' said Danny Kortchmar. 'It was just a matter of when. And when he finally did make it he didn't change much, but he also didn't go in a closet and hide. At first he really got a kick out of being a star and enjoyed living life to its fullest. But he never forgot about the people close to him and he always remained the same down-to-earth guy.' Sometimes, Taylor would pick up an album and run his finger over his name printed on it. It was his way of reassuring himself that he really was living this rise to fame.

It was no longer a daydream. He realised that he was a star after reading a glowing review of his album in *Rolling Stone*. He read the piece over and over. Throughout most of his career, Taylor has tried to read every article written about him. Whether he likes what is being said about him or not, he spends hours poring over every word. Later on, after the breakup of his first marriage to Carly Simon, he was furious because some of the tabloids were writing terrible things about him. He tried to shrug off the critical comments. But he still read most of the articles, regardless of how accurate they were.

Some of the articles painted an unflattering portrait of Taylor's personal life, making him out to be wild and damaged. He enjoyed, they said, the opportunity to exploit his fame to pursue the three major interests rock stars were renowned for – sex, drugs and rock 'n' roll.

The flurry of attention Taylor received caught the eye of the editors at *Time* magazine. The time was ripe, they decided, not only to devote a full length feature story to the man behind the myth, but also to put him on the cover. The issue appeared on 1 March 1971.

Taylor was excited that his face would appear on the cover of America's best-known and most powerful magazine. He told his friends and family the news. Then he waited eagerly for the magazine to appear on the newsstands. *Time* had conducted a series of interviews spread out over several days. The magazine made sure that Taylor was very aware of the conditions of the interview before they decided to go ahead with it. There were to be no restrictions on the questions asked and Taylor had to promise not to try to conceal information.

Taylor's manager, Peter Asher, excitedly awaited the article's publication. Asher knew the value of the cover of *Time* magazine, especially because Taylor had started working on a new album that would be released shortly. Asher tried not to overestimate the article's worth to Taylor, for fear that it would make Taylor nervous. But inside Asher's head, the dollar signs were rolling. He would calculate the millions of dollars in record sales and publicity that the *Time* article would bring in. He knew that Taylor, now an enterprise, would skyrocket.

Executives at Warner Bros were also happy; being on the cover of *Time* was like winning an Oscar. It was the best publicity an artist could ever hope for. Better than being on *Johnny Carson*, better than being on the cover of *Rolling Stone*.

Taylor knew that a lot of his colleagues would resent him for appearing on the cover of *Time*. He understood that the flip side of success in the music business has always been envy, which opens the door to a parade of armchair critics and backbiters. Taylor's fear was valid. He did receive harsh words from people in the music business and the public shortly after the article was released. Indeed, a huge debate broke out among executives at rival records labels, fellow musicians, members of the media and the public over whether Taylor's story was worthy of being on the cover of *Time*.

'When Taylor got the cover of *Time* I'm sure he made a lot more enemies than friends,' said Victor Maislin, a New York session musician who eked out a living back then playing jazz cafés in Greenwich Village for thirty-five dollars a week. 'I remember reading the story and feeling sorry for myself and all the other musicians I knew who had similar stories to his but were struggling to earn a dollar. From a musician's point of view I didn't care too much for his music, because it was basic three chord folk songs. Even though he had some depth in his lyrics, more than a lot of other artists, I never really quite understood what all the fuss was about. So what, he was some rich kid who did some smack because he got bummed out with life. If that was *Time*'s criteria for doing a story on someone, I could have provided them with a thousand James Taylors.

'I remember thinking to myself how unfair it was that a guy like James Taylor was on the cover of *Time* instead of somebody who was a true musician, somebody who had a similar hard life to his but had been around for years and made dozens of albums. Somebody like Miles Davis, Freddie Hubbard or even Nancy Wilson.'

Over the years Maislin worked with such music legends as Barry White, Joe Cocker and the late Marvin Gaye. He said he changed his mind about Taylor when he met him years later. Maislin happened to walk into an elevator at a music conference in New York. James Taylor was already in the elevator and politely asked him which floor button he could press.

'I introduced myself to him and he was extremely polite,' Maislin said. 'I told him that I'm a musician and he was very interested in finding out about what I do. When I told him I'm a jazz player, he said that he loved jazz and was really into John Coltrane and Charlie Parker. I remember thinking to myself that this guy is real and is not as self-absorbed as most of the pop stars I've worked for and met over the years. Since then I've bought a couple of his albums and have actually gotten into some of it. I play some of his more recent stuff when I need some easy-listening music, like when I'm entertaining dinner guests or just trying to relax. I really do appreciate a lot of his lyrics. When I saw him on TV being honoured by *Billboard* magazine I agreed with their choice. I thought, "Hey, this guy might not be the greatest technician, but he deserves it because he's managed to stick around for so many years in a business in which people pop off like flies."'

As expected, when the article appeared on the news-stands, Taylor's management received a flurry of calls from all over the world. Dozens of electronic and print journalists, a couple of Hollywood scriptwriters, and even a US senator called to inquire about Taylor's availability. Everybody seemed fascinated by his story. Titled 'One Man's Family of Rock', the lengthy feature story was a well-chronicled, in-depth account of Taylor's rise to stardom. It dealt with his upbringing and the troubles that had plagued him for so many years. For the first time, America knew what was really behind the man who, during the past year, had captured their hearts and imagination with his unique folk style. *Time* wrote:

> What Taylor intones is far more artful than it seems at first. For if his voice is spare and strangely uninflected, his guitar fingering lends sudden lights and shadows to the barest melody. Musically, Taylor is a fusion of the three black and white mainstreams of pop: the lonely twang of country, the pithy narrative of folk, and the rhythmic melancholy of blues. Beyond that, Taylor's use of elemental imagery – darkness and sunlight, references to roads travelled and untravelled, to fears spoken and left unsaid – reaches a level of both intimacy and controlled emotion rarely achieved in purely pop music. He can, says one of his campus admirers, 'turn an arena into a living room.'

In the end, the only person who wasn't happy with the article was Taylor himself. He thought it revealed too much about his personal life and heroin habit. He particularly didn't like the parts about his erratic emotional past and his family. Overall, the article focused more on his dark side than on his music:

> Like so many other troubled, dislocated young Americans, Taylor may at first seem self-indulgent in his woe. What he has endured and sings about, with much restraint and dignity, are mainly 'head' problems, those pains that a lavish quota of middle-class advantages – plenty of money, a loving family, good schools, health, charm, and talent – do not seem to prevent, and may in fact exacerbate. Drugs, underachievement, the failure of will, alienation, the doorway to suicide, the struggle back to life – James Taylor has been there himself.

 Even today, Taylor is frequently asked in interviews to comment on the

Time story. Usually he responds that it was too long ago to really remember the specifics of the article, but that it had a huge impact on his career. He describes the article as fair. In a 1979 *Rolling Stone* interview, however, Taylor voiced his indignation to writer Peter Herbst.

'The press want something that'll sell copy,' Taylor said. 'They pick up on the mental hospital, family stuff, try to invent some category of rock that I belong to, or perhaps they pick up on my drug problem. But it gets to the point sooner or later when you start to think about your kids: "What does your daddy do for a living?" "He plays the guitar and he talks about his drug problems." It's embarrassing to read the drivel that comes out of your mouth sometimes. So I guess maybe the question is, why am I doing this in the first place? And honestly, I suppose I'm doing it because I'd like to promote my record.'

Taylor told Herbst that after the *Time* article, he lost most of his trust in the press. From that time on, he avoided giving interviews unless he needed to promote a new album. Taylor has always felt uneasy around journalists because he doesn't like to have to regurgitate his turbulent past. He's not one to shy away from controversy, yet he worries that whatever he says will be blown out of context or misinterpreted. He says he's been burned by the press so many times over the years that he prefers to say nothing than to reveal something that might be used against him. But he does concede that being on the cover of *Time* when he was just 22 years old was one of the highlights of his career.

'Not many musicians get to see their face on the cover of *Time*,' Taylor said. 'If someone had told me a year before the article appeared that I would be on the cover of *Time*, I would have never taken them seriously. I thought only politicians and famous people got the cover. It all happened so fast. It was quite an honour. All my friends and family were really proud of me.'

The story endeared Taylor to a broader audience of fans. The extraordinary paleness and thinness of so many of the people who showed up at his concerts suggested that they shared with Taylor an acquaintance with the needle and spoon. Some heroin addicts in the throes of kicking the habit looked to Taylor as a beacon of hope for recovery.

'After I read the *Time* article he became the artist I was able to best relate to,' said Sean Roth, a former '60s hippie who for years battled heroin addiction and, like Taylor, spent time in a psychiatric hospital.

'We all knew that so many of our music heroes were doing hard drugs, but most of them tried to hide it. Taylor was honest. He wasn't afraid to come out and open himself up. I'm sure a lot of people resented him for doing that. But a whole lot of other people admired him because he was speaking for a generation of people who had similar problems to him. After I read that he had been in a mental hospital it inspired me to get help, too. I needed somebody to tell me how to try to seek some answers and balance – and he seemed to be the chosen one.

'His music spoke to me better than the words of the psychiatrists who tried to help me. My best therapy was listening to him sing. A few years later, I finally kicked heroin. To this day I can honestly say that it was James Taylor who helped me more than anybody else. Nobody I can think of was able to use their art to express the difficulty and strain of growing up in America they way he did.'

Taylor was on top of the showbiz world but his attempt at drug rehab was to stall again. Shortly after the *Time* article, Taylor disappeared for several days. He had begun the long slide into another bender. For several weeks, he indulged in some of the excesses that are the hallmark of so many rock stars. His self-control deteriorated with the use of more and more drugs. He flitted in and out of frenzied affairs with women. Soon, his friends noticed his increasing disturbance. He stopped shaving and washing himself. At one point, he wore the same clothes every day for three weeks, because he felt the blue denim shirt and jeans could somehow 'protect' him from the demons in his mind.

Taylor's personality had snapped. Beneath his haggard, unshaven countenance was true desperation. His paranoia and anger were running riot. Taylor no longer needed ego stroking or a gorgeous young babe to go home with as a remedy for his lingering depression. He knew that what he needed most was to come to terms with his inner self and his career. Instead, he was drilling his life to rock bottom. Taylor realised that performing and posturing for millions of people was not the way to understand his personal malaise. He inadvertently revealed to reporters some of the issues he was grappling with in psychotherapy.

'The idea that I have to perform makes me angry,' Taylor once told a reporter. 'And I think that anger is in ways inexpressible because it's not really at anything specific. It's like an old anger. And in that way recording an album might have made me very angry and might have made me turn to drugs as an alternative . . . as a way to stomach that anger. Obviously, if you can't express it, you'll have to swallow it somehow.'

Taylor was also alarmed that his parents seemed headed for divorce. Taylor begged and pleaded with his father to try to save the marriage. Taylor had always felt closer to his mother, and he didn't want to see her get hurt. As their relationship took its final tailspin, Taylor negotiated between his mother and father. He refereed late-night phone calls and emotional encounters until he could no longer stand the pain it caused him. He felt he had been left alone when his parents divorced.

There were rumours that Isaac might be having an affair with a woman who worked at North Carolina State University. Trudy and Isaac often slept apart, and sometimes Isaac wouldn't bother to come home at night. He denied the affair, but Taylor trusted his mother's intuition. Trudy had overheard phone conversations. She had spotted the early signs when her husband started to take extra care with his grooming. But most of all, she just knew.

Isaac, by all accounts, was not an exemplary father or husband. He seemed to be more concerned with himself and his career than his family. It took almost a lifetime for Isaac to understand the full impact of his neglect. Years after his marriage to Trudy had dissolved, he expressed his profound regret about the way he acted: 'There were lots of times when I knew I was negligent. If I had the chance to do it all over again there would be a lot of things that I'd do differently. Trudy is a remarkable woman and she definitely deserved better. She deserved a man who would have been more devoted and taken her out dancing or to dinner more often. She sacrificed so much for the sake of the family. There were times when I felt so bad for her but I didn't know how to express my feelings of sorrow to her.

'Our children were all wonderful. They were so compassionate, loving and respectful toward their parents and older people. If I had been around more often, maybe I could have prevented some of the bad things that happened in their lives. Alex was a great kid but he had trouble dealing with certain things in life. He needed some guidance, somebody who had a wise and strong character to help point him in the right direction. I always felt bad that I wasn't around more for him. There were times when I tried to help him, but it was difficult to get his respect because he was sensitive to the fact that I wasn't around a lot and that I had my own share of personal problems to deal with.

'I was always proud of all my children and the times we had together at Martha's Vineyard where they grew up. They were some of the most cherished moments in my life. No matter what they got themselves into,

I never lost an inch of my love for them. I just had a tough time showing it. Trudy was always the one who made people feel at ease to talk about everything in their life. She believed that self-disclosure was the best remedy for personal problems. I was the one who was a bit more closed-minded because I was raised in a family that didn't always bring things out in the open. There's no question in my mind that the kids' openness today is a result of Trudy's liberal values.'

Trudy had fought for communication and stability in their family for years, and she was devastated by her husband's failure to give her the attention she deserved. She told Isaac that she thought they should separate. Their marriage had become nothing more than a convenience; now that the children were grown up, there was no need to continue the charade.

Isaac became even more withdrawn. He devoted most of his time to his work, and finished most evenings with a late-night drinking session. All they seemed to do together was trade insults. They were both unhappy with their marriage, and they both knew there was no chance of resuscitating it.

'James had become a star and the other children had grown up, so they had to make a decision about what to do,' said one of the family's close friends. 'Everybody was still a bit mad at Isaac because he never seemed to be there when push came to shove. He also had trouble understanding his kids' emotional problems, and it drove him to do a lot of drinking. His drinking created more resentment and distance from the children. If he had reacted differently, maybe the marriage could have been saved.

'I always felt bad for Trudy because she was such a devoted mother and wife. But it was the kids who suffered most. They went through so much and their father often was not there. I admire Trudy because she had the courage to confront Isaac and give him an ultimatum to shape up or ship out. Trudy was the type of person who never was afraid to speak her mind.'

The separation of his parents had a powerful impact on Taylor. He lost a lot of respect for the principles of marriage and what it stood for, and told friends that he seriously doubted he'd ever get married. He promised himself that even if he met the right woman, he would think very hard before making any sort of commitment.

'Sometimes I feel as though I'd rather be married to my guitar,' Taylor said. 'When you get involved with someone there's so much that you have to try to understand about the other person, and sometimes it's not easy to do. You're different people with different goals. The idea is to find some common ground and to respect each other's ideals. Otherwise, it's not going to work.'

Taylor's efforts to find the perfect companion in his life were stymied by his drug habits and his penchant for dating several women at a time. 'I was quite a bit screwed up and it made it difficult for me to properly devote myself to a relationship,' he said. 'I was a tough guy to be around because I had so many things to deal with in my own life. But I had to experience what I was living back then. If I had done things differently, who knows, I might never have even written 'Fire and Rain'. Not that this justifies my actions, but I'm not one to look back and regret what I did.'

It didn't take long for James to realise that the weight of his very name could be a burden. At parties, nightclubs, or restaurants, or even on the street, when people found out who he was they often tried to hit him up for cash or get him involved in some crazy scheme. Once at a Beverly Hills restaurant, a waitress – who was also an aspiring singer – got on top of Taylor's table and started belting out 'Fire and Rain'. Everybody in the restaurant turned around to watch the bizarre spectacle. When they noticed that Taylor himself was in the house, they didn't leave him alone for the rest of the evening. People bombarded Taylor with questions about his life and career and asked him for autographs. Another time he was mobbed in a supermarket when the zealous manager announced on the PA that James Taylor was in the store.

'I realised early in my career that there was a price to pay for fame,' Taylor said. 'There were lots of times when I wished that I could go out like a regular person and enjoy myself. When people always recognise you, your life is never your own. You might not be in the best of moods but you still have to try to put a smile on your face. People are usually nice, but there are some who try to take advantage of who you are and try to get you to do things that sometimes aren't very legitimate. I like to lend my name and associate myself with worthy causes. But I learned early in my career to be very careful of who and what I associate myself with so that it doesn't backfire.'

Despite all his success, Taylor, now 23, still felt like an outsider. He found it difficult to find peace and resorted again to drugs and alcohol. It had been close to 18 months since Taylor last shot up. Being a star created new pressures. He had always wanted to be accepted by his friends and family, but now he feared that people sought him out only because he was famous. He was more confused than ever. He only found peace when he played his guitar and sang. People often made him feel uncomfortable because they preferred to talk about his career and successes instead of being interested in more meaningful things like personal struggles or relationships.

Throughout his life, Taylor had been driven by his need for approval. By now his career had taken off and even gone into overdrive, but he felt more alone than ever. He found it difficult to be in a business with people who were so self-absorbed and self-deluding. Taylor desperately needed someone who could really understand him and be a true friend.

The only drug Taylor had taken in recent months was methadone. He'd first used the drug at the urging of a physician friend in Chicago. The doctor feared for Taylor's life and wanted to help relieve his addiction to heroin. But now that James felt like he was again losing control of his life, he reverted to his old lifestyle. He obtained more heroin and, as usual when he was using, just dropped out for a time. His body always welcomed back the first few delicious hits of heroin.

'It's an amazing downhill slide,' Taylor recalled in an interview. 'It's fast, too, but the initial thing is trying to get away from a feeling that you cannot control and that in any way you cannot express. That's at the basis of most addictions. Either it's anger or fear or a combination of the two.

'The other thing about addiction is that it's consistent. What the junkie is looking for when he picks up his syringe or goes out to cop is something that will be the same every time and that will completely supersede all other goings-on. And smack does that. It's the circumstances around it that kill you. Heroin maintenance has worked well in England. But it's like being dead. It knocks out your sensitivities at the same time that it gets rid of the suppressed emotion you can't stand anymore.'

12

JONI MITCHELL, THE WOMAN HE LOVED TOO MUCH

Taylor wasn't about to acknowledge to his colleagues the fatigue and despair he had been feeling in the past few months. When friends and family, who had been worried about his state of mind, inquired about how he was doing, he'd quickly go on the defensive. He told them that he never felt better and that there was no basis for their concerns. Taylor always had a knack for persuasion and negotiation. His endearing personality usually helped him charm everyone. But inside, he was far from recovered. In public he was able to put up a good façade by maintaining a rather dignified and serene persona.

Privately, he was an emotional wreck. He had become thoroughly disheartened. He seemed to be on the verge of a nervous breakdown. He was unfit to work and asked his manager Peter Asher for some time off. 'I just need a few days to get myself together before we continue working on the new album,' Taylor told his manager. 'Everything's happened so quickly and I haven't had a chance to just sit back and realise what has happened. I'll be fine and ready to go again after a bit of a rest period.'

Taylor needed to find something that would revive his spirit and his will to live. For the first time in months he had thought about suicide again. He seemed incapable of maintaining any stability or love in his life.

Outside of his music, most of Taylor's time was spent trying to assuage the pain of not being able to find the right woman. Despite meeting dozens of beautiful, eligible women every week – many of whom lusted after him – Taylor was unable to form a relationship with any of them. There was nobody he met with whom he had a spiritual and profound connection. He had dallied with many women but forgotten them all. Maybe it was because he couldn't get himself together, let alone become involved with a woman. Maybe it was because he was never in one place long enough to develop any strong feelings for a member of the opposite sex. In the past he'd been able to get by with a lot of one-night stands, but now they made his stomach churn. When he woke up the next day, he felt empty and lonely. He was convinced that a meaningful relationship would get his life back on track.

A young Canadian girl with a face of amazing tenderness answered Taylor's wishes in late 1969. Joni Mitchell, then 26, had already become one of the biggest names in music by the time she met Taylor. Taylor saw Mitchell on several occasions at the Troubadour Club in Los Angeles, where they both performed regularly. Taylor fell for Mitchell the first time a mutual friend introduced him to her. They shared a similar circle of friends, and it seemed that they were destined to wind up in a relationship.

No woman he had ever been involved with inspired him remotely the way Mitchell did. Her beautiful long, blond hair, her poise and smile, her aesthetic air swept Taylor off his feet. He had finally met the woman of his dreams and showed his gratitude by showering Mitchell with poems and love letters.

Besides being major recording artists, Taylor and Mitchell had a lot of other things in common. They both did drugs and were emotionally fragile. And they had both grown more than a little weary of the music business. Mitchell had threatened to quit several times because she wanted to pursue painting, which she thought would be much less stressful than the daily grind of the music industry. 'There's too many phonies and crap in the music business,' Mitchell said. 'I'd rather do something that's in a more natural setting and doesn't sap up so much of my creative energy.'

The two singers shared similar backgrounds and had been through a lot of the same kinds of experiences to get their start. Mitchell was born Roberta Joan Anderson in Fort Macleod, Alberta, Canada. Her father, an officer in the Canadian Air Force, was always being transferred to new postings. Most of Joni's childhood was spent in the spectacular prairie lands of Saskatchewan. Like Taylor, she got her introduction to folk music listening to Pete Seeger records and hanging out at coffeehouses.

After finishing high school, she moved east and gained some recognition playing in folk clubs in Toronto's Yorkville Village, which had launched the careers of Gordon Lightfoot, Neil Young and Buffy Sainte-Marie. In 1965, when she was 22, Joni married folk musician Chuck Mitchell and headed for New York's legendary folk hub in Greenwich Village to try to obtain more recognition south of the Canadian border. Their marriage was short-lived. From the day they exchanged vows, the couple argued about everything from music to the food they ate. They were verbally abusive toward each other. Their numerous conflicts couldn't be resolved. Mitchell relaunched her career on her own and in a matter of months was signed by Reprise Records. She released her first album in 1968 and was well on her way to fame and fortune, becoming the new golden princess of American music.

Before she became involved with Taylor, Mitchell had been through a string of relationships with other musicians, including Jimi Hendrix and David Crosby of Crosby, Stills, Nash & Young. Mitchell accused Crosby of being overly possessive and broke off the relationship shortly after touring as an opening act for Crosby's band. Mitchell was infuriated when Crosby commented publicly that 'Joni Mitchell is about as modest as Mussolini'. Despite the bitter end to their relationship, Crosby, Stills, Nash & Young sang a cover version of one of Mitchell's best-known songs, 'Woodstock', which captured the spirit of the legendary music festival in the summer of 1969.

'If any two people in music were destined to meet, it was James Taylor and Joni Mitchell,' said music critic Martin Smith. 'They seemed to be each other's soul mates. Both of them were shy and introverted and were getting extremely messed up on heavy drugs. They were also the two biggest up-and-coming stars on the folk circuit at that time. I don't think that anybody during that time, including Dylan, was writing more straight from the heart than James or Joni.'

The shy and laid-back Mitchell had heard some disquieting things about Taylor's long history of one-night stands and his dependence on drugs before she met him. Of all the great folk stars of the late '60s, Taylor had one of the most questionable reputations. Still his easygoing hippie style quickly allowed her to cast her doubts aside. 'He wasn't very well known when I first met him, but the things I did hear were a bit conflicting,' Mitchell said. 'But I fell for him right away because he was very easygoing and free-spirited. We shared a lot of similar interests and common ground.'

It took Taylor a while to get used to being around Mitchell; many of his previous girlfriends weren't as perceptive or *au courant*. In fact, a lot of his friends and even family had referred to a few of his past girlfriends as lightheaded bimbos. At first Taylor felt intimidated by Mitchell, his intellectual equal.

Yet he admired everything about her. He thought she was one of the most gifted musicians he had ever met. Taylor loved her looks, her little body, and her waist-long corn-silk hair. He also bragged a lot about how well Mitchell performed in bed, according to several of his close friends.

'She's so sensual and free with her body,' Taylor said. 'She's a real artist who likes to search down deep. And she's not afraid to experiment. She's like a goddess, a goddess of love. A real true goddess. Being with Joni is so pleasurable. We share a lot of common ground. We're very compatible.'

For several months Taylor and Mitchell were almost inseparable. They slept together, jammed together and got high together. The two were mesmerised by each other's presence.

On 29 October 1970, Taylor and Mitchell performed together at London's Royal Albert Hall. Peter Asher thought it would be interesting to have the celebrated couple team up for a special show that would be recorded by BBC Radio. This historic concert remains a very popular bootleg item, usually under the title *You Can Close Your Eyes* or *In Perfect Harmony*.

In London, Taylor and Mitchell spent lots of time partying and catching up with old friends. But the whirlwind romance was about to take a bad turn. Mitchell realised that Taylor had a disconcerting habit of looking at other women, even when he was with her. Many times she would catch his eyes travelling over her shoulder to peek at other women. Despite her freewheeling style, she was jealous. Taylor simply couldn't get enough of the attention of attractive women. Even though he never ceased declaring his love and admiration for her, the temptation proved irresistible. He slowly began sliding back into his old habit of taking advantage of what was being so freely offered. Over and over Mitchell found telltale signs of his errant ways, and she became increasingly angry. Arguments and screaming matches soon followed, and their once-perfect relationship began to fall apart.

At first Taylor tried to hold onto Mitchell by being overly caring when they were together, but he was unable to keep up the solicitous façade for long. Eventually he broke it off and returned to his old life, dating several women at the same time and getting involved in a flurry of late-night partying.

Tellingly, Taylor never gave much thought to Mitchell once they had split up, according to several people close to both of them. Mitchell told several friends that she thought Taylor was selfish and never really had any intentions of developing a long-term relationship with her. She was devastated. Always the sensitive artist, Mitchell chose to use the pain to write many new songs.

She even once went to see a psychologist to try to overcome her heartbreak. Her self-confidence was shattered when she thought that Taylor dumped her because she wasn't pretty enough. She also decided to take a long break from all the glitz and glamour of being a music star and retreated to her isolated home in Laurel Canyon in the Hollywood Hills. It wasn't a sudden decision. Mitchell didn't seek the limelight, but lived her life slipping into and out of the spotlight, uncomfortable when it shone on her. After she became famous she preferred spending time in vast rural areas like the land of her childhood, away from the noise and pollution of big cities.

Joni often directed subtle messages to James in the interviews she gave after they broke up. She wanted him to get the message that she was still angry and in no mood to forgive him. She told *Rolling Stone*: 'You lose all your peripheral view of things. It has its reward but I don't know what the balance is – how much good and how much damage there is in my position. From where I stand it sometimes gets absurd, and yet, I must remain smiles, come out of a mood where maybe I don't feel very pleasant and say "smile". Inside, I'm thinking: "You're being phony. You're smiling phony. You're being a star."

'I was very frightened last year. But if you're watching yourself over your own shoulder all of the time and if you're too critical of what you're doing, you can make yourself so unhappy. As a human you're always messing up, always hurting people's feelings quite innocently. I'll find it difficult, even here. There's a lot of people you want to talk to all at once. I get confused and maybe I'll turn away and leave someone standing and I'll think – "oh dear" . . . I'm getting very defensive. I'm afraid. You really have to struggle.'

She also delivered her strongest message to Taylor in the songs she wrote after they split up. She poured out her heart and soul on her 1971 *Blue* release. Taylor appeared on three of the album's songs singing backup vocals and playing guitar, even though they had broken up by the time the album was released. The songs on *Blue* were written with Taylor in mind. On 'All I Want' Mitchell spoke about her desire for emotional fulfilment. She sang: 'All I really want our love to do is bring out the best in me and you . . . I want to make you feel better, I want to make you feel free.'

Perhaps because of the emotional punch behind it, many critics felt that *Blue* was the best album Mitchell ever released. Mitchell said that she needed to record it to come to terms with all the emotional turmoil she had recently gone through.

'At that period of my life, I had no personal defences,' Mitchell said. 'I felt like a cellophane wrapper on a pack of cigarettes. I felt like I had absolutely no secrets from the world, and I couldn't pretend in my life to be strong.'

On the inside sleeve of her *For the Roses* album she stood naked, surrounded only by wilderness. She was trying to show how free and secure she felt again. On the track 'Lesson in Survival' Mitchell sang: 'I am looking way out at the ocean, love to see that green water in motion, I'm going to get a boat, and we can row it.'

'A lot of her songs were written because of her relationship with James Taylor,' said Roberta Spehr, who used to book bands at a café Mitchell once played at in Greenwich Village and has been a devout Mitchell fan and follower since 1966. 'Joni's name was always being linked to famous people but she was never in love with any of them the way she was with James Taylor. Even when she moved in with Graham Nash, she said that she felt like she was married to him, but it didn't compare to her feelings about Taylor. Taylor was the only man she ever felt that she had a lot in common with and she really thought they would settle down together. When he broke off with her she was devastated and the only thing she had to turn to was her music. You'd be surprised at how many songs she wrote for him after they broke up. Some people say that even some of the songs she wrote in the early '80s were about him. I don't think she ever really got over him.'

For a long time Taylor and Mitchell stopped speaking. On several occasions, she ran into him at music-industry functions. Every time, she forced herself to avoid him and look the other way. They both appeared on Carole King's celebrated *Tapestry* album, considered to be her best work ever. But Mitchell couldn't put behind her the anguish and embarrassment Taylor had caused her. The two kept a safe distance during the studio sessions.

Mitchell was asked by a reporter in 1974 if she felt that her relationship with Taylor had helped boost her career in any way. She quickly said no. 'I don't think so, not in the time that James and I were spending together anyway,' Mitchell said in Canada's national weekly magazine *MacLeans*. 'He was a total unknown, for one thing; maybe I helped his career? . . . But I do think that when creative people come together, the stimulus of the relationship is bound to show. The rock-'n'-roll industry is very incestuous, you know, we have all interacted and we have all been the source of many songs for one another. We have all been close at one time or another, and I think that a lot of beautiful music came from it. A lot of beautiful times came from it, too, through that mutual understanding. A lot of pain too, because, inevitably, different relationships broke up.'

When Mitchell finally came to terms with the grief she felt in her life without Taylor, she realised that it was unfair to put the entire blame on him for their breakup. In fact, she admitted, when she met James she was young and naive, yet she already had a history of jumping from one bad romantic escapade to the next. Even her romances after Taylor, she continued, included a fling with actor Warren Beatty that went sour because she wasn't ready to settle down with one person. She needed to come to terms with who she was.

But Mitchell still had trouble forgetting Taylor and couldn't resist delivering indirect messages in her songs to her former lover whenever she had the opportunity. It was part of her healing process. Usually she would refrain from naming Taylor directly, because she didn't want to generate any more publicity for their lost relationship. To her close friends and associates, however, it was obvious whom she was referring to. On *For the Roses*, which received much critical acclaim, Mitchell used her title track to deliver a strong message to Taylor.

Overall, *For the Roses* was meant to remind Taylor how things were before he met Mitchell and how they quickly changed after they became lovers. 'Joni wanted Taylor to know how much he hurt her,' recalled journalist Julian Walsh, a longtime Mitchell follower. 'It took her a long time to get over him. She let it all out on this album. What a way to get back at him. I'm sure he wasn't too pleased.'

Another track on the album, 'You Turn Me On' – in which Mitchell likens herself to a radio and invites her ex-lover to tune in to her message – was perceived by many to also be dedicated to Taylor.

'Joni was very bitter and ambivalent after their relationship dissolved,' said Myra Dorfman, a concert promoter in the early '70s. 'If you read between the lines of a lot of the material that Joni put out after they broke up, it was pretty easy to figure out that a lot of the heartache and pain that were prevalent in her songs was because of the rough time she went through after her relationship with Taylor. And it really hit home because so many women, myself included, went through tough relationships and could relate to everything Joni was singing about. No woman had challenged males before the way Joni did in her songs. Today we have people like Alanis and Tori Amos singing about how shitty men treat women, but it was Joni who was the first person to do this. She paved the way for the whole women's movement in popular music, and a lot of it came out because of the heartache she went through when she was involved with James Taylor.'

Many of Taylor's devout followers thought that when Mitchell criticised the man, it might have been sour grapes because he'd dumped her. Time and again during Taylor's career, critics made character assessments of him that his fans insisted were more flippant than true. For more than 30 years now, Taylor has managed to retain an extremely loyal following. His fans have stuck by him with unwavering support throughout his years of hardship.

'You'd always hear crazy rumours and stories about James's personal life,' said Ernie Greene, who has been both a Mitchell and a Taylor worshiper since 1968 and has bought all of their albums. Greene has also attended over one hundred of their concerts. 'So what if he screwed around with Joni Mitchell. Does that make him a weaker person, and should we stop buying his albums if he was a jerk to her? It's very easy in this business for people to go to the media to try to retaliate. Mitchell was rumoured to have slept with many rock stars and actors around the time she went out with Taylor, so anybody who thinks that she was some innocent prima donna in the whole thing is extremely naive. I love Joni and certainly sympathise with her, but it doesn't mean that she shouldn't take any less heat than Taylor for their bad relationship. Even if she did get dumped and if Taylor was a prick to her, she should have just moved on and not sound like she's trying to say bad things about him in her lyrics and songs.'

Greene continued, 'It's important to look at the overall picture. Taylor had way more class than Joni because he never bad-mouthed her in the press, in his music or in public. He was too much of a gentleman to stoop to her level. The media made too much of their affair and were very unfair to Taylor. Remember, you're talking about an artist who has bent over backward so many times to help people less fortunate than himself, and who has done so much concerning environmental issues. Everybody knew that Mitchell was a bit screwed up back then. It was very unfair that Taylor got condemned after they broke up. And despite the attempts of so many people to make him look bad, it sure didn't hurt his career. He went on with his life with much more class and less bitterness than Mitchell did.'

After Mitchell threatened several times to retire permanently from the music business, she put her stamp on several glorious and highly acclaimed releases. But her great success would come only after she came to terms with the end of her relationship with Taylor. Her work by then seemed more mature and stronger, partly because of her strong, spare lyrics combined with the use of unusual instrumental effects, which Mitchell had avoided in the past. She became more heavy, at times even melodramatic. Her playing was more thorough and more nuanced.

'There was a lot of affection in those relationships,' Mitchell said in a 1979 *Rolling Stone* interview. 'The fact that I couldn't stay in them for one reason or another was painful to me. The men involved are good people. I'm fond of them to this day. We have a mutual affection, even though we've gone on to new relationships. Certainly there are pockets of hurt that come. You come a little battered out of a relationship that doesn't go on forever. I don't live in bitterness.

'I'm a confronter by nature,' she said. 'I have a tendency to confront my relationships much more often than people would care. I'm always being told that I talk too much. It's not that I like to, but I habitually confront before I escape. Rather than go out and try to drown my sorrows or something, I'll wallow and muddle through them. My friends thought for a long time that this was done out of masochism. I began to believe it myself. But at this time in my life, I would say that it has paid some dividend . . . Even psychiatrists, mind whores for the most part, don't have a healthy attitude toward depression. They get bored with it. I think their problem is they need to be deeply depressed.'

Eventually both Joni and James got beyond their pain and anger, and found they were happy to be friends again. They had shared so much together in their youthful passion, and the bonds between them were still very strong. A series of long, intense phone calls – arranged by

Peter Asher, who had also become Mitchell's agent – led to a joyful reunion in the early '80s. But more than this, the two began talking music together. They had always greatly respected each other's musical skills, and it was exciting for them to begin thinking about collaborating on a grand scale. The two of them had been successful in a couple of previous collaborations and both were convinced that reuniting their talents would be truly magical.

And so their professional relationship began in earnest. This collaboration would give both deep satisfaction over the years. In some ways, Taylor said, it was even more meaningful than love to be able to collaborate together musically. Although these were not some of their best-selling works, *aficionados* of both cherish their music together as collector items.

The new series of collaborations made them regain respect for each other, marking a new beginning to their once-troubled relationship.

In 1981 Taylor was busy helping out his longtime backup vocalist and close friend David Lasley on Lasley's solo project *Misssing Twenty Grand* (Lasley was also a successful songwriter in his own right who had written for such well-known singers as Bonnie Raitt, Anita Baker and Boz Skaggs). Before they embarked on a tour of Japan, Lasley asked Taylor if he would become a guest on his album. Of course, Taylor obliged; he has always been a big supporter of the solo projects of the members of his band.

Ironically, fate was about to throw Taylor and Mitchell together again. Taylor walked into the impressive surroundings of A&M studios in Los Angeles in March 1981. He headed for Studio A where Lasley was at work. Directly across the hall, Joni Mitchell was recording *Wild Things Run Fast*, her debut on David Geffen's highly hyped new label, Geffen Records. When Mitchell asked him to play on her album, Taylor agreed and spent the rest of his time hopping back and forth between studios.

The former lovers also collaborated on Mitchell's seminal *Dog Eat Dog* album in 1985. Taylor figured prominently among the handful of guest artists with famous names on Mitchell's fourteenth album, including Don Henley, legendary saxman Wayne Shorter, and even actor Rod Steiger, whom Mitchell hired to play the role of an extremist right-wing evangelist on 'Tax Free.' With synthesiser-laden bands like the Eurythmics and A-Ha at the top of the charts, Mitchell tried to work her way back into the mainstream by combining modern synth sounds with her usual free-spirited style of politically inspired lyrics.

Critics weren't too kind to her new album, however; they found it too formulaic and artificial.

'The synthesiser was irresistible,' Mitchell said. 'It puts a whole orchestra at your fingertips.'

Perhaps the biggest fan she had for her new style was Taylor himself. He sang background vocals on the albums' title track, 'Dog Eat Dog', and couldn't stop raving about how innovative his ex-girlfriend had become. Taylor got a huge thrill out of working with Mitchell again. It inspired him to adopt some of the modern synth sounds she was using into his own music. 'Her music isn't whimsical, transitory, or momentary,' Taylor said. 'When I worked on her album, I said to myself, "That's the stuff".'

It's the haunting sound of their voices mingled together in the soulful melodies Mitchell arranged that delighted many of their fans. 'They had very similar interests and styles,' said former Grateful Dead leader Jerry Garcia. 'Both of them were big innovators in the modern folk movement. I could listen to Joni's albums over and over and keep finding new things in her music every time I put it on. And the same can be said about James Taylor. And the times they sang together were very uplifting moments. Everybody who was into the whole thing of the peace-and-love movement in the '60s bought their albums. They were the two artists we could all relate to because they were doing drugs, making love and living the lives every hippie out there could only live in their dreams.

'Hey,' Garcia added, 'we were all a bit screwed up during that period. So when Joni and James sang about how fucked up their lives were, it sure hit home. Listening to their music was spiritual. It was almost along the lines of being therapeutic.'

13

'YOU'VE GOT A FRIEND'

In April 1971, Taylor, 23, was in a great mood. He was *en route* to New York to make several promotional appearances for an upcoming North American tour. He had hired the members of Danny Kortchmar's band Jo Mama, along with Carole King, as backup musicians. Kootch's band was a perfect fit for Taylor. He appreciated the members' ability to play tight, and they were also his good friends. One thing in particular impressed concert promoters around the country about Taylor: He didn't leave many seats empty. Taylor and his band embarked on a 27-city tour that had been sold out in advance. Critics labelled it a 'must-see,' making it one of the hottest tickets on the arena circuit.

'This is a dream come true,' Taylor told a member of his band. 'If you'd told me two years ago that people would be lining up to hear me play, I would have said that you're nuts. This is what it's all about, making music and having a blast. There's nothing else that could be better than this.'

Taylor was in high spirits because during the past few months he had managed to stay sober and drug-free. He had grown tired of his erratic lifestyle and desperately tried to change. Determined to put the past behind him, he was in the process of trying to clean himself up. A few of his close friends, including Peter Asher, had confronted him about his drug use. When he heard the same recommendation from his entourage, he had to stop. The people at Warner Bros were worried as well; Taylor was their best-selling artist, and they didn't want him to become the next rock-star-turned-casualty. Warner's first concern was for Taylor to stay clean and sober on this tour.

'Taylor's records were flying off racks,' said an ex-Warner Bros employee. 'Most of the artists were stoned out of their minds back then. What Taylor was doing was not anything out of the ordinary. But he was one of the label's most important and popular artists. Everybody at Warner liked him because he was such a nice guy. Nobody wanted to see him destroy himself. The people who ran the show at Warner feared that the drugs might cause him to burn out before he was 25. They talked to his people and asked them to try to do something to help straighten him out.'

Asher had several long talks with Taylor, trying to convince him to get help and clean up his act. Taylor seemed to achieve some kind of emotional maturity. He realised that all the drug taking and womanising had begun to take its toll. He finally admitted that it was time to forsake his past lifestyle if he wanted to stay alive. He was very excited about finishing the new album he had started recording, *Mud Slide Slim and the Blue Horizon*. But first he needed to get his head together. Taylor told friends that he would work hard on the album in the hope that he'd have no free time to devote to his destructive drug habits.

Everybody in Taylor's camp thought that it was possible that the new album might shatter the sales figures of *Sweet Baby James*, because Taylor seemed to pour himself into writing the material. Solo artists like Jackson Browne and Cat Stevens were enjoying much-publicised revivals, so it wasn't difficult to predict that Taylor's new album would see massive media exposure.

'All eyes were on Taylor to see what he could do as a follow-up to the enormous success of his previous album,' said pop critic Martin Smith. 'And I'm sure that a lot of people wanted to see him fall flat on his face. But when I heard the new album, I was blown away. I couldn't believe that he was able to top the performance he did on the *Sweet Baby James* album. There were so many rumours being bandied about his personal problems and his drug habits; many people expected that his work would suffer greatly. But it didn't. I think the new album wound up being one of my top three favourite albums of the '70s. The thing that struck me right away when I first heard *Mud Slide* was the way James had matured musically. It was very apparent that all those gigs and recordings he'd done in the past couple of years had paid off. If you listened to his music two years before and compared it to what he was doing at the time of *Mud Slide*, it was apples and oranges. This album is the reason why his career lasted so long. It set the stage for the rest of his career. It's an album that is still considered by many a pop classic. Very few albums in the history of pop music had as big an impact as this one.'

But for Taylor, his feeling about making music had changed. He later told *Billboard* editor Timothy White that by the time he started working on his third album, he had become quite disenchanted with the music business; making music wasn't as pleasurable as it used to be. 'When I made my first and second albums it was basically unknown terrain, and I was still working, somehow, from a very pure place. After *Sweet Baby James*, I knew what it felt like to work for a living and be this sort of hypothetical entrepreneur with a record company, agent, manager, whatever.'

Before *Mud Slide* was finished, Taylor's camp faced a new crisis. Chip Taylor (no relation) announced that he was going to release the *James Taylor and the Original Flying Machine* album he had produced a few years back. Before he realised the implications, James Taylor didn't seem to mind that his former producer was trying to capitalize on his fame. The other members of the Flying Machine didn't object, either, because it meant that they would finally get some royalty cheques for the work they'd put in. But Peter Asher was livid. He thought there was a good chance that *Flying Machine* would interfere with record sales for the new album. Asher desperately tried to persuade Chip Taylor to postpone his plans. But Chip made it clear to everybody that all that he wanted to do was try to get a return on his investment.

'I put up a lot of my own money to produce that album, so why shouldn't I try to get some of it back?' he said. 'This album is important because it's the first one James made, and it will have good sentimental value to his fans. They deserve to hear it. I'm not trying to interfere with his other albums, but I have the right to release this album because I own the rights.'

Without James's support, though, Chip Taylor wasn't able to market the album properly. He released it on his own label in the hope that Taylor fans would buy it out of sheer curiosity. Initially record sales were very low because it was overshadowed by the release of *Mud Slide Slim*. Throughout the years, however, the album has been re-released several times with a variety of covers and label names. Sales and popularity among Taylor fans increased enormously when it was released on CD in 1996 on the Gadfly Records label, even though Chip Taylor was harshly criticised for digitally rearranging several songs. He was seen by some as a self-righteous opportunist who would do anything to pad his own pockets.

Lahri Bond blasted Chip Taylor in a March 1997 column in *Dirty*

Linen. 'In reissuing this album, producer Chip Taylor has created one of the cardinal sins of the modern CD world,' Lahri said. 'He has messed with the sequencing of the original album and has added new versions of old songs at the beginning of the disc, rather than at the end, where they can be perceived as bonus tracks to a much-beloved album . . . The reissue begins with a new version of ["Night Owl"] that has been remixed with a recently added bass, drums and percussion parts. "Knockin' 'Round the Zoo", a peculiar pop tune about Taylor's self-imposed exile to a mental hospital for nine months before his move to New York, is given a similar, unwelcome updating. . . . Yes it's nice to have this landmark album on CD. Yes, it's nice to hear it without all the crackle, pops and skips that most of us have grown used to, but please, please, don't mess with what was a perfectly good album to begin with!'

Meanwhile, Taylor had forged ahead with several other side projects, including his first attempt at acting. He was well aware that the popularity of musicians who were able to land major film roles increased immensely. And so did their record sales. In early 1971, well-known Hollywood film director Monte Hellman approached Taylor to star in his upcoming film *Two-Lane Blacktop*. It was an epic about two wild car freaks drag-racing across the southwestern part of America in a grey 1955 Chevy. Taylor thought it was an irresistible opportunity to break into Hollywood. Throughout the years, several people had suggested to him that he would be a good actor, because he was good-looking and charismatic.

Hellman took a special interest in Taylor because he was fascinated with the things Taylor had gone through and experienced in his young life. Hellman had gained notoriety for directing underground classics like *The Wild Rebels* in 1967 and *Ride in the Whirlwind* in 1965. He chose Taylor for the role of the driver who was challenged by a character named GTO to race to Washington, DC. The first one to arrive won the loser's car. On the journey, the lives and bizarre personalities of the drivers and mechanic are brought out.

Two-Lane Blacktop got mixed reviews and did poorly at the box office, despite having some of the best racing scenes ever shot on film. Taylor's performance was singled out as one of the few bright spots in the film. On the set Taylor and his co-stars became fast friends. He palled around with the Beach Boys' Dennis Wilson, who played the mechanic, and Warren Oates, who played GTO. The actors and crew loved working with Taylor and were proud to become associated with one of the nation's best-known artists. Most of the cast and crew were already fans.

'The day he set foot on the set you could tell that everybody was a bit in awe of him. They couldn't wait to meet him and tried to bend over backward to make him feel at home,' Hellman said. 'They all knew who he was and were aware that it was his first big film project, so they went out of their way to make him feel comfortable. By the end of the shoot, he was already acting like a seasoned pro. He was a natural. The performance he gave was strong, and he got very good reviews. There was never a doubt in my mind that he was right for the role. If you watch the film closely, it would be very difficult to tell that acting wasn't his day job. He really played his part with authority and conviction.'

Meanwhile, Taylor had a different take on the Hollywood experience. It had been a physically demanding role, and he was exhausted by the time the shooting wrapped. He told his friends that he enjoyed being on set but he didn't realise how tough it was to be an actor; he was in no hurry to audition for another role. Despite its lack of success the film remains a popular selection in video stores for James Taylor fans.

Shortly after returning from shooting the film, Taylor put the finishing touches on the new album. *Mud Slide Slim and the Blue Horizon* featured guest appearances by several people close to Taylor, including his sister, Kate, and Peter Asher. Joni Mitchell appeared on three songs doing backup vocals, even though their intimate relationship had ended. Carole King played keyboards and sang, and penned the song that became one of Taylor's all-time biggest hits, 'You've Got a Friend'.

On the album's cover, Taylor's sombre look was reflective of his music. He appears to be in pain, with a haunting look and a stone-cold facial expression. Mustachioed and neatly dressed, he holds the suspenders on his pants. There is a slight aura of Bonnie and Clyde. Never raising his voice and accompanied by his usual dose of autobiographical lyrics, James' music is darker than usual and deals with a wide range of underlying melancholy topics, ranging from loneliness to self-doubt.

The first time Taylor heard Carole King sing 'You've Got a Friend' live at one of her concerts at the Troubadour Club in Los Angeles, he got goosebumps, and tears started to roll down his face. He was able to relate the lyrics to the crippling depression he had suffered for so long. King, whose songwriting Taylor had long revered, was flattered when he told her after the show how much he liked the song.

Indeed, he had connected so strongly with the song that he soon asked King if he could cover it on his upcoming album. King, who had already agreed to perform on the album, seized the opportunity to lend him her trademark song. And musical magic was about to happen.

Almost everyone who grew up in the '70s has a story about how Taylor's version of 'You've Got a Friend' affected their lives. Taylor admits that he never intended to be the voice of a generation, but each album he released seemed to have a few songs that were able to strike a chord with society's downtrodden. After Taylor, Kootch and bassist Les Sklar laid down the final guitar tracks, everybody in the studio had a feeling the song would be big – but nobody could have predicted how big. 'You've Got a Friend' became an anthem for millions of people around the world who needed a dose of confidence to snap out of their loneliness. It also became one of the most popular standards to learn for anyone who picked up an acoustic guitar.

New York City guitar teacher Greg Bahnsen says, 'When I start teaching a new student, I always ask them to name a few tunes they want to learn. Nine out of ten times they name a James Taylor song, and usually it's "You've Got a Friend". It's a pretty basic tune, but there's a lot you can learn if you master its chord progression. And it's a lot of fun. Some students get discouraged and give up playing if you throw at them a more difficult jazz tune like "All the Things You Are" or "Autumn Leaves". A lot of great guitarists, including my own kid brother, have started out by learning Taylor's music. I'm not saying his music by any stretch is for beginners, because I truly believe that the man's a genius, but it's more fun and easier to learn when you're starting out.'

'You've Got a Friend' succeeded in gaining the approval of even his harshest critics. Taylor didn't get along too well with several members of the music press, who were more eager to dig up facts about his personal problems than to discuss his music.

'Taylor needed an incredible song to follow up on the success he had with his previous album,' recalled music critic Martin Smith. 'A lot of critics were waiting for him to fall flat on his face because he had a reputation for not being co-operative with some members of the media. Not too many people thought that he'd be able to top or even come close to the success he had with "Fire and Rain". The first time I heard

"You've Got a Friend" I told my girlfriend right away that it was going to be a monster hit even though it was such a simple song. And I was right. To this day it remains a classic. So many of the old songs from that era died after a year or two because they sounded like everything else being put out back then. Nothing remotely came close to sounding like Taylor's version of "You've Got a Friend". It's a pretty simple song but I predict that in a hundred years people will still be listening to it because it's a song everybody on this planet can relate to.'

Shortly after it was released, 'You've Got a Friend' was placed on heavy rotation by radio stations across the country and hit number one. It also won Taylor a Grammy for best male pop vocal performance and brought Carole King song of the year honours. *Mud Slide Slim and the Blue Horizon* peaked at number two and was selling at a record pace.

'Long Ago and Far Away' examined lust and longing and was by far the most daring track on the album. Taylor liked to experiment with various styles and usually included one or two songs on his albums that were different. Taylor later explained to journalist Timothy White his thought behind writing 'Long Ago and Far Away'. 'That's the type of song that comes straight out of the melody, but long ago and far away is not part of the lyrics. What I actually say is long ago, a young man sits and plays his waiting game. It's a simple song about how things don't turn out the way you planned for them to, a melancholy song about the nature of people's dreams and the cold hard realities that have a habit of blowing in on them . . . The most coherent part of that song for me is probably the second verse – Love is just a word I've heard when things are being said . . . It's a musing on the nature of expectations, and how they don't last.'

The B side of 'Long Ago', entitled 'Let Me Ride', earned notoriety as a message Taylor was trying to deliver to the people close to him. In the song he asked to be let alone to do his thing, even if people didn't always agree with it. His sister, Kate, sang background. James kept reworking it again and again; he wanted to make sure that it delivered the message and captured his mood. In vintage Taylor fashion, he didn't mince words.

Peter Asher was delighted with the cascade of royalty money. He quickly became the most sought-after manager in the music business. He was bombarded with other project requests. He was easygoing, well liked and shrewd. Not since the days of Brian Epstein or Colonel Tom Parker had someone created a buzz about his client the way Asher did for Taylor. Indeed, he was to become a legend in the music industry. In the meantime, concert promoters around the world lined up to book a Taylor concert, Hollywood came calling and endorsement offers poured in.

A shrewd businessman, Asher ran the day-to-day operations of Taylor's career with a tight fist. He would sit in his office all day listening to the piles of unsolicited demos he received, trying to find the next big star. Being a good judge of character played a large part in his career. It was common for people to show up at his door unannounced, begging to jump on board with him. He was very careful about whom he hired. He was well aware that one or two bad moves in the music business could destroy what he had worked a lifetime to accomplish.

'From the person who answered the phone to the musicians he hired in the band, Peter Asher was responsible for every move in Taylor's career,' said one of his close aassociates. 'He wasn't as authoritative as someone like Colonel Tom Parker, but he took care of business in his own quiet way. Not many managers were capable of protecting their artists the way Peter Asher protected Taylor. He was aware of every trick in the book and was very hard to suck into a new project unless it was something that would be guaranteed to benefit his client.'

Although Taylor's record sales kept the cash register ringing, Asher had to work hard to make sure the books balanced. The huge overhead of carrying a full band on tour and the costs of major nationwide promotional campaigns ate away a lot of the budget. Asher was ambitious and knew how to cut corners to ensure that everybody made a good penny.

'Asher liked to spend a lot on the production both in studio and live performances,' said Allen Walker, a respected recording studio engineer. 'Taylor's concerts were usually sold out but they had a lot of expenses. Taylor always used the best equipment and had a reputation for carrying some of the best backup musicians in the business. Asher was very particular about everything that went on before, during and after the show. I've worked for some artists who show up and seem to be more interested in getting the performance over with and getting paid. Asher was a perfectionist. If a microphone wasn't turned on properly or if a light was out of place, he'd hit the ceiling. He didn't care about how expensive the show was to put on. He cared about giving people the best possible value for their entertainment dollar.'

Asher never lost his desire, friends have said, to keep improving

Taylor's artistic talents even as the money poured in. He was just as committed to artistic integrity as he was to making money.

'Each time Peter produced an album, he wanted it to sound fresh,' said Richard Hewson, who worked for Asher doing music arrangements. 'He was a real innovator who was always trying to be a bit different than everybody else. That's one of the major reasons why his artists were so successful and were able to have such long careers.'

14

THE BIRTH OF A ROCK FAMILY

In the spring of 1971, Taylor's mission during his 27-city sell-out tour to support *Mud Slide Slim and the Blue Horizon* was to try to stay clean. He had made a firm commitment to himself and his management team that he would try to avoid taking drugs. During previous tours many people who worked with him hit brick walls when they tried to get him drug-free. This time there was cause for rejoicing. His band mates had often been concerned that his live performance wasn't up to par when he was whacked out on heroin. Kootch and the rest of the band did their share of marijuana and drinking, but they didn't go near the hard drugs to which Taylor was addicted.

For 23-year-old James Taylor, it wasn't easy to make a major change in his lifestyle. He found it excruciating to withdraw. He tried to keep his condition to himself, because he didn't want to alarm the rest of the band. He had no idea how long he would be able to stay clean without falling apart.

His father told a friend that Taylor should have never gone on tour at that time because he was very unstable. According to the friend, Isaac said, 'He looked terrible and seemed very desperate. Everybody was giving him advice how to straighten himself up but they didn't tell him to stop touring, because he was selling out everywhere he played. I felt so bad for him because he needed to be getting help instead of being out on tour. During that tour with Kootch's band he went through so much pain because he was suffering from withdrawal. When he went onstage he looked frail and confused. It was amazing that he was even able to stand up. I felt so sorry for him because he was putting the desires of his money-hungry handlers ahead of his own well-being. That's the type of person James always has been. He always wanted to make people happy, even if it meant he had to suffer.'

On the road, Taylor devised some desperate tricks to try to stay clean. He would lock himself in his hotel room and try to sleep off his cravings for heroin. If he couldn't fall asleep, he called a family member on the telephone and talked until he felt tired enough to doze off. His handlers also supported his effort. Moments before a concert, he was whisked off to that night's venue. Minutes later, he was performing.

Onstage, Taylor was a physical and emotional wreck. The withdrawal symptoms overwhelmed him. He began to rely on uppers to avoid collapsing. He didn't feel right. By the end of the first few songs of his set he felt like passing out. When he'd stepped onstage in the past, most of the time he was high. Without drugs he didn't have the buzz he relied on to make it through a whole concert without feeling like he was about to die. Taylor was no longer comfortable performing straight.

One of his biggest supporters was Carole King, the brilliant songwriter who accompanied him on keyboards. King had experienced her share of personal turmoil and drug abuse while she was married to Gerry Goffin, her songwriting partner in the '60s. Together, King and Goffin penned dozens of mega-hits like the Shirelles' 'Will You Love Me Tomorrow?', Bobby Vee's 'Take Good Care of My Baby', and Aretha Franklin's 'Natural Woman'. But their marriage was doomed shortly after they became successful. The press heaped ridicule upon them after reports that their relationship was marred by jealousy, nasty arguments and infidelity.

After their marriage broke up, King went through an ordeal of considerable inner pain. She had difficulty accepting the fact that neither she nor Goffin had lived up to their marriage vows. King needed a long time to fully recover from a relationship that she later admitted was a tapestry of broken dreams.

Although Taylor pressed on during the tour as if he were invincible, King sensed that he was a mess. She noticed the classic signs of withdrawal. Taylor appeared helpless, dismayed and dominated by quick mood changes. She confronted him after a show in Chicago and offered to help him. Taylor took in every word as King spoke for hours about the tough times she had gone through. Listening to King's stories about her own experiences made Taylor feel like he was not the only person on the planet who was screwed up. It has often been said that without King's support and inspiration, Taylor might not have ever made it through that tour.

'Carole was the type of person who was able to make people forget about their problems,' said Los Angeles rock critic Al Taylor (no relation). 'She was used to being around male musicians who had lots of problems, especially problems that were drug-related. And she knew how to deal with the situation. She wouldn't quit a project because somebody was fucked up. She'd try to help. Carole was one of the strongest people ever in this business, 'cause she had gone through so much shit in her own life.

'When she was on tour with James Taylor in 1971, she was the person who held that band together. The other members in the band were party animals and weren't able to understand what Taylor was going through the way Carole did. Through her own experiences she was able to give him hope and was one of the only people he felt comfortable to open up to, to tell how lousy he was feeling.'

During the tour, ugly stories about Taylor's personal life began to surface in the media. Writers had a field day discussing his drug problems and his affairs with women. They were more interested in asking Taylor to comment on his personal past than the songs on his new album. His drug use and womanising were laid out in major feature stories across America. The *New York Times*, *Rolling Stone*, and *Time* all ran features reporting on Taylor's wild lifestyle. King advised Taylor to deal with it by taking some of the things the media said with a grain of salt. She said that the best tonic for his troubles was work.

'In music you gotta just keep learning and evolving,' King said. 'It's a lifelong pursuit. Just 'cause you have a hit record it doesn't mean that you should stop learning things like more advanced chords that will help you become a better all-around musician. You shouldn't get caught up in the hype – otherwise you'll start believing that it's true.'

Despite some of the negative press, Taylor's fans stayed on his side. If anything, it made them more compassionate toward their hero.

According to Al Taylor, Taylor's record sales soared whenever a journalist tried to discredit him. 'A friend of mine was working at a radio station in San Francisco and he told me that the most requested song was "You've Got a Friend". This was in the early '70s. I remember speaking to him shortly after a *Rolling Stone* story appeared about Taylor's personal life. It painted him as being very unstable and heavily into drugs. The story was pretty accurate but was a bit too explicit for my liking, because it didn't focus enough on the brilliance of his songwriting. My friend said that after the story came out, the lines lit up with requests for "You've Got a Friend". Taylor's fans wanted to give him a clear message that they were with him and didn't care what was said about him by his detractors. Almost 30 years later his fans' loyalty is just as strong. Usually in the music business fans abandon their heros when negative stories about them start surfacing. Just look at people like Michael Jackson, M. C. Hammer or even Frank Sinatra, whose records didn't sell like they used to after negative reports about their personal lives started to be reported in the media.'

After what seemed to be a strategically decent interval, Taylor took some time off. When his 27-city tour was over, he escaped to his favourite hideaway, Martha's Vineyard, to catch up with old friends and family. He was especially eager to learn about the musical endeavours of his brothers and sister. Taylor received a hero's welcome. His celebrated career was the talk of the island. Tourists flocked to his cottage to try to catch a glimpse of him. His mother worried that the family's privacy would be interrupted and considered moving to another location. Taylor wouldn't have it. He told his mother that he owed it to his brothers and sister to try to stay in the place they had all grown so fond of. Indeed, Taylor wanted to settle permanently on Martha's Vineyard and was willing to pay the price of being recognised wherever he went.

'You couldn't have met a nicer man,' said Barbara Thompson, who was vacationing on the Vineyard with her husband in 1971 when she met Taylor at a grocery store. 'I was picking up some vegetables and I noticed him a few feet ahead of me. I couldn't believe it. I knew he lived there, but I never thought that I'd get the chance to meet him. I approached him and told him I was a big fan. Never have I met a nicer and more down-to-earth person. He recommended several sites to visit and suggested a couple of good bars to go to. He knew everything about Martha's Vineyard. I had read about his problems in the newspaper but when I met him it was hard to tell he was the same person. He was so polite and seemed to be very happy.'

Taylor discovered that he wasn't the only talented member of his family: the music of his brothers and younger sister had found many receptive fans as well. Everyone except his brother Hugh released albums in 1971, including debuts by Alex and Kate. Alex's *With Friends and Neighbours* was released without much fanfare but managed to attract a cultlike following, largely out of curiosity because of the success of his brother. Kate Taylor's *Sister Kate* received a little more attention and airplay. Everybody was anxious to hear how James's sister sounded. 'She has a beautiful voice,' James told several members of the media. 'She has potential to go very far.'

Livingston's *Liv* showed respectable sales and has been re-released several times. At age 20, Livingston signed with Phil Walden's Capricorn label. Jon Landau, who later managed Bruce Springsteen, produced Liv's first two albums. Like his brother's, Liv's music was laid-back and autobiographical. He'd spent time in the same mental hospital as his brother, which was the source of a lot of his artistic inspiration. Doctors called his condition 'adolescent turmoil' but Liv preferred to say, 'I had the blues.' In a *Rolling Stone* interview in 1970 he said: 'While I was sitting around at McLean, I saw a lot of people who were very depressed and unhappy about life in general and had nothing to do, and I said to myself, "Man, I'm not gonna spend my life that way."'

The Taylors displayed little of the sibling rivalry that tore apart other '70s musical families like the Jackson Five, the Beach Boys and the Osmonds. It was common for the Taylor kids to help each other out on their albums and at their concerts. Many times they appeared at each other's performances, accompanying on guitar and lending backup vocals.

In a 1980 interview in the *Dallas Morning News*, Livingston said that he was not so foolish that he would try to be like his brother, who had become one of the world's top-selling artists. 'I have never sold a million records. I don't know how that feels, but I don't feel bad about what I do. Indeed, contrasted with James, my success is modest. But take away that comparison and the success is just fine.'

Livingston tried to downplay his relation to his famous brother. He was determined to make a name for himself. James's other siblings also started attracting some media attention, mainly due to the success of their famous brother. *Time* magazine said the Taylor kids were emerging as America's 'Family of Rock'! 'James's rivals may also soon include a few more individual Taylors. Thus far Livingston, Alex and Kate have openly, though in Livingston's case not always willingly, ridden on James's coattails. Yet the tendency to see Livingston merely as an "up" imitation of James's "down" is unfair and misleading, as anyone will know who listens to the deft melodic twists and musical good humour of Livingston's first LP.'

The Taylor offspring transformed Martha's Vineyard into a folksy celebrity magnet, giving it a fairytale reputation. The highlight of the summer occurred when James and his siblings performed live. Most longtime Vineyard residents agree that without the allure of the Taylor musical dynasty it might not have become such a popular getaway; it would've been just another summer resort with a pleasant climate and prohibitive prices.

'Anybody who says that people who don't come to Martha's Vineyard because of James Taylor doesn't know what they're talking about,' said William Cohen, whose family rented a cottage there for several years. 'Every summer I've bumped into people who came wanting to meet James, or one of his brothers. I think that most people come to meet James, but it's surprising how many people are familiar with the music of his brothers and sisters. Whenever they performed here the concerts were always sold out.'

Alex Taylor affected an almost paternal role with his famous brother. More than anybody, he was responsible for getting James started in the music business. In later years James repeatedly credited his older brother with helping him learn music, as well as being there for him when he went through several rough periods. Unfortunately, Alex had less success with both his own life and career. His drinking and drug problems, along with his fiery temper, did not remain a secret for long, and record executives became hesitant to sign him. Many people in the music industry felt that Alex was the most talented of the Taylor kids, perhaps even more talented than James. But for executives banking on his future, he was too much of a risk.

Legendary record executive Morris Levy once said: 'James Taylor's family was talented but they seemed to have too many drug problems. His older brother was very talented and he could have capitalised on the fame of his brother. I was interested in signing him but the A&R people were not in a hurry. They warned me not to do so because of his chequered past. There's no doubt in my mind that the family was fascinating and that their talent was unbelievable. But the rumours about their personal problems were a deterrent.'

Alex's songs wandered a misty terrain of self-disclosure and romantic yearning. His distinctively dark ambience and acoustic guitar were usually at the centre of his music. His lyrics had a rebellious undertone that questioned the basic tenets of society. 'He definitely had something to say,' James Taylor said. 'Alex was very sensitive to what was going on in the outside world and his feelings about certain things in life were brought out clearly in his music.'

The Taylors insisted that sibling rivalry was a foreign concept to them, on or off the stage. Still, their similar folk-music styles dictated that their careers would be put on collision courses. For one Taylor to do well, he or she had to show better record sales than the others.

As for grudges, Livingston Taylor did not think one existed among his siblings. The disintegration of their parents' marriage proved so devastating that they vowed to support one another even more than before. 'We went through a lot of ups and downs together, and if anything it brought us more together,' Livingston recalled. 'In the music business there's room for everybody. I wouldn't want one my brothers' or sister's careers to suffer because of me. I want us all to do well and find our own niche. Sometimes we might have joked with each other about whose album was getting more attention, but it was all in good taste. The music business is tough; you're only as good as your last album. A lot of people might have thought that James's success would have opened doors for the rest of his family. Instead we seemed to have more pressure to live up to the high standard that our brother set. In a way it was good, because it made us become better musicians.'

Not all of the Taylor youngsters displayed Livingston's positive attitude. Alex Taylor, who might have been watching James's triumphs with delight, was actually in despair. During the height of James's fame in the early '70s, Alex considered quitting the music business. Confronted by the constant comparisons with his famous brother, Alex was reluctant to record another album. But he never held a grudge against James. In fact, he stood up for him. During a concert one night on Martha's Vineyard in 1971, Alex became irate when, in the middle of a tune, a member of the audience shouted out from the back of the room, 'Your brother sucks.' Alex, very upset, stopped cold and stared down the man. 'Some people just need to get a life. If you don't like my brother or my family then you shouldn't be here in the first place,' Alex responded, before launching again into his song.

A lot of people were cynical and waited for the Taylor kids to fail. Critics knocked them as much for things they did not do as for what they did.

'There was a time when people were very critical,' Livingston Taylor recalled. 'Some people couldn't accept the fact that we were all into similar styles of music. They expected us to be very different and to be as successful as our brother. I've always known that I have my own voice, and when people get too critical I try not to let it bother me. I keep a positive attitude.'

'Alex's music was very personal to him, and he resented that critics were always comparing him to James,' said musician Joel O'Brien. 'It was tough for him because he was extremely talented and his music had its own merits, but in many ways he was forced to live in his brother's shadow. If he hadn't had to bear the Taylor name, his career might have taken off sooner and he wouldn't have always had to worry about the comparisons. Many people knew him more as James Taylor's brother than as Alex Taylor. But people who listened to his music closely knew him first as Alex Taylor.'

15

ENTER CARLY SIMON

In April 1971, 23-year-old James Taylor was about to finally change his luck with a new, solid love relationship. He became involved with Carly Simon, the 27-year-old singer. The tall, blond, curly-haired beauty with luminous skin and curvaceous hips made heads turn wherever she went.

Taylor and Simon bumped into one another several times at folk concerts when they were growing up. Their relationship was cordial at best. They began dating after being more formally introduced by Carly's brother, Peter, who knew Taylor's younger brother Livingston. Shortly after, they encountered each other again on the street. At first Taylor didn't recognise her, because she was all dressed up.

'I followed her, thinking she was another woman,' Taylor told a reporter. 'I was thinking, "What a fine-looking woman that is." Then I discovered it was Carly.'

Simon recalled how she lusted for Taylor after their first real meeting. 'It was his eyes, looking out from under long brown hair. His eyes looking half-crazed and totally romantic. I remember looking at him and thinking he was magnificent in some strong sense of the word . . . It seemed as if we had known each other and lived in the same place before.'

Taylor and Simon were two of the most eligible catches in the country – both rich, famous and good-looking. Although Taylor was plagued by severe emotional and psychological problems, Simon fell head over heels in love. It was the start of a relationship that would dominate both their lives for the next decade. They became known as rock's quintessential couple. The celebrity relationship was played out in the media for years; the couple's romance, escapades and legendary bitter feuds were grist for the gossip columns.

Simon's formula in the past for trying to meet the right man had been playing hard to get. She quickly abandoned this when she met Taylor, practically throwing herself at him. Taylor might have been four years her junior, but she had never before found anybody as fascinating.

They married on 3 November 1972. That same night, Taylor announced during a midnight concert at Radio City Music Hall that earlier in the evening he and Simon had been married. The capacity crowd congratulated the newlyweds with thunderous applause. According to Carly, they had decided to get engaged one afternoon after Carly jokingly suggested earlier in the morning that it was time for them to get married.

'I mentioned one morning to James in London that I thought we should get married, and James was kind of hesitant in his response,' Simon told writer Stuart Werbin. 'He said, "Oh well, there's really no reason to get married. We love each other and we've been living together." And then later on in the afternoon, James said, "You know, I've been thinking about it, and maybe we should get married." I said, "Well, what's happened between this morning and this afternoon?" He said, "This afternoon it was my idea."'

Many people close to the couple doubted that their marriage would last. They both had unstable personalities and had not been successful in maintaining long-term relationships.

'When I heard they got married, I remember thinking to myself that it wouldn't last longer than six months,' said Bonnie Platt, a New York artist who knew several people in both Taylor's and Simon's families. 'They were two of the flakiest people you could ever meet. I always thought Carly was a bit weird and I couldn't have imagined anybody living with her for a long period of time. She was very fussy and demanding and had a reputation for being very hard to be around. If you look at both of their backgrounds, they were a bit spoiled and didn't seem to want to ever grow up. They were always getting into some sort of trouble. They were two of the most screwed-up young people you could meet. Both of them had their share of encounters with psychiatrists, drugs and booze. Nobody who knew them could have seriously thought that marriage would be the answer to their long history of problems. If anything, we all thought it would make them more confused.'

By the time Taylor became involved with Simon, he was trying to sort out his life. He had recovered from the relationship with Joni Mitchell that had ended more than a year before, yet he often wondered if the right woman would ever come along. In Simon he had finally met his match.

She was a woman with a complex temperament and an equally complex sense of humour. Like Taylor, she was totally self-absorbed. She seemed able to extract whatever she wanted from life. And, like Taylor, she used art and music as a direct expression of her innermost self. She wrote songs about the love, anger and petulance that had dominated her young life.

'Carly was best able to bring out her true feelings about life when she wrote songs,' said her longtime friend and songwriting collaborator Jacob Brackman. 'She seemed to have many different personalities when she was offstage because of her many insecurities. She was able to put on many masks, depending on what she thought someone wanted from her. She transcended her ongoing search for self-identity and meaning in her music. By doing this she was more able to realise who she actually was.'

Like Taylor, Carly Simon came from a secure, established family. She was born the third daughter to parents who were among the wealthiest ten per cent in the country. Her father, Richard Simon – a founder of Simon & Schuster Publishing – was the most inspirational figure in her years growing up. This proud, domineering man was determined to offer his daughter a world of culture and education. He wanted her to pursue something creative. He encouraged her in his liberal values and devotion to practising and developing the arts. It was regular practice for her father to bring famous dinner guests to the family's mansion in Riverdale, New York. He introduced Carly to famous authors, artists, athletes and intellectuals, including legendary editor Max Eastman, baseball great Jackie Robinson and playwright Lillian Hellman. Richard Simon was a promoter of culture and education and intensely fought against America's high rate of illiteracy. When once asked what his major goal in life was, he answered, 'To live to see the day that every American can pick up a book and read it.'

Carly's mother, Andrea, made sure that art and culture were the focal point of the education of her three girls and one boy. She hired the best private teachers to teach her children music, painting and sewing. 'I knew the children were artistic and I provided the materials,' Andrea Simon said. 'They sang before they talked. My husband was an absolutely brilliant pianist; and I sang to them during the nursery period. I used to stand outside Carly's room, crying with joy, as she sang.'

Before she met Richard, Andrea Simon was very poor and had to work double shifts as a buyer for Altman's Department Store to help her family make ends meets. She often went without proper meals and weighed only 87 pounds when she was hired to work as a switchboard operator at Simon & Schuster. When she met her handsome six-foot-five boss, it was love at first sight.

'I knew it was going to be something,' Andrea told Jane Shapiro. 'Certainly as a child I lived with terror and terrible insecurity and little love but you develop great resilience and maturity, you develop a set of values very sensible, sound and intelligent, and wise, wise, wise. Because when you live the kind of life I did your priorities are down-to-earth.'

While they were growing up, Richard Simon lavished his daughters with expensive clothes, trips and gifts. Andrea was concerned that he was spoiling the children. She used her harsh past experiences to help keep them grounded and to keep their expensive tastes within reason.

'We were brought up with the best of everything,' recalled Carly's older sister Joanne. 'Our parents were wonderful but sometimes I wonder what it would have been like growing up in more modest surroundings. Many times we took things for granted. We got too used to having whatever was in style, things that most other kids had to earn. We had more than most other people but it seemed that we weren't always too happy. Our mother was instrumental in bringing us back down to earth whenever things got out of hand. She had a rough life growing up. When she made us aware of it, we became more appreciative of how blessed we actually were.'

Carly's tendency to clown around and be prone to mischief distinguished her from the rest of her family. She feared that being the youngest daughter would make it difficult for her to carve out her own identity.

'My older sisters had their own personalities,' Carly recalled. 'Joanne was sophisticated and distinguished. Lucy was the shy one who got everybody's attention because she was cute and sweet. I had to find out who I was and I had to make a decision which way I wanted to go. I decided to go the comedic route. I used to make a lot of funny faces to try to get everybody's attention. I tried to be funny. I didn't really know what I was doing at the time but I was definitely doing it for a reason. A career in show business.'

Whatever her motives, Carly's constant quest for attention gave much pleasure to the rest of her family. 'When things were a bit stagnant, Carly was usually able to make us all laugh,' her mother said. 'She was always getting involved in some new project or scheme. There was never a dull moment when she was around.'

In the fifties, Carly's father, Richard, became very sick. He suffered two heart attacks and several strokes. After Richard Simon died of a third heart attack in 1960 when Carly was only 16, his passing completely changed her life. She started to rebel. She became live-in lovers with writer Nicholas Delbanco, who was five years her senior. 'I felt abandoned, and I was angry at the thought of being abandoned by him [her father]. At the same time as I was abandoned by Daddy, I was abandoned by God, because losing my father also meant losing my faith in God . . . I feared his death incredibly, and in fearing his death, moved away from him fearing that I might die.'

As a child, Carly admitted, she was neurotic. She had several anxiety attacks, including her first at only eight years of age, when she was staring into a bowl of Cheerios. She was constantly teased by the kids in her class because of the way she stammered out words. 'Kids made fun of me in school, and I couldn't read out loud,' Simon said. 'It made me not want to go to school. I developed side symptoms, a lump in my throat that made me gag every time I started to speak.' After her father died, Nicholas Delbanco helped Simon get over being self-conscious about her stuttering by convincing her that it was 'unique and sexy'. He convinced her to do what many of her shrinks had failed to – to be herself.

Growing up, Simon also had constant nightmares and was very paranoid. All this led up to much-needed therapy.

'I've been in analysis since I was 11 – not straight, that's when I went to see my first shrink,' Simon told journalist Joyce Wadler. 'I've seen a number of different gurus . . . I've done biofeedback, I've done hypnosis . . . It's like what it says in the song: "She's looking for a cure, she doesn't know exactly what it's for."'

Carly spent her childhood summers surrounded by the pristine beauty of Martha's Vineyard. She was first brought there when she was just two months old. She has often said that going to Martha's Vineyard was the highlight of her adolescent years. It was the place where she felt most comfortable, where she felt free to explore nature's pleasures. 'I'm a pure product of the Vineyard soil,' Simon said. 'I rose from it, and here I am today. It's the only place I've ever called home.'

While the other children there were busy fishing or playing in the sand, Carly immersed herself in reading and writing. She had an insatiable appetite for learning new things. 'I've always liked to try to grow,' Carly recalls. 'One of the best ways is by learning. When you stop learning, you stop living.'

Ever since she could remember, Carly was drawn to excitement and adventure. When she was nine, her parents became worried when they couldn't find her for several hours. She had gone hiking on the outback of the island and returned with a tick bite and poison ivy. When she was 11, Carly fell more than ten feet out of a tree in her parents' backyard. Badly bruised, she got up and walked away as if nothing had happened.

'When we were growing up, Carly was adventurous and was usually not afraid to try daring things,' said her brother, Peter Simon, a respected photographer. 'She was a bit of a daredevil. She was really into learning new things. When she was young, she liked to hang out with my friends and wasn't afraid to participate in sports and activities that girls her age might have been reluctant to try because they required a lot of stamina.'

Carly discovered she loved music in her early teens. She and her sister Lucy used to sing at folk jams and hootenanny nights on Martha's Vineyard. The pair were billed as the Simon Sisters. But back then Carly was not the talented singer she would eventually become.

'She usually sang off key,' said Mitchell Amar, a New York professor who saw the Simon Sisters perform a couple of times. 'I never thought she had what it took to become a star. She was nowhere near being in the same class as some of the good women singers. But she had looks, and thank god somebody out there had the brain to figure out that she was marketable. Heck, I remember seeing her perform one night and every guy in the place was giving her the eye, hoping she'd go home with him. She couldn't have been a day over 17 but she was downright hot.'

Taylor remembered seeing her perform and admits he fancied her, but he didn't think she would go for him. He told Stuart Werbin: 'I thought she was quite attractive, but she was, and still is, four years older than I was, so back then when she was 18 and I was 14 she was a bit less approachable than she was when I was 24.'

Carly spent two years at Sarah Lawrence, an exclusive college in New York. Then she was approached by Bob Dylan's manager, Albert

Grossman, to sign a record deal. Grossman believed that Simon would become the female version of Dylan. This idea failed miserably, because critics resented the fact that Grossman was trying to compare his new discovery to a living legend. Even after Dylan rewrote the lyrics she sang for Eric Von Schmidt's 'Baby, Let Me Follow You Down', Simon clearly wasn't ready to become a singer. The woman who'd never dreamed of being a musician until she started singing with her sister Lucy did not yet have the sharpness and clarity that would make her a star a couple of years later.

'Grossman was trying to cash in too soon,' said music critic Martin Smith. 'If he had waited a bit longer, he would have made a fortune. But he thought he would be a bit clever and try to rush Carly's career. It severely backfired and he didn't make a dime off her. Carly showed promise but she needed a lot of seasoning. She couldn't sing a tune with conviction. She needed to loosen up a bit onstage and the only answer was for her to do a lot of gigs. Most people who heard her sing didn't think she had a hope in hell of ever selling a record.'

Undeterred by her sceptics, Simon continued to plug away at a music career. In 1969 she wrote commercial jingles for an agency whose clients ranged from several banks in New England to Bonnie Bell Cosmetics. 'I wanted to get experience,' Simon says. 'And I was willing to take advantage of any opportunity that came up.'

In 1969 she joined the funky rock band Elephants Memory, which John Lennon joined after the Beatles broke up. Simon didn't get along with a couple of the band's members, who seemed more interested in getting her into bed than her singing. After she left the band, Simon became embroiled in a bitter legal dispute with them over publishing rights to several songs she wrote. One of her tunes, 'That's the Way I've Always Heard It Should Be', was an unexpected hit. 'Some of them resented me,' Simon said. 'They saw me as the rich girl who wouldn't carry the amps.'

But even that bitter experience led her farther along the path to success. Later that year, a smooth-talking New York promoter, Jerry Brandt, took notice of Simon and signed her to his Brandtworks production company. He recorded a demo with her and got Elektra Records' Jac Holzman to listen to it.

'Jac was convinced that Carly was the female version of Mick Jagger,' Brandt said. 'He was really taken with her music and offered her a deal right away. He was convinced that she'd be a star and he wanted to be her guiding light.' Holzman arranged for Simon to do some recording at a local studio and put together a full promo package for her that included photos and a bio.

Finally, Simon received national attention in 1970 with her megahit 'Elektra'. She became a popular club booking. She opened for artists like Cat Stevens and Kris Kristofferson. And like Taylor, she gained a reputation as a solid talent in the music business playing at the Troubadour Club in Los Angeles.

'Carly had something very special I had not seen in many artists who played here,' said Doug Weston, the club's owner. 'She had a very powerful presence. When she got up onstage it was hard to take your eyes off her. Sometimes she made mistakes, but nobody seemed to notice or care. The audience was very taken by her. It was easy to tell that it would be only a matter of time before this beautiful young girl broke loose. The first time she ever set foot in the Troubadour I knew that magic was in the air.'

From her Troubadour Club days, Carly Simon fell deeply in love with Cat Stevens, who was known then as one of rock's biggest playboys. Simon was an easy target for Stevens to get between the sheets. Stevens was attractive, successful, and sexy; she was mesmerised by his star presence. It was Stevens to whom she dedicated her big hit, 'Anticipation'. 'He found a quality in me that has not been tapped since,' Simon said in a *Rolling Stone* interview. 'A kind of fragility.'

Women found Cat Stevens strikingly handsome. He reputedly could make love for hours at a time. His dark, piercing eyes could call to beautiful women in the audience to share his bed. Women even said that he smelled good. Some said his satiny, curly hair was a turn-on. For whatever reason, Stevens exuded a strange magnetism that attracted women to him. The swarthy singer was desirable to every woman he met. And he was not ready to commit to just one woman.

Stevens dumped her and Simon was shattered. He had cheated on Simon several times before finally telling her it was time to call it quits.

Doug Weston, who hired and worked with both performers, put it bluntly: 'Cat was new on the LA scene and he was really attracting the female crowd. Carly wanted something a bit more serious and it didn't figure at all in Stevens's plans. Cat was one of the biggest womanisers in the music business and he had trouble keeping his dick in his pants. That's why he quit music at an early age and turned to Islam. His abusive attitude toward women caught up to him and he wanted to stop sinning.'

A broken Carly Simon was left in the wake of Cat Stevens's conversion.

She found consolation in the arms of Kris Kristofferson, whose gravelly, sultry voice was comforting to her. He had great charm and warmth. But he, too was a magnet for women. Girls practically threw themselves at his feet, which made Simon extremely insecure. Their relationship did not survive the threat of infidelity, ending after six months.

'It was very difficult because I couldn't help but feel like Kris was going to fall for another woman,' Simon said. 'Our attraction to each other was very strong but I always felt like I was walking on eggshells. The pain and insecurity made me write more songs than I had ever written in any previous relationship.'

Until she met Taylor, it seemed unlikely that Simon would ever settle down with one man. According to Doug Weston, Simon went around with more men than any other female musician who performed at his Troubadour Club. 'I felt bad for her because most of the musicians were male and it was almost expected that she had to go home with somebody at the end of the night.'

If Simon had a strong reaction to her failed romances, she tried to disguise it. She often told people close to her that she liked to live and learn. But in reality, she was taking heavy hits to the heart. To succeed as a singer she had to compete professionally with other performers, yet on an emotional level she was being used and dumped like a groupie.

'Carly wasn't the sweet, innocent girl that her record managers tried to make her out to be,' said one of her longtime close friends. 'She was ambitious, naive, and would do almost anything to help move along her career. The fact that she went to bed with so many rock stars was no coincidence. Before she married James, she was linked to almost every major male recording star. She had a big ego ever since she was a kid. She liked to get the men who were almost impossible for other women to get. She liked the fact that the press and the public talked about her bizarre love life. It made her feel like even more of a celebrity.'

Between affairs Simon and Taylor reunited several times. They appeared destined to wind up together.

'It was pretty obvious that they would settle down together,' Doug Weston said. 'Despite all the rumours, many of which were true, about the many affairs they had with other musicians, they really did need each other. They had a certain magical chemistry. It just took them a while to realise it because there were so many obstacles and distractions. They had become famous and with that came a lot of people who pursued them. They needed to experiment before making the big decision to commit to each other. They were both very liberal people with a keen taste for adventure. James seemed more ready to settle down than Carly. In the early '70s almost every male in the music business dreamed of being with Carly, and it was difficult for her to resist some of their advances – no matter how much she cared about James.'

A year before they married, Taylor almost lost Simon again after introducing her to pop's biggest star, Mick Jagger. Taylor had struck up a friendship with the Rolling Stones' sex god through Peter Asher, who was good friends with Jagger during the late '60s when he worked in London. During a trip to London in late 1971, Taylor wanted Jagger to meet the new love of his life, Carly Simon. Jagger became intrigued with Simon the first time he set eyes on her. The fact that she had become Taylor's lady was not a deterrent; Jagger had had affairs with some of the world's top beauties, regardless of whether they were attached. His philandering eventually ruined his marriage to his wife Bianca, who went ballistic when she found out he was having an affair with Simon. When Mick returned home to the south of France, Bianca was waiting. She confronted him with a revolver and threatened to kill him. After some tense moments, Bianca reconsidered. Still furious, she threw his belongings on the street and locked him out of the house.

Bianca told friends how much she resented Simon. She had become used to hearing about Jagger's numerous dalliances with other women, but she'd hoped that he would eventually grow out of it. She felt more threatened by Simon than any of the other women with whom Jagger had cavorted. Simon was more sophisticated and intelligent. For the first time, Bianca had a true rival. Jagger told bandmate Keith Richards that Simon was a most sensuous and pleasing lover.

'Mick was involved with so many women behind Bianca's back, but it seemed that he was starting to get bored until he met Carly,' said Richard Dunn, a business associate of the Rolling Stones. 'Carly's wit and sophisticated air rejuvenated Mick's spirits. You could tell by the expression on his face. It lit up whenever Carly's name came up. Mick had become used to dating all kinds of bimbos and it seemed that he was getting bored of the whole thing. Carly challenged him and didn't go gaga over Mick the way all the other women did. If Mick had not been with Bianca, I'm sure that Carly would have become Mrs Mick Jagger.'

Bianca told her pal Andy Warhol that Simon was ruining her marriage. She feared that Mick was going to leave her. Warhol told Bianca that she should considering leaving Jagger if she didn't want to have to look over her shoulder for the rest of her life. Warhol had never before seen Bianca get so riled up and jealous. And he agreed she had good reason. 'Carly Simon is intelligent and has the look Mick likes – she looks like Mick and Bianca.'

Back in Los Angeles, word reached Taylor that Simon was cheating on him. He confronted her during a telephone conversation, begging her to come back to him. They racked up thousands of dollars in London–LA telephone bills as they negotiated. The frantic calls ended when Simon finally admitted to Taylor that she was having an affair with Jagger. She insisted that she needed some time on her own to make a decision.

'Carly was so confused, she didn't know what to do,' said Martin Smith. 'She loved Taylor but had trouble resisting the fun and excitement that accompanied her and Jagger wherever he went. With Taylor, life was a bit slow and too predictable for Carly. She needed adventure. Jagger made her feel as if she was living her life right out of a movie.'

By the time Simon released her album *No Secrets* in early 1972, her affair with Jagger had ended. He had told her there was no hope for a future together – he didn't love her. Toward the end of their relationship, Jagger was seen in public with several other beautiful women. Carly Simon was confused about love yet again. She reunited with Taylor. She had decided to return to the comfort of the more homespun life she had with Taylor.

'After Jagger, Carly realised that she needed some stability,' said her sister Lucy. 'James had his share of problems but he was more committed to Carly than anybody else. They both had experienced a lot of bad luck in relationships and were tired of getting hurt. They both were in desperate need of some stability in their lives and got back together with hopes of making it a lasting relationship. A lot of people, including myself, were sceptical. But we all hoped and prayed that their bad experiences would make them realise that it was time to settle down.'

Simon's hit single on the new album, 'You're So Vain', was best known for the controversy it created about its subject. Most people thought Simon wrote it for Jagger, who sang backup vocals on it. At first Taylor thought it was about himself. Over the years, Simon has told several conflicting stories about the song's inspiration. She told her producer Richard Perry that 'You're So Vain' was dedicated to actor Warren Beatty, with whom she had been involved before she met Taylor. She told a New York journalist that she didn't really have anybody in mind, but that some parts were influenced by her relationship with Jagger. All this created so much speculation that several radio stations across the country ran contests asking listeners whom they thought was the subject of Simon's song. The most popular answer was always Jagger.

'If you examine the lyrics closely, it's obvious that Carly was singing about her affair with Mick Jagger,' said author Esmond Choueke, who has covered both Taylor's and Simon's careers for more than 25 years in several major North American newspapers and magazines. 'The way she says, "Your scarf it was apricot . . . you watched yourself gavotte . . . the wife of a close friend . . ." was her way of delivering a final message to Jagger. She was madly in love with Jagger and was devastated that their relationship ended. Carly is the type of person who always tries to get the last word in, especially after she's been humiliated. If she says the song was about Warren Beatty, I really can't see the connection. The lyrics and imagery she uses have nothing to really do with Beatty, James Taylor, or any of the other numerous lovers she had around that time. It's all Jagger. When the song was first released, Jagger bragged to his friends that he was the subject of Simon's song. I think that when Simon found out she was incensed and refused to admit that the song was about him because she didn't want to give Jagger the satisfaction.'

Simon denied to the *Washington Post* that 'You're So Vain' was about Jagger and hinted it was written for Beatty. 'It certainly sounds like it was about Warren Beatty. He certainly thought it was about him – he called me and said thanks for the song.'

Taylor was crushed by all the publicity surrounding 'You're So Vain'. He felt betrayed by Simon's penchant for sneaking behind his back with Jagger and other famous rock stars. He told friends that he wasn't sure if he would be ever be able to trust her again.

'It was tough for James because he thought he had finally met his soul mate in Carly,' Taylor's producer and good friend Don Grolnick told a reporter. 'James tried and eventually succeeded in working things out with Carly but I don't think it was easy for him to erase it from his mind. He seemed reluctant to introduce Carly to some of his other famous friends after the Jagger incident. It's amazing how they got back together, put it all behind them, and got married only months after the whole thing was plastered in every newspaper in the country. Not many people would be able to forgive and forget as easily as Carly and James. They were both very strong-willed and liberal in their values. And it seemed like they had a special magnetic attraction to each other. No matter how crazy things got, they always got back together.'

It was not the best time for Taylor to be publicly cuckolded. His *Mud Slide Slim* was one of the year's best-selling records. His artistry was expanding, his career taking off in new directions, but wherever he went people seemed most interested in asking about his tempestuous affair with Simon.

'James Taylor was always a bit uneasy because journalists were more intent on asking him about his drug problems than his music,' said Martin Smith. 'When it seemed that he had finally silenced his critics and that it was time to focus more on his music, Carly Simon popped into his life and created a media storm. Her flamboyant lifestyle coupled with his long string of personal problems made them ripe for gossip columns across the country. Journalists followed them everywhere with hopes of catching them off guard. Readers couldn't get enough of the dirt on them. It was almost like they were being staked out the way Prince Charles and Lady Diana would be a decade later.'

A woman who always had had high ideals for herself – even though she wasn't always able to live up to them – Simon was bent on becoming the best-known female artist in the music business. She worked tirelessly on her wardrobe and looks to gain more exposure. As her career progressed, her party life intensified.

A Martha's Vineyard friend remembered her as a big party animal. 'She loved to have a good time and to just go wild. She attracted more men than anybody I knew because she had a certain type of artistic mystique. Lots of the local men claimed to have had sex with her and one of them told me how much she enjoyed having sex. He said they did it four times one night on the beach under the stars. When she married James everybody was a bit surprised, because Carly usually dated older men. But she always did have a thing for famous men and being with a rock star boosted her ego more than ever. At one point early on in their marriage, it seemed as if Carly was getting a bit out of control. I saw her on TV being interviewed and she looked out of it and seemed to be a completely changed person. In later years she reverted back to her old self, after many wild and crazy incidents in her life.'

The Taylor and Simon entourages seemed shocked when the pair decided to marry. 'Who knows how long it will last?' Taylor's father said to a close friend. 'If they want it to work, then they'll both have to tone down their lifestyles considerably.'

Simon told her mother that she was tired of playing the field and wanted to settle down with Taylor – the only person, she believed, who'd ever fully understood her. 'We're madly in love,' Simon said. 'I finally found the peace and happiness that I've dreamed of finding for so many years.'

It was clear from the outset of her marriage to James Taylor that Carly Simon was intent upon making it work. Carly had always lived a carefree life, and allowed herself to exercise her many whims. She also regularly fell into deep emotional depressions, feeling that she'd failed everyone around her including her family. It was time for her to show the world that she was capable of leading a normal life. She spent thousands of dollars equipping her new home with everything from blankets to European cookware. Carly Simon was the envy of every salesgirl when she shopped. 'She showed excellent taste,' said Elizabeth Christensen, a former sales-clerk in Maine who served Simon. 'She spent a lot, she bought only the best-quality things. It was kind of cute. You know, like a young newlywed feathering the nest.'

Simon tried to stay out of Taylor's way when things got hectic. 'We have our share of problems that every married couple has,' she commented to a *Circus* magazine reporter early in her marriage. 'But ours is a relatively comfortable relationship based on our respect and affinity for each other. More than anything else, when James is recording or touring, he wants my total support at home.'

During the first couple of years of their marriage, Simon and Taylor collaborated and performed together regularly, becoming the most spotlighted couple in the music business. Still, Carly started to feel insecure with Taylor. His drug habits, wild libido and immense self-doubt bordered on self-destructive.

'It was very harrowing for me,' Simon said. 'In the beginning of our relationship, I didn't really understand the extent to which James was addicted or needed drugs. It just kind of confused me that there was a wall up between us and I didn't know exactly what it was, because I had never been close to anybody who was really addicted to anything before. I was aware of remoteness with James, that I couldn't depend on him. In a sense, he could depend upon me more, but I was terribly confused . . . there seemed to be this barrier that I couldn't break through.'

Simon dedicated herself to helping Taylor get off drugs, but he refused to speak to her whenever she tried to bring up the subject. First he would suggest she was imagining things. Then he would deny he took drugs, and finally he would stomp off. Sometimes he would shut her out completely, even refusing to sleep in the same bed with her.

'There were times when he stopped communicating and it was very difficult to figure him out,' Simon said. 'It was frustrating because I loved him so much and I felt like I was up against a brick wall. I felt bad for him and desperately tried to get him help 'cause I didn't want anything bad to happen to him. I also wanted to save our marriage.'

Taylor had been clean for over a year when he embarked on a solo tour to support his *Mud Slide* album. He became lonely and depressed after only the first week on the road and quickly reverted to his old nemesis, heroin.

'When Carly found out he was using hard drugs again, she hit the ceiling,' said one of her former band members. 'She took it the wrong way. She thought he was doing drugs again because he was bored with being married to her. It was a bit selfish of her to think that way because James was an addict, and addicts are liable to have a relapse at any time. Usually she always stood by his side and supported him through thick and thin. Suddenly, she threatened to leave him if he didn't shape up. She even tried to dissuade him from doing any further touring. Meanwhile, she was working harder than ever writing music and recording albums. She threatened to leave him several times that summer. The lady could throw a momentous fit. Then he would promise whatever she wanted just to put a stop to her. But he never meant it. You could see he was just trying to placate her.

'I think she was envious of his success and had an ulterior motive. If she was so concerned about him doing drugs, I can tell you for a fact that she wasn't exactly innocent herself during that time. It turned into a complete circus. The musicians and producers who worked in both of their camps never knew what was going to happen next. One day they'd say we'll be doing one thing and the next day they'd change their minds and throw us something else. During the whole time they were married it was very difficult to predict what would happen next.'

In 1972, at the age of 24, Taylor released his *One Man Dog* album, which wasn't as well received as his previous work. Many of his fans say that it was one of his worst albums. It had been 21 months since Taylor had released a record, and his manager Peter Asher was pressuring him to produce some fresh material. Taylor took a long time with *One Man Dog* because he was putting most of his energy into kicking heroin. He recorded the album in three different places – New York, Martha's Vineyard and Los Angeles – in an attempt to get motivated. He couldn't concentrate.

'So much was going on in our lives at that time,' Carly Simon said. 'It wasn't always easy to keep focused because of all the distractions.'

Rumours flew that Taylor was forced to put out the album after Warner Bros head Mo Ostin and Peter Asher pleaded with him to finish it. They were afraid that his star was waning. Asher especially feared that his absence from the public eye would jeopardise Taylor's career. The plan was for *One Man Dog* to sell on the virtue of Taylor's previous hits. The majority of music critics were not amused. They heavily criticised the new album, and it flopped.

Pop critic William Ruhlmann said: 'What a letdown. *One Man Dog* contained 18 tracks, some of them instrumentals, many of them running less than two minutes. A lot of it was sketchy and seemingly unfinished, and none of it had the impact of the best songs on the last two albums . . . it disappointed fans. . . . Taylor was bypassed by the singer-songwriter movement, becoming more of an easy-listening cover artist (his next hits were remakes of "Mockingbird" and "How Sweet It Is").'

The only track on *One Man Dog* to receive attention was 'Don't Let Me Be Lonely Tonight,' which made it to the Top Twenty. But its melody and chord structure were nowhere near as catchy as Taylor's previous hits.

By this point Taylor and Simon had established a pattern that would shape their lives for the next several years. They spent weeks in the studio recording, hoping that one of their albums would take off. The gamble usually worked. One of the their records would get good reviews and sell, while the other's wouldn't do as well.

When Barbra Streisand and Kris Kristofferson remade *A Star Is Born*, many believed that it was based on the careers of Taylor and Simon.

'The market was getting tougher because more and more artists were releasing albums,' said author Esmond Choueke. 'In the case of James and Carly, it was almost a sure bet that one of their albums would take off. And if they both did well, it was a bonus. Their markets were very similar. It was good for them because it almost guaranteed that one of them would bring home some bread. In this business, for some reason or another, so many artists' albums bomb and they're forced to go through a lot of dry periods.'

16

WALKING MAN STUMBLES

Carly Simon was making no headway in her attempts to get Taylor off drugs. She thought starting a family might be the only way he'd settle down. One of Carly's dreams since she was a little girl was to have children. 'She would flip a magazine to an ad page with a picture of a baby,' remembered one friend. 'She would show James and coo to it as if to a baby just to see his reaction. She would stop, look into the window of a baby store, and twitter at the cute little dresses and hats. You could see the mothering urge growing in her.'

'Children are the most innocent people,' Simon said. 'I always enjoyed being around them. I always dreamed of meeting the right man, settling down and raising a family.'

At first Taylor was reluctant to have children because of the couple's hectic schedule. He liked the idea but thought they should wait a couple of years. Simon promised him that his career would not suffer and that she would free up her schedule and devote most of her time to playing housewife.

'It was amazing how determined Carly was to start a family,' Doug Weston said. 'She had turned out several hits in a row and was at the height of her career. Now she decided to practically give it all up. She kept recording but stopped touring for a long time. I think that turning 30 scared her a bit, because most of the friends she grew up with already had children and were leading much more stable lives. The thought of raising a family had to be scary because he was a renowned junkie. I don't think many women in America would have wanted their children to be raised by him. But whatever it was that motivated her, Carly usually got her way.'

Simon enjoyed her pregnancy. She grew big and healthy. She ate well. She wanted a beautiful healthy baby. Her dream came true in

January 1974, when she gave birth to a gorgeous baby girl, Sally. Several months into Carly's pregnancy Taylor made a promise to stay off drugs. Everything seemed to be finally falling in place. Shortly after Sally's birth, Simon and Taylor collaborated on the hit song 'Mockingbird', which appeared on Simon's *Hotcakes* album.

The period of Simon's greatest artistic growth occurred while she was married to Taylor, and she credited her husband with inspiring her to extend the boundaries of her vocal range and artistic expression. Simon was eager to branch out. But she didn't win over her critics. *Hotcakes* peaked at number three. It didn't come close to matching the success of *No Secrets*, which stayed at number one for weeks. Simon's confidence was shattered. She had hoped that her new album would have finally given her the same artistic respect that critics offered to Joni Mitchell and Joan Baez. Meanwhile, some Simon copycats signed with major labels and sold millions.

'I was distraught,' Simon told journalist Roger Friedman. 'That number three wasn't enough for me after number one. I thought, "Oh my god, I'm slipping." One of the terrible things about success is that you're always trying to live up to yourself. It's very, very pathetic.'

If the record sales were not as high as they had once been, their little girl was always their number one concern. Both Simon and Taylor were caring parents. The two spent hours with their daughter.

'After they had children [son Ben was born in 1977] everything changed,' journalist Martin Smith said. 'The albums they put out weren't greeted with the same enthusiasm that they had enjoyed earlier in their careers. In the music business artists are sometimes perceived to be over the hill when they have kids and settle down. I think that the best work both of them did at that time was the music they collaborated on, like "Mockingbird". Taylor in particular seemed to lose a bit of his ability to write lyrics and melodies that were close to the edge. I think he mellowed quite a bit to try to become a good father and family man.'

Being a father did make Taylor more settled. It seemed he enjoyed being with Sally more than he liked working. He stayed clean and became a very good dad. But there were some who suspected that he wouldn't be able to keep it up for long.

'Taylor had made a commitment to keep recording and touring. There was no way that he'd be able to be around for Sally as much as Carly was,' said a close friend of his. 'It was difficult because when he was around Sally he was a different person. I had never seen him happier. He wasn't looking forward to leaving her behind when he went out on tour.'

In August 1974, Taylor released his first major album without Peter Asher as producer. *Walking Man* was produced by well-known New York arranger and guitarist David Spinozza. It was also the first time Taylor collaborated with his longtime close friend Don Grolnick. Taylor insisted that he had brought in Spinozza only because Asher was too busy. Gossip suggested a major falling out. There were reports of first Asher, then Taylor stomping out of recording sessions. Asher reportedly slammed a door hard enough to break the glass in it. But for business reasons, only the very best face was put on the Taylor–Asher relationship.

'Peter and I will always be friends and we'll still work together,' James said. 'A lot have things have been going on lately and the time was right for a change. Peter has been busy working with other artists and it wouldn't have been practical for him to have to free up so much of his time to produce my album. I felt that it would be good to take a break and to work with someone else. David Spinozza's a very good producer and it was very enjoyable to work with him.'

According to Steve Bellows, however – a pop-music archivist who has followed Taylor's career for years – Taylor and Asher needed a break because of too many artistic clashes.

'They started to have different outlooks. One of the backup musicians in Taylor's band told me around that time that the atmosphere in Taylor's camp started to get very stale because Asher seemed only interested in putting out very commercial hits. Taylor was more interested in gaining artistic respectability and wanted to stay away from Asher's formulated way of making music. If it was up to Asher Taylor would keep writing songs in the style of "Fire and Rain" and "You've Got a Friend". Taylor didn't feel that it was appropriate to go that route at this time in his life. His marriage to Carly Simon and the birth of their daughter changed his life. He always wanted his music to be an extension of his life. It was time to express himself differently.'

According to Bellows, Taylor considered quitting music if Asher didn't step aside. 'By all accounts, Taylor was at a big crossroads with Asher. He told several people that he felt Asher was becoming a bit of a dictator, and that it made him lose focus on his music. Asher had a reputation for wanting to call all the shots. There's no denying he was one of the best in the business, but it was easy to see where Taylor was coming from. Most artists I've met change their producer after one or two albums. John Lennon once told me that when he worked with Phil Spector and several other producers after being with George Martin for so many years he vowed never to work repeatedly with the same person again. Lennon said after one or two albums it all became redundant and it limited his creative outlook immensely.

'I think that the last album Asher produced, *One Man Dog*, clearly showed that Taylor needed a change. It didn't sound as fresh and as brilliant as some of his previous works. He realised the only way he could bounce back and win over his critics is if he brought in some new energy. Spinozza was very cutting-edge and Grolnick was a musical genius. When it was announced that they'd all be working together, it sparked quite a bit of curiosity among JT's fans because nobody knew what to really expect.'

But the Spinozza, Grolnick, Taylor synergy did not translate onto the tracks. The change away from Asher's influence was not the musical renaissance Taylor had hoped for. *Walking Man* was doomed from the start.

The album resulted in the worst reviews Taylor ever received. Critics said he was slipping; some wondered if his career might be finished. The *All Music Guide* said *Walking Man* was:

> A more considerable effort than its predecessor that managed to be just as trivial but even less interesting. As a result, it became the worst-selling album of Taylor's career. Somehow, a songwriter who had seemed in 1970 to have as precise an idea of the national mood as Bob Dylan had had in 1965 now seemed to be a man without a country . . . *Walking Man* sounded like the statement of a songwriter who either had nothing to say or didn't know how to say it.

Nothing seemed to go right on *Walking Man*. Taylor developed throat problems and had trouble singing. He had included one song as a commentary to the Watergate scandal. 'Let It All Fall Down' flopped when Richard Nixon resigned a day after it was released in July. Any chance for the song to be a timely hit disappeared with the disgraced president.

'JT's luck ran out on him,' Steve Bellows said. 'Everything he did seemed to fall apart. Everybody was disappointed. They thought that working with a new team would get him back on track. I think the big problem was that his heart was not in it anymore. He didn't have the passion he used to because he was working too hard. His commitment to his family, the time he spent touring, the studio hours, it all finally caught up with him. A lot of people thought it was because of drugs but I don't buy it. In the past he had performed very well even when he was on drugs.

'Even though a lot of people criticised him, JT persevered and didn't give up. A lot of other people might have called it quits, put over the coals the way he was. Music critics placed very high expectations on JT. If those high expectations weren't met, they would not be afraid to knock the hell out of his work. Not many other artists were put under the microscope the way JT was. The only other one that comes to mind is Paul McCartney after he left the Beatles and started Wings.'

But Taylor refused to let the album sink. He still hoped that *Walking Man* could do well.

On 13 July 1974, Taylor, then 26, embarked on a three-week tour to support his new album. Joining him as opening acts were the Manhattan Dirt Riders and Linda Ronstadt. While not as influential as Taylor, Ronstadt was an excellent singer with a wide range. And, like Taylor, her lyrics bit hard.

'Linda was the star attraction of the tour,' Martin Smith said. 'Taylor didn't perform at all close to what he was capable of. Maybe he had a lot of things going on in his life at that time. He couldn't properly focus. A journalist friend of mine who reviewed one of the shows said that if Ronstadt had not been on the bill, a lot of people would have asked for their money back. Every artist has their ups and downs and this was clearly a low point for JT.' Ronstadt carried the show. Thanks to her powerful voice and haunting melodies, the tour went ahead as planned.

Only a few years before, Taylor had introduced and popularised a unique style of music folk rock. Now many people were saying that he was finished. Taylor was confused. He turned to his wife and partner Carly to guide and comfort him.

'He was really hurt because on *Walking Man* he had tried hard to do something different, something a bit more gutsy,' Don Grolnick said. 'We worked hard and the atmosphere was positive, but something did seem to be missing. It was almost as if we kept going ahead with the project and everybody knew that something was missing but they just didn't want to come out and say it. If I have to pinpoint it, I think that JT was a bit wary of doing another album at that time because his previous one bombed. He was worried that it might happen again. So what did he do? He tried really hard to do something different and in the end it got worse reviews than the last album. I was a bit shocked because even though I knew something was missing I still thought the album had a lot of strong points. "Daddy's Baby", "Let It All Fall Down", and "Fading Away", were very strong tunes, and they probably would have done better if they were released by another artist. The problem was that everybody had certain expectations of JT and they weren't willing to let him sway from the style that made him famous. There's no way that this album was worse than his previous one, which a lot of critics claimed. It was total bull what a lot of people were saying. One critic even admitted to me that the album was good but that he gave it a bad review because it wasn't as good as *Sweet Baby James*. That's totally unfair. Artists should be judged on the merits of their work, not on what they did several years ago.'

Taylor was typecast. 'It's like having every part of you rejected, but one,' he told Don Grolnick.

He retreated to their home on Martha's Vineyard. He was only happy when he was playing with his daughter Sally. Meanwhile, Carly Simon was trying to boost his morale and to keep their home life happy and the family intact. She supported Taylor through his phases of gloom and crying. Eventually, though, his neediness took its toll on their marriage.

17

THE GEFFEN FACTOR

James Taylor's career had by this time grown less eventful with the dwindling of his record sales, but the public's interest in his private life had risen to a fever pitch. Reports were rife that his marriage to Simon was in serious trouble. In February 1975, several tabloids ran stories suggesting that their days together were numbered. There were also persistent rumours that Taylor was unfaithful when he was on the road. According to several members of his band, these rumours were completely false. They claimed that while Taylor had beautiful women offer themselves to him almost every night, he never succumbed. 'I would have been ecstatic with just half the women James threw over,' said one. 'But he was faithful to Carly. He would sooner call home and talk to his daughter and his wife than go chasing women.'

'When he married Carly he was ready for permanence,' Don Grolnick said. 'The tabloids were coming out with all kinds of crazy things about them. Unfortunately some people started believing the lies. I'm sure they had the regular problems that most couples have, but when they were together they seemed very happy. The only time I noticed anything wrong was when they would record together in the studio. Yes, sometimes they did have screaming matches, usually about what lyric or melody to use in a section of a song. They are two of the most obstinate people you'd ever want to meet. They both liked to get their own way and if they didn't, all hell would break loose.'

By the time Taylor finished promoting *Walking Man*, Simon seemed intent on living a more private life. For a long time she had been torn between fame and privacy. She enjoyed both. She found it difficult to give up being the centre of attention. But the media's hostile attitude toward her relationship with her husband convinced her that if she didn't try to lead a more private life her marriage might be doomed.

'Carly and JT were worried because the media was following them everywhere they went,' Don Grolnick said. 'They'd be at a restaurant or in a movie theatre and all of a sudden camera flashbulbs would be going off in their faces. They needed to do something to lead a more private life. JT was worried that his daughter wouldn't be able to grow up like a normal child. He didn't want his child to have any part of what was going on in the press. Same with Carly. They were both very protective of little Sally. They didn't think it was fair the way the media harassed them and their daughter. JT once said that it was getting to the point that he couldn't even walk out of the house without having to dodge a cameraman or a reporter. The press became obsessive, and if anything, that caused a lot of anxiety for the Taylors.'

One rumour was true: Taylor was doing hard drugs again. Simon had tried yet failed to help him kick his addiction.

'I really thought drug addiction was like a virus, that he would get rid of it,' Simon told journalist Roger Friedman. 'I was in a constant state of denial about it. I didn't want to see it. I didn't want to know how serious it was . . . I just wanted to help, to do anything for him I possibly could.'

Simon had tried anything and everything she could think of. Some nights, she could see from his introverted behavior that he was feeling vulnerable, that he might be tempted. She would try to distract him at first. If that didn't work, she would help him get to bed early and wait until he was asleep. In the past, he had some times awakened at night dressed silently in the dark, and slipped out into the Martha's Vineyard night to get drugs while she slept. By now, though, Carly had found a way to outwit her husband for his own good. Once he was sound asleep, she would slip into bed next to him. Then she would gently tie one end of her silk bathrobe sash to one of his ankles and the other end to her own ankle. He could not sneak out of the bed without waking her. Eventually, Taylor caught on to this trick. Simon would awaken to find that he had slipped out of his end of her sash and was gone. He would return home hours later, still drugged or crashing.

Once, Simon obtained the phone number of someone she was sure was Taylor's drug supplier. Boldly, she dialled the number. There followed a heated exchange with Simon eventually screeching she would expose and destroy the pusher. The voice on the other end of the line replied: 'Lady, if I go down, your husband goes down with me!'

And Taylor continued to use. He would promise her not to do drugs anymore. He would try not to, but eventually, the monkey on his back would tap him on his shoulder. According to several people close to him, Taylor started doing drugs again because he was distraught about his career. Although Sally had brought him new focus and purpose, he had trouble dealing with his abysmal record sales.

'It was difficult for him to accept what was going on in his career,' said Don Grolnick. 'He seemed to be going through a midlife crisis and needed to take drugs again to soothe his fears. He needed to regain the feeling he had a few years earlier. Once he had been able to combine his manic energy of youthful angst with his soft, gentle touch that became the trademark of his music. It was sad to see him have to go through this because Carly had worked so hard at getting him to rehabilitate himself.

'JT was committed to being straight when he was around Carly and Sally. But when he went on the road he couldn't resist the temptation of partying. He was messed up because his career was going downhill and he also missed being away from Carly and the kid. Several people who were close to him tried desperately to convince him to get help again, but he wasn't interested. He said that he was just going through a rough time and that he'd snap out of it once things around him calmed down. Nobody knew whether or not to believe him. We were all worried because he seemed to be so weak and fragile.'

Simon put on a bold face and tried to carry on as if things were normal. She told her husband that nothing would please her more than him taking a break from music.

'It's destroying you,' a former baby-sitter overheard Simon tell Taylor. 'It's destroying us. Every day it seems that you're fading more away. The pressure is getting to you and I think it's time that you take a much-deserved break. If you can't do it for your own sake, then do it for Sally. There's nothing worse than having a father around who's a junkie. What will you tell your daughter when she's old enough to understand that her father was always high when he held her in his arms when she was little?'

Taylor felt bad that Carly had to endure his bad habits day in and day out. When he had relapses he would apologise to her profusely. But he couldn't agree to stall his career.

'If I was him I would have just laid back and taken a break,' Steve Bellows said. 'Can you imagine what Carly must have been going through? It must have been sheer hell.'

Midway through 1975, the Taylors relocated to Los Angeles. They rented a $3,750 a-month Beverly Hills mansion whose previous occupants had included Sonny and Cher, Elizabeth Taylor and Mick and Bianca Jagger. Taylor and Simon were urged by their handlers to come to Los Angeles to work on their new albums.

'We needed a change of scenery and the idea of going to Los Angeles seemed right,' Simon recalled. 'But it turned out to be a nightmare. Nothing seemed to go right. There were a lot of distractions. It just never felt right being there. I think what we really needed was some time on our own, without all the record and showbiz people around us. After a few months there I started to feel very uneasy. I thought we were starting to get too caught up in that whole Hollywood scene. It wasn't healthy for our marriage or for our daughter.'

Simon was working on her *Playing Possum* album while Taylor was putting the finishing touches on *Gorilla*, which featured a remake that turned out to be one his biggest hits ever: 'How Sweet It Is to Be Loved by You'. Another track, 'Sarah Maria', was dedicated to his daughter. Taylor told friends that his daughter inspired him to write 'Gorilla', and that he wanted to dedicate a song to her. He credited little Sally for making him realise for the first time since he grew up in North Carolina how important it was to have a family. In fact, he said the most relaxing time he'd had in many years was spent time with his daughter.

For the first time Taylor opted to work with two producers, Lenny Waronker and Russ Titelman. They told Taylor that they would get him back on top of the charts by reverting to his soft, adult-contemporary style of music.

'This was almost a do-or-die situation for him,' said critic Martin Smith. 'If he didn't achieve at least marginal success with this album, he would have really been labelled as washed up because of the poor record sales of his two previous albums. He worked with two veteran producers who had the right focus. They decided to do a cover version of "How Sweet It Is", a song covered by several artists in the past, including the legendary singer Marvin Gaye. It was obvious to everybody that Taylor sang this song as a tribute to his wife. Simon sang backup vocals on it. "How Sweet It Is" was considered his best cover since "You've Got a Friend". Today, it still gets a lot of radio airplay on adult contemporary stations.'

Smith continued, 'There is no doubt that this album revived his career. Waronker and Titelman were able to bring out in Taylor that soft, mellow, folksy style, which was the vital cog making him into a star earlier in his career. The album flowed very well and there were at least three or four tracks that got considerable airplay, including my favourite, 'Mexico'. It seemed a bit weird to me because there had been rumours that Taylor was using drugs again. The albums he released when he was off drugs were complete bombs. I remember thinking to myself that maybe there was truth to the popular belief that some artists need to be high to express themselves. Just look at the Beatles, the Rolling Stones and Jimi Hendrix. They wrote some of the best popular music of all time while under the influence of heavy drugs. Like Taylor, when Paul McCartney and Mick Jagger stopped using heavy drugs, the quality of their songwriting went completely down. Even the jazz great Louis Armstrong needed drugs to stimulate him. He claimed that he smoked marijuana every day of his life from when he was a teenager to help get his creative juices flowing.'

While Taylor's *Gorilla* soared up the charts, many critics criticized Simon's *Playing Possum*. They said that its music didn't live up to the fortune Richard Perry had put into producing it. Perry indeed spared no expense on Simon's album, budgeting well over a hundred thousand dollars for studio time and backup musicians including Ringo Starr, Rita Coolidge and Dr John. According to Perry's girlfriend at the time, actress Gwen Welles, everything was chaotic in Simon's camp because of all the high spending.

'Richard spent lavish sums when he produced people like Martha Reeves and Carly Simon,' Welles said. 'I think Carly just went along with Richard even though she often hinted that she wanted him to try to tone down the expenses. Her husband was recording an album at the same time as she was that didn't cost nearly as much. Because her album was so expensive, everybody expected it to be her best ever. And it turned out that it wasn't. This created a big rift between Richard and Carly and was the reason their working relationship was beginning to dissolve. Carly always seemed to be a bit uncomfortable when she was in LA. The pressure of working with Richard started to get to her. It wasn't easy for her because her husband wasn't able to be there for her when things got heated. James was working long hours in the studio on his own album.'

During their time spent in Los Angeles, Simon and Taylor often fought. Simon called her mother in New York several times and broke down in tears. She feared that her husband's old habits had taken possession of him again. She was going to end their marriage. Simon found it hard to understand the complexity of her husband's lifestyle. A year later, in 1976, she told a reporter that the first few years of her marriage were very difficult and at times she wasn't sure it would last.

'In a sense, our marriage has been helped by the fact that the beginning was as rocky as it was,' Carly said. 'James was still a junkie at that time, and I'd never known him off junk . . . The beginning of our marriage really went through a lot of pain. But I suppose if you start from that position, it had to work its way up.'

Playing Possum's lyrics, which in effect criticized relationships, exposed Simon's more cynical side. It prompted critics to speculate that her marriage to Taylor was foundering. Simon would not deviate from her new dark style for the next several years, until her marriage to Taylor started to collapse in earnest.

She told writer Alison Steele that it was a release for her to reflect on her relationship in her music: 'It was seen as your husband or your boyfriend policing your life, or at least the projection that he is doing that, and seeing the husband as the cop because a misdemeanour has been committed. A good description of me is an emotional reporter. I kind of spy on emotions. I'm interested in the motivations of personalities.'

Simon's image as a sex symbol put even more pressure on Taylor. It made him uneasy to be with her in public; he would often make excuses not to accompany her when they were supposed to attend various functions. James was jealous, both of the men around Carly and because once he married her his own status as a male pop star and sex god seemed to evaporate.

'At one point Carly was the most sought after woman in Hollywood and Taylor had a tough time dealing with it,' Steve Bellows said. 'Men all over the world drooled over Simon the same way they did for other famous women who were knockouts, like Raquel Welch and Julie Christie. It made Taylor feel more emotionally unstable than he already was. Everyone knew that it was a roller-coaster marriage. The fact that Simon had men chasing her wherever she went didn't help. In public, Taylor was always looking over his shoulder because he thought somebody might try to steal his wife. If their marriage didn't work out, Carly could have had any man she wanted. Taylor knew it and it clearly bothered him. He wanted a wife who would sit home and nurse him to help him conquer his drug addictions. Simon tried to do that but she was also able to stand very well on her own feet.

'I remember seeing them at a music awards party in 1975 and Carly looked dazzling. Every male in the room had their eyes on her. It made Taylor very uncomfortable and for the whole night he tried to keep Carly engaged in a conversation with him and his producer. He made sure that nobody would be able to get close enough to her to get their attention. I remember thinking to myself that I couldn't blame him for being possessive. How would anybody feel if they were married to a woman who once had affairs with Mick Jagger, Kris Kristofferson and Warren Beatty?'

Simon appreciated her legion of admirers and relished the attention. But she tried to downplay the public's interest to her jealous husband. She would repeatedly reassure him that he was the only man for her and that no matter what happened she would always stay by his side.

'I don't see myself as a sex object,' Simon once said. 'That's the way other people see me. But it doesn't bother me. I like myself now – physically, sexually, but not to a narcissistic degree. People go through stages of hibernation. I'm moving not so much out of James's shadow but my own.'

Ironically, a record company merger in the mid-'70s was to make deep inroads into the Taylor-Simon marriage. After Elektra joined Asylum Records, David Geffen became Carly's new boss. Her love-hate relationship with Geffen was legendary. Geffen tried to dictate to Simon every move she made, including the lyrics in her songs and how she dressed onstage. Geffen's attitude infuriated Taylor. He warned his wife to be wary of the man, who had a reputation for being a playboy and control freak.

Simon recalled in a *Rolling Stone* interview how Geffen had created friction in her life. 'I went through a period where I wanted to leave the label because I felt that David Geffen's interests were too divided and that I was not – since he hadn't discovered me, there was no way of being sure that he liked me, and there were several incidents in which I got my feelings hurt.'

Geffen had publicly said several negative things about Simon, including that he thought she was a spoiled rich kid.

'I don't know if any of it is true,' Simon said. 'But they seemed vitriolic.'

A lot of people said Geffen resented Simon because she was married to Taylor; Geffen had heard many negative things about him from his ex-love, Joni Mitchell. Geffen managed Mitchell and signed her to his label. Taylor and Simon were worried that Geffen was giving priority to Mitchell over Simon because he didn't want to offend his biggest star.

Simon told *Rolling Stone*, 'I felt in a sense it was a little bit like an ego trip for Dave Geffen to have three major artists [Mitchell, Simon, and Bob Dylan] released at the same time, and that he capitalised on that rather than on catering to the individual artists . . . He explains it by saying that at that time, his life was very much involved with Cher's and that he was so one-track minded, it was like falling in love for the first time. He was completely enmeshed with Cher's life and he was neglecting his duties as a record company president.'

Taylor warned Simon not to sacrifice her artistic freedom to Geffen. He was worried that Geffen's conflict of interest might hurt his wife's career.

'He was managing the woman who was the leading lady in Taylor's life before Carly arrived on the scene,' said Hollywood reporter Cal Blumenthal. 'Can you imagine how Taylor must have felt? Mitchell was still bitter toward him, and if she wanted to get back at him this was the perfect opportunity. Geffen would do anything Mitchell asked him to because Mitchell was his star attraction. Lots of people said that the whole thing made Carly feel very paranoid that Geffen might have ulterior motives. If he pulled a fast one on her by not supporting her albums properly, her career would be ruined. All this made Taylor very uneasy. He would have preferred that his wife was associated with another record label to avoid what seemed destined to become a very messy situation. In the end Geffen and Simon worked out their differences. But before they did it was very unpleasant for both Taylor and Simon. The last thing they needed at this time was something else that would add chaos to their lives, which were already very disrupted.'

18

CARNEGIE HALL, A NIGHT OF MAGIC

Carly Simon bent over backwards to please her husband. She was determined to keep their marriage alive. She cooked his favourite dishes. She kept the house clean, had it smelling sweet, kept the lights low, and played his favourite music in the background. And she gave him the best sex of his life, anytime he wanted it. Because of the way the media portrayed his wife as a sex symbol, Taylor found it difficult to completely trust her. Simon was well aware of his insecurity and tried to assuage his fears by being dutiful, domestic and always available.

Martha's Vineyard was her home turf. During the school year, the Taylors lived in a town house in New York. But it was on Martha's Vineyard where Carly felt she could make miracles happen. If their marriage could be saved, this was the time and Martha's Vineyard was the place.

'After their experience in Los Angeles, James and Carly needed to escape to Martha's Vineyard for a period of rest,' musician Don Grolnick said. 'It wasn't easy for James because he was always worried about whether or not he could trust Carly. Many times he asked his close friends question like "Do you think I can trust her?" or "Do you think it's going to last?" If anything, he was walking on eggshells. No question they loved each other, but Carly's popularity made JT feel uneasy. Carly was committed to making the marriage work, even if it meant sacrificing her career.'

Grolnick added, 'She once told me shortly after Sally was born that nothing she had ever experienced came close to being a mother. She said she didn't want her and JT to be like some showbiz couples who had nannies looking after their kids while they toured around the world.'

Carly was ready to become a full-time mother while Taylor recorded albums and toured. She felt that the only way her daughter could be raised in a normal way was at home. JT was pleased with Carly's attitude. He also felt the same way. He was more intent on continuing his career than Carly was, so they both decided that she would become a full-time mother.

Grolnick said, 'I think a lot of their decision was based on the fact that Carly still dreaded performing live. Carly had waged a lifelong battle with stage fright. Also, JT had made plans to record a couple of more albums. JT has never been the selfish type. He often said that if ever Carly decided it was time to get back into music, he would give her his full support. He would have been willing to look after Sally while Carly was in the studio recording.'

Taylor and Simon re-examined their love and their life as they tried to recuperate from their soul-grinding experiences in Los Angeles. Meanwhile, the media were having a field day. Several tabloids reported that their marriage was over.

'It couldn't have come at a worse time,' said author Esmond Choueke. 'Carly was putting all her energy into trying to make the marriage work and to helping Taylor get off drugs again. The media reports were the last thing they needed. They went back to Martha's Vineyard and renewed their commitment to each other. The time they spent in LA was just too hard on the relationship. They weren't getting along at all and were usually at each other's throats. When they went back east things might have gotten better but by then it was already too late. Some of the media were speculating that it would be only a matter of days before divorce papers would be filed.'

Both Taylor and Simon recognised the seriousness of their situation. He could read in her voice what she wanted. One night after a particularly heated argument, James walked out into the backyard. It was past midnight, and a full moon lit his steps as he paced back and forth. Inside, Carly Simon was watching him from the patio door. She knew that James could be pushed only so far; he had to make for himself the major decisions in his life. She could only watch and hope that all the love she had shared with this man would throw the balance in favour of their little family. He slipped back into their home later that night. Carly was already in bed, asleep, but he had made a decision – to make it work. The next day, he laid down the law to Peter Asher and his management team.

'JT told everybody that his family came first,' Steve Bellows said. 'He said he'd still tour and do albums but he made it clear that Carly and Sally were his first priority. Even though they both worked so hard at making it work, they were both willing to sacrifice multimillion-dollar careers for the sake of a good family life. They always had to answer questions about the bad things that were being said about them in the media. JT never complained about the criticism but it was not difficult to tell that it upset him. He once told me that the best way to avoid being affected by it was by ignoring it. And he was right. Could you imagine if he and Carly had responded to every report about how awful their marriage was? They wouldn't have had time for anything else.'

In 1975 Taylor, 27, continued to perform in venues across the country while Simon stayed at home, in her new role as full-time housewife. As usual, most of Taylor's tour dates were sold out, and he received rave reviews. The highlight show of the year for Taylor occurred on 30 May, when he played New York's Carnegie Hall with special guests Carole King and David Crosby. Taylor had never imagined he would ever set foot onstage at America's most famous performance venue. 'When I lived in New York several years ago I used to pass by Carnegie Hall and would always look up to see who was on the marquee,' Taylor said. 'Carnegie Hall always had the top performers. The first time I played there I felt like I was in a dream. I couldn't believe I was performing in this place that had so much history. I was standing on the same stage music's legendary greats had stood to perform. I kept thinking that maybe I'd wake up and realise it was all a dream.'

That night, the show went magically. At one point the audience hushed, waiting for the next song. Taylor teased with a few notes. Then a surge of recognition swept the room. The music swelled as Taylor and King launched 'You've Got a Friend'. The crowd screamed its delight. The duet received a standing ovation. This recording was released years later on King's 1994 release, *The Ode Years*.

'After the Carnegie Hall show JT's spirits were really up,' said music critic Martin Smith. 'He was very well received, better than I think he ever expected. Even though by this time he had made it very clear that his family came first, he talked about the Carnegie Hall show for years after it happened. I think it was a big turning point for him. It made him realise for the first time how important his music had become. His music was at the centre of American folk history. He had become a living legend.

'He had started a family. He seemed less erratic than he did several years before and his passion for performing was still very strong. He still had a lot to say, and marriage and family were not going to slow him down. I think the reason why Carly let him continue focusing on his career while she stayed at home with Sally was she knew that if JT stopped touring, he would probably be a miserable person to be around. He's one of the few artists I've seen who could survive so much turmoil and adversity and still manage to play every gig like it was the last one he would ever play. It was amazing. With all the wild rumours about his marriage to Carly and his drug habits he was able to put it all behind him and still deliver a top-notch performance. Obviously he's an artist who needs to perform, and that's why 30 years later he's still touring nonstop. He's often said that the best therapy for him is to pour out his heart and soul.'

To friends and family it seemed that Taylor and Simon loved each other more than ever. At a 1975 Christmas gathering they appeared perfectly happy. According to a Simon family member Taylor was happy that Simon had given up her career to tend to family matters. 'He always wanted Carly to be a devoted housewife,' Lucy Simon told a friend. 'When Carly said that she would slow down her career for James, it was a dream come true. No matter how much he denied it, everybody who knew him well knew that he was insecure about all the attention Carly received. I always thought it made him jealous because for a long while his career had been declining. The media reports that came out were mostly false but there's no denying there was a kernel of truth there. Carly had broken down many times because she wasn't happy with the way James was going about things. She wondered how much longer she would have to wait for James to give up drugs. Several times she told me that she was considering leaving. If they didn't have a baby daughter, I think their marriage would have been history by the beginning of 1976.'

A few nights before Taylor embarked on his July 1975 US summer tour, he and Simon threw one of their famous outdoor parties on Martha's Vineyard. As usual there was plenty of booze, exotic foods, and an open jam session with the many musicians who attended. Drugs – especially cocaine and quaaludes – were passed around like candy. Some couples were enjoying open-air sex behind the bushes in the Taylor's backyard. One guest had brought a very young, very shapely aspiring actress. The girl wore a tight, low-cut blue satin dress.

'Everyone at the party kept eyeing this gorgeous girl,' said Rina Fleming, a fashion photographer who attended the party with one of Taylor's friends. 'At one point, she and the guy she was with went back toward the bushes. We could just see her long legs and the blue high heels, but we could hear her moaning and talking sexy to him. Next thing you know, this rock star – this guy was top of the charts – saunters over to them and suddenly she's doing both of them and really moaning it out! I saw this girl after she had made it as an actress – she was playing a virginal type – I can't say more or you'll know who it is, but you'd laugh, too, if you had once seen her with those legs in the air with two guys. Those were crazy times.'

Despite the high jinks that night, Taylor and Simon were gracious hosts. They mingled with the guests till the early hours of the morning, refilling their glasses with beer and hard liquor, and inviting whoever stayed till the end to crash in one of their guest rooms.

'It was always easy to tell when there was tension between them,' said a close friend of Taylor. 'I remember seeing them together at their summer party and they never seemed to be happier. James looked a bit worn out because he was trying to juggle his music career with being a husband and father. But there didn't seem to be much substance to the rumours that we had all heard about in the press. The parties Carly and JT threw were always pretty wild. I once saw a couple openly fucking on their kitchen floor. There was always a lot of drugs. It was a scene you could only picture in a movie. Carly usually wore a revealing dress that would attract the attention of every male in the room. But it was clear that she was still committed to JT and that she only had eyes for him. At that party they were almost inseparable for the entire evening. They danced and kissed and held hands while their guests partied. JT told me that he had never been happier and that being a father was the greatest thing that ever happened to him.'

In September Taylor headed off again, this time on an eight-city solo tour. He tried not to let on that his marriage was in trouble when Simon's name came up. In every interview he gave, Taylor went to great lengths to praise his wife and dismiss the rumours. 'She's the most incredible person on earth,' Taylor told a radio reporter. 'Our marriage has never been more solid.'

Meanwhile, Simon was becoming increasingly concerned about her husband's whereabouts and his recurring drug habits. She told Taylor's good friend and attorney Natt Weiss that she feared she was becoming a single mother. She was also upset that his handlers at Warner Bros were giving him a busy touring and recording schedule, leaving little time for him at home.

'Toward the end of 1975 things started to get out of hand because Taylor's busy schedule didn't leave him enough time to spend with Carly and their daughter,' said rock critic Al Taylor. 'There were a lot of conflicting reports about what was really going on in their relationship. It was obvious that no matter what Carly said she wasn't happy just being Mrs James Taylor. Sure, she told everybody that she wanted to be a good wife and mother, and that her career wasn't as important as her family. But as soon as her husband went off on tour, her attitude changed. A close friend she confided in told me that Carly was fed up and if she didn't have a daughter with him she would have left him ages ago. She often felt like she not only had to be a mother to Sally but also to Taylor. In public they appeared happy. Carly loved being in the spotlight. When she decided to take on more of a domestic role, it made her miserable. When she found out from several people that her husband was partying hard on tour, she was livid. She confronted him and said that if he continued abusing himself then she would absolutely have no choice but to leave him.'

After Taylor's solo tour, Simon demanded that he take a long break to try to clean himself up. Despite strong objections by his management, they finally came to an agreement that he would spend more time with his family and stop touring. He agreed, however, to continue working on a new album that Warner expected him to release in mid-1976.

'He looked very tired and torn,' Al Taylor recalled. 'But he came to his senses and stayed with the decision that his family was more important than his career. There were a lot of people around him who were trying to manipulate him. If Taylor stopped making music, it would affect a lot of people who relied on him to make a living. His handlers were worried that if he took too much time off, he wouldn't be able to come back. It had happened before to so many other musicians. Taylor's career had just received a much-needed shot in the arm with the success of his last album, *Gorilla*. His career was in full motion again. The last thing his management needed was for him to have another personal relapse and to take more time off. The last time he did it hurt him immensely.'

Taylor's reputation was starting to catch up to him. 'JT was always one of the nicest and classiest guys in the business, but when he started doing drugs again it was difficult to work with him,' says a musician friend, who worked for Taylor for several years during the mid-'70s. 'He was temperamental and often seemed like he was on the verge of self-destruction. Many of the musicians who worked for him offered to help him but he didn't seem to want to snap out of it. For a while, after JT and Carly had a daughter, it seemed that he was intent on becoming more responsible with his life. When he started doing drugs again it was bad for himself and everybody else around him. I felt really bad for him because he was so fragile. Without Carly's support he probably would have ruined his life. It was sad to see him become such a mess again.'

After resisting the pressure to tour, James found some peace. He spent several months relaxing with Carly at their home on Martha's Vineyard. Many people detected a radical change in his personality.

'Whenever he spent a considerable amount of time away from touring, it always seemed to do him good,' said Paula Gill, a longtime Taylor groupie. 'The hotels on the road were a big distraction because Carly wasn't around. JT was able to do whatever he wanted without anybody watching over him. His band members have always been wonderful people but like in any business it's hard to control your boss. One time in late 1975 I went to a concert of his in Florida, and he looked terrible. I was surprised because with his new daughter and the success of his album I would have assumed that everything would be going very well. I talked to a member of his crew who told me that he had never seen JT so fatigued and depressed. I felt terrible because I had thought that his drug problems were finally behind him. For the first time I thought that maybe those rumours about his marriage troubles with Carly were true. I was supposed to go to another concert of his a few nights later in South Carolina but I cancelled my trip because I couldn't bear to see him in that condition. When I heard that he was taking a break I breathed a sigh of relief. If anybody in the business needed time off, it was definitely JT.'

19

THE BIG MATCH: COLUMBIA VERSUS WARNER

The year 1976 was pivotal for James Taylor, who faced another big crisis because he was fed up with the way Warner Bros was handling his career. By the end of the year, he would seize an opportunity to sign a multimillion-dollar contract with Columbia Records, Warner's biggest rival.

After several months off, Taylor, started to feel withdrawn. He feared that he might lose his sanity again if he didn't start working on a new album. Carly Simon sympathised with him and gave him her blessing to resume his career. Their relationship had improved during the last few months. Taylor had assumed more responsibility around the house. He was a happy family man again. He had straightened out, and spent a lot of time playing with little Sally. Simon still chided him for his reckless drug habits. She wasn't sure he would be able to avoid drugs again if he was alone on the road, but she also knew it was time for him to get back to work.

'Carly was always his biggest supporter,' said Martin Smith. 'When things got rough, she would ask him to take some time off so they could work out their differences. But she would always encourage him to make music. Carly knew that making music was the best therapy for him. If Taylor wasn't playing his guitar and singing then Carly would have one miserable camper loafing around the house.'

In May 1976 Taylor, who had turned 28, released his seventh album and final effort for Warner Bros *In The Pocket*. On the heels of *Gorilla*'s huge success, Taylor decided to rehire producers Lenny Waronker and Russ Titelman. After months of diligent work, the album was released to mixed reviews. Several critics charged that Waronker and Titelman's production was too slick, and that Taylor's trademark laid-back style got lost. People who followed Taylor's career were disappointed not to find that acoustic and raw feel Taylor was renowned for.

'I think they became a bit complacent,' said music critic Al Taylor. 'Expectations were very high and they didn't live up to them. It was disappointing for Taylor, because he had had some bad experiences with several producers before he teamed up with Waronker and Titelman. But now he had to start from scratch again because it clearly wasn't working out.'

Despite the bad reviews, *In the Pocket* still spawned the mega-hit 'Shower the People', Taylor's best-known original song in over four years. 'Shower the People' hit number one on the easy-listening charts and peaked at number 22 in the pop category.

'The only bright spot on the album was the fact that Taylor finally showed that he was still capable of writing a hit song,' said pop-music archivist Steve Bellows. 'Most people who followed his career thought he was keeping it going by covering other people's songs. A lot of people blamed it on his drug use, which they suspected might have severely damaged his train of thought. 'Shower the People' silenced his critics and confirmed once and for all that all the personal problems he had endured over the years did not diminish his songwriting skills.'

Waronker and Titelman wanted to follow up Taylor's hit cover 'How Sweet It Is' with Bobby Womack's 'Woman Gotta Have It'. Disappointingly, it failed to make the pop charts, though it hit number twenty in easy listening. It was the only cover song on the album, a move that surprised many.

'In the music business if you have success with a certain formula, it's smart to stick with it,' said former Warner Bros executive Joe Smith. 'Taylor was successful doing cover versions of people's songs but I think that, like a lot of serious artists, he wanted to do his own material. I couldn't blame him. He was definitely a person who had a lot to say. Sometimes it's difficult to tell what will work and what won't. You spend big bucks thinking that a certain thing will make the album successful and all of a sudden something you never really considered becomes the focal point of the project. In Taylor's case I think that he was such a good craftsman that it would not have done him justice if he just did cover versions of other people's material.'

Most of Taylor's songs on *In the Pocket* took on an autobiographical approach, especially 'A Junkie's Lament', 'Family Man', and 'Daddy's All Gone', which was a message to his daughter describing how difficult it was to be away from her when he was on the road. Several guest artists appeared on the album, including Stevie Wonder, who co-wrote and played harmonica on 'Don't Be Sad 'Cause Your Sun Is Down', and Art Garfunkel, who sang backup on 'Captain Jim's Drunken Dream'.

For Wonder, it was a pleasure to work with an artist he had long admired and respected. 'James Taylor is one of my favourites,' Wonder said. 'I've listened to his music for years. There's nothing phony about him. He has lots of soul and continues to make music that moves the masses. I can't think of too many people who have continued to stick around as long as he has, putting out hit after hit without diverting too much from the soft, gentle folk style that made him famous. When he asked me to play on his album it was a big thrill for me because I got an opportunity to work with an artist whom I greatly respect.'

On 3 July Taylor was joined by saxophone virtuoso David Sanborn on a four-week tour. It was one of the summer's biggest concert draws, bringing in more than a million dollars in gate receipts. It was obvious that Taylor's appeal had not been diminished by bad record reviews. Fans still flocked to see him.

'A lot of people thought that he might not get the crowds he was used to because *In the Pocket* wasn't doing as well as Warner Bros had hoped it would,' said concert promoter Shelly Finkleberg. 'Many artists have to play small theatres and clubs if their album isn't flying off the shelves. But not James Taylor. Even when he put out an album that had mediocre sales, it didn't at all seem to matter. He had developed an extremely devoted cult following. Unlike most performers, Taylor's a sure bet when it comes to playing live. Rarely does he have a bad show. That's why he doesn't have to rely on the success of his albums to fill seats. His reputation as a great live performer has followed him for years. He's able to bring in the fans. He's one of the few artists who could sell out big venues even if he didn't have a new album out.'

In November 1976 Warner released a twelve-song compilation of Taylor's greatest hits. The album went platinum. It would be Taylor's last release on Warner. He then stunned the music industry with the most significant move in his career: a few weeks later Taylor signed with Columbia Records.

The move to Columbia was a huge coup for its president, Walter Yetnikoff, who'd had a long-standing feud with Warner head, Mo Ostin.

Yetnikoff first came up with the idea of snatching Taylor away from Warner at a recording arts convention in Florida. There, he had quietly chatted up Taylor's good friend and attorney, Nat Weiss. Yetnikoff and Weiss agreed to meet secretly in a room at the Diplomat Hotel. Both men were seasoned deal makers, and the stakes were high. Yetnikoff had waited a long time to get back at Ostin and Warner Bros for taking several big-name artists away from him, among them Van Morrison, Black Sabbath and Randy Newman. Taylor's contract with Warner would soon be due for renewal. It was a good time for Yetnikoff to lure away his archrival's biggest star, and he was ready. The two men talked late into the night, ordering room service meals and eating while they worked out a deal.

After a round of negotiations, Weiss excused himself from the room and phoned Taylor from a public phone. 'I think I know a way to get a million dollars an album,' Weiss said.

Taylor thought he was joking. After so many years of success, he never thought the day would come when he would sever ties with Warner. He had made many close friends at the company, too, and was reluctant to leave them.

'It sounds good but I'm not sure if it's a good idea,' Taylor told Weiss. 'I don't want to turn my back on people who helped me make it. It's not that easy. What if I go to Columbia and they don't give me the support that I got at Warner?'

Weiss convinced Taylor that the offer Columbia made might not come up again. It was now or never. The offer Yetnikoff made was indeed one of the most lucrative ever proposed to a recording artist: he was willing to guarantee Taylor $1 million per album with a hefty $2.5 million advance on signing. The deal would make James music's richest solo act.

'Yetnikoff made the offer at a time when we were at war with each other,' Warner's Mo Ostin later admitted. 'He knew that if he signed Taylor it was the perfect opportunity for him to convince other major acts to follow. We were not at all pleased with the way things worked out but there was no way we were able to compete with the kind of money Walter was offering. It would set a scary precedent.'

Ostin and several other people at Warner begged Taylor to reconsider. The singer broke down several times and cried in front of Weiss and his manager Peter Asher. He was hesitant to leave.

'James Taylor has always been a very loyal person to his family and also to his colleagues,' Peter Asher said. 'When he had to make a big career decision it was never easy, because so many things had to be taken into account. JT always took into account the feelings of the people involved. Especially if they were his friends.'

Taylor discussed the situation at length with Carly. One option remained. It was tempting. Almost irresistible. Taylor would give Warner a final chance to match Columbia's offer. If they did, he would re-sign with them; otherwise, he would switch to Columbia. After another lengthy meeting, Ostin refused to match Columbia's offer. James and Carly finally agreed that he would sign with Columbia. Taylor's representatives made Yetnikoff promise not to interfere with his creativity. They also demanded that his career would not take a backseat to any other artist's.

'We're not offering him a deal like this so he can sit around and wait for things to happen,' Yetnikoff told Weiss. 'We want to make him much bigger than Warner made him. We're going to get behind him in every way. At this point, he can't even imagine how much we intend to support him. We won't try to change his style at all. Leave the music end of it to him and the marketing to us.'

The deal was set. The fine print had been worked out. The signing took place at Nat Weiss's Upper East Side Manhattan apartment in December 1976. At the last minute, however, the deal almost fell through: Taylor did not want to betray his good friends at Warner. It took several hours before Peter Asher could persuade him to go to Weiss's apartment. They were supposed to arrive for the signing at 11 p.m. but showed up more than an hour late. Yetnikoff was furious. Several times he clenched his right fist and looked like he was going to throw a tantrum. He couldn't believe that Taylor was thinking of pulling out at the eleventh hour. 'I've worked so hard to get you this deal,' he told Taylor, waving a check for $2.5 million in front of his face. 'Offers like this are not made every day.'

Taylor broke down in front of everybody. He admitted that he didn't think he could go through with the deal. He told Yetnikoff that friendship and allegiance were more important to him than money. 'You have to respect James's feelings,' Peter Asher told Yetnikoff and Weiss. 'It's a very big decision for him.'

'What about my feelings?' Yetnikoff said. 'I've bent over backward to get him this deal. Before I came here tonight I was told we have a deal. Now is not the time to back out.'

Taylor stood his ground. He told everybody that he needed a little more time to think about it. Yetnikoff agreed to leave the room to allow Asher and Weiss to pour on the pressure. After several more hours of hard persuasion, Taylor finally told Yetnikoff that they had a deal. He signed the contract just after four a.m. There was no champagne popping or celebration. Taylor's divided loyalties had left everyone too exhausted. They all went home to sleep.

'Leaving Warner was the hardest thing for Taylor,' said journalist Esmond Choueke. 'He would have stayed with them if he wasn't put under so much pressure by Nat Weiss and Peter Asher, whose eyes were rolling with dollar signs. Taylor was not one to ever try to rock the boat. He has always stayed loyal to the people who work with him. He doesn't like to shake up his personnel. Everybody from his manager to his backup musicians have worked with him for years. He got along well with Mo Ostin, so it was a very hard move for him. He also knew that he had got caught up in the middle of a power struggle between Warner and Columbia, which made him feel more uneasy about the whole deal. He knew that in a way he was being used by both sides. He's not the type of person to get off on that. He has always liked to take things gradually, especially when it comes to the business side of things. Sure, he likes to make a good living, but he's not like some other artists in the business who will prostitute themselves to make an extra fifty cents. Taylor has high business ethics.'

Yetnikoff bragged to his colleagues about Taylor's signing. For months, he gloated how he had stolen Warner's biggest solo act. Yetnikoff's celebration, however, didn't last long. A year later Ostin got even by signing Paul Simon, one of Coumbia's biggest acts. Yetnikoff was furious. A lawsuit filed by Paul Simon in November 1978 accused Yetnikoff of planning to 'destroy Simon's professional career out of anger and retaliation' because he had deserted Columbia.

'James Taylor's signing with Columbia started a big war between Columbia and Warner,' said former music executive Robert Katz. 'Both labels were out for each other's blood. They put millions of dollars on the table to try to sign each other's big-name artists. It resulted in a flurry of lawsuits and in the end nobody wound up victorious. A lot of the artists who signed didn't bring in the profits that were anticipated. The only one who did well was Taylor. No matter whom he recorded for, his fans were not going to desert him. It was probably the smartest business decision Columbia made in the whole '70s.'

The brouhaha surrounding Taylor's move to Columbia attracted the attention of media around the world. Many journalists thought it was the right thing for him to do.

'Yetnikoff was known to be a big talker but he had never offered anybody that kind of money,' Robert Katz said. 'There was no way he was going to pay somebody 2.5 million bucks and not make sure that they didn't put out a good product. Everybody was eagerly awaiting Taylor's newest incarnation. The only question left was whether or not Columbia would try to divert Taylor from the easy-listening folk style that he had become known for. A lot of artists were reinventing themselves with the growing popularity of electronic music. If Taylor decided to go that route he might have risked alienating a large part of his strong fan base.'

Like many men who had started with nothing and made the bulk of their money suddenly, Yetnikoff was a shrewd businessman. He didn't want to tamper with Taylor's artistic talents; the singer's fans might feel betrayed. What he wanted to do was increase Taylor's marketability.

'Walter was no idiot when it came to making big decisions,' said Robert Katz. 'There was no way he would make a stupid move with Taylor's career after investing all that money. A lot of people at Columbia were tossing around all kinds of ideas, but Walter got the last word. He didn't want to lose the fan base Taylor had worked so hard to build up. What he wanted to do was expand it with some aggressive marketing. He realised a lot of people had still not been exposed to Taylor's music because it had not received a lot of airplay in several years. Walter huddled closely with his staff and decided to target those people who were not too familiar with Taylor. It was a very smart business move.'

After finally coming to terms with the fact that he no longer worked for Warner, Taylor geared up. Within weeks, he fell in love with the new people he worked for. It wasn't the same old chummy atmosphere that he had enjoyed at Warner, but it offered what he wanted most, respect. Yetnikoff ordered that his staff treat Taylor as if he were a god. Peter Asher got in on the act, too: Yetnikoff felt it would be good if Asher produced Taylor's albums again, and James agreed. He was happy to work with the man whom he credited for producing the best stuff of his career.

'It was a real no-brainer,' Robert Katz said. 'Taylor had been tinkering with several other producers for years when the most qualified man to do the job was the man behind the whole operation, his manager Peter

Asher. When Taylor started using other producers, it wasn't the same. Asher was able to capture the real essence of his music. He brought out in Taylor what others had failed to – that soft, easy-listening sound that was a cross between Paul McCartney and Bob Dylan. Yetnikoff was no fool. He did his homework. With Asher, it was almost guaranteed that Taylor's music would strike gold. With anybody else it was a big risk.'

20

TWO GREAT HITS: LITTLE BEN AND 'YOUR SMILING FACE'

In 1977, everything seemed to settle down for Taylor. It was a year of many personal triumphs. To begin with, Carly was pregnant again. Taylor prayed she would have a boy. He told friends that he wanted Sally to have a little brother. 'As long as the baby's healthy, I'll be happy,' he said. 'But I'm hoping for a boy.' Simon's second pregnancy was also a healthy one. 'They were both so happy,' said a family friend. 'He took such good care of Carly. Just like when she was pregnant with Sally. He would huddle up next to Carly's big pregnant belly, lift up her top, and run his hands over the smooth skin. They would both sing to their child in there. Those were lucky babies, to be wanted so much and to have two of the world's biggest stars singing to them while they were still inside.' When his son, Benjamin, was born, Taylor was ecstatic.

Taylor was also excited about the release of his Columbia debut album, *JT*. When it was released on 24 June, critics hailed it as his best work since *Sweet Baby James*. Taylor was in heaven.

'Finally, Taylor silenced his critics,' Martin Smith said. 'No ifs, no buts, it was a first-class album. By working again with Peter Asher, he was able to recapture the spirit of his work the way he did in the early '70s. Nobody was second-guessing him anymore. He was considered a genius again.'

JT went double platinum. Taylor and Asher respectively captured Grammies for best pop vocal performance for 'Handyman' and producer of the year. It was a major highlight in both their careers. Asher said, 'This is the biggest honour we can receive. When we started working on this album we knew we had good material but we never expected to receive such big awards. It feels great to receive this after so many years of hard work put in working with each other.'

Music critic William Ruhlmann said, 'Taylor had made the transition to craftsmanlike pop music, abandoning the shadows of his earlier work . . . the Columbia work is so well crafted, forcing you to acknowledge what a good singer Taylor is.' Well-known DJ Arnie Schaffer declared, 'Columbia scored big when they signed this megatalented superstar . . . the new album demonstrates true class and professionalism . . . Taylor's songs are so appealing . . . Nobody out there delivers a song with the same eloquence. And nobody has done it over and over for so many years the way he has.'

Taylor and everyone associated with him became a hot commodity. They were asked to every cool party, every charity affair.

On 20 September, *JT*'s second big hit was released. 'Your Smiling Face' was instantly put into heavy rotation by stations around the country. Today, it remains one of his most popular songs. Yetnikoff's plan had snowballed.

'The first time I heard it, I knew that it was going to be big,' Robert Katz said. 'The production was first class and Taylor's voice had never been in better form. The smartest move Taylor ever made was to put his name on that contract the night in Nat Weiss's apartment. Yetnikoff managed to completely turn around his career.'

Taylor finished off his big comeback year with a US tour. Back at home, though, Simon was worried she was losing her husband to his work again. Whenever Taylor went out on tour, the rift between them started to widen. Carly couldn't tolerate being alone. She hated the long periods of separation.

'Carly encouraged him to do his thing but she was always a bit apprehensive,' said a close friend of Taylor. 'She didn't completely trust him. Sometimes she would call him 20 times a day to check up on him. She feared that he might be up to his old tricks. She also didn't like the fact that she was left to raise their two kids alone. Even if he left for only a few weeks, the minute he walked out the door Carly started getting nervous. She never knew what to expect from him when he was out of her sight. The combination of all her previous bad relationships mixed with Taylor's bad habits made her very paranoid.'

But Taylor's career was in high gear. Carly wanted to do right by both her husband's career and her children's home life. She knew that Taylor also suffered when he was away from his children.

Taylor continued to sell out large venues across the country. The birth of his son, however, finally made him understand that it was really time to grow up. He told *Rolling Stone* magazine that Ben's birth had transformed his life.

'It has totally changed it, 180 degrees. People say you don't change that much. It's taken my horizon from two months from now to 20 years from now. Not only am I thinking about what kind of role model I am for my kids; the first two years of their lives, what you're doing is trying to keep them alive. I want to spend time with them, and I feel bad if I don't. It also kicks you upstairs. You can't be a kid anymore, in a sense. You can; it's sort of like a little of both. It reacquaints you with what that frame of mind is. Musically, all I listen to is kids' records . . . but at the same time, it takes away freedom . . . for instance, if I wanted to stay out until three o'clock and get down and get crazy and make some music, I've got to think about what's going to go on two hours later. And if I wanted to get really drunk and all fucked up, I'd have to worry about whether or not I would hear the baby crying if she fell out of the crib.'

The Taylors had a highly sensitive security system installed at their New York home. Every door, every window even the perimeter of the property was covered (unlike their property on Martha's Vineyard, which they left wide open). But beyond the safety of herself and her children, Carly had other, deeper fears. And James knew that for those fears, he and his behaviour were the only sentinel.

Taylor tried to help Simon overcome her anxiety while he was on tour. He would call her after every gig from his hotel room and talk to her for hours, reassuring her that he was being a good boy. He promised her that when they got off the phone, he would go right to sleep.

'After he signed his new record contract he really tried hard to combine marriage and work,' said a longtime member of Taylor's band. 'He knew that if he did anything that would slightly set Carly off, it would probably mean the end of their marriage. It was so intense being around him because he had so much to deal with and at times it seemed like he was going to fall apart. The thing that kept him together was that he always kept in the back of his mind the fact that he had a family waiting at home for him. If not for this, I'm sure he would have been tempted to use hard drugs again. Several people in the band were doing it and he knew it. He never said anything – he never judged anyone – I think he was tempted to join in.'

Taylor had an almost perfect relationship with Columbia for the first year. Yetnikoff was more than pleased with the sales of *JT*. He gave several bonuses to Taylor, one day taking the singer to lunch, then to a luxury car dealership. 'Pick any car you want, it's yours,' he said. Taylor refused. He told Yetnikoff that he preferred driving the beat-up old yellow taxi he had bought in New York. He said the car had history. If Yetnikoff was attempting to both please Taylor and to polish his star's image, the plan backfired. Taylor was as loyal to cars as he was to friends.

'It was quite a sight to see a big rock star cruising around in a taxi that looked like it was going to conk out at any second,' said Adrien 'Patches' Henderson, a New York photographer who spotted Taylor in it several times. 'He looked so goofy. It was almost right out of a Cheech and Chong movie. I wondered if the taxi was made out of marijuana. Only a person with a bizarre character would do that.'

Yetnikoff's only concern was that Taylor would not co-operate with the media. Between 1973 and 1978 Taylor granted only one major interview, *Stereo View* magazine. *Rolling Stone*'s Peter Herbst commented, 'He trusts only these things: playing music in front of an audience that asks only that he be himself; working with musicians he admires; writing songs; and most of all, being with his family.'

Exhilarated by his recent US tour, at the beginning of 1978 Taylor vowed for the umpteenth time to spend more time with his family. He agreed to take on one family music project, however – producing his sister, Kate's, new self-titled album. He had helped convince Columbia to give her a record deal. He also helped arrange Kate's songs and wrote 'Happy Birthday Sweet Darling'. Like his other siblings, Kate was blessed with talent but found it difficult to break out of her brother's shadow.

'His sister and his brothers were also very serious artists,' pop critic Neil Adams said. 'But it was tough for them to get recognition because people in the business then were hesitant about family acts. It seemed every big artist had a brother or sister who was also a singer, and most of them were nothing to write home about. If the Taylors had collaborated from the start as a family act, like the Osmonds or the Beach Boys, they would have had quite a career. Because they were all solo acts people were only interested in the most famous member of the family. For Kate and her other brothers, it meant that they would be forced to struggle hard to make any impact. Today, Livingston continues to record album after album, and plays to reasonable-sized crowds. He sounds a lot like his brother. If he wasn't James's brother,

I'm sure he would have sold at least ten times the amount of records.'

The success of his brother was instrumental in making Alex re-evaluate his own career. He was jealous that his famous brother had gone to his sister's side and not his own.

'It hurt both Alex and Livingston, who both were struggling with their careers,' said Phil Newman, a musician who knew Alex. 'Alex was definitely happy for his sister, but in the back of his mind he wondered when it would be his turn. James was always supportive of his siblings' musical endeavours, but I think he should have tried harder to get them all record deals. They definitely deserved them, regardless of their connection to him. I wouldn't have wanted to be in their shoes. Nobody would take them seriously without thinking that they were a spin-off of their brother.'

James's shadow seemed darkest when it fell on Alex. It would take ten years before he produced another album. Like his famous brother, he became dependent on heroin, a habit that would eventually take his life.

'I'm telling you, Alex had all the ingredients that were necessary to make him a star,' Phil Newman said. 'Very few people I ever heard had a voice as distinct as his. The big problem was escaping his brother's shadow. Maybe if he'd dropped the Taylor name and changed it to Hughes or Walker, his career might have taken off. I remember hearing him jam one summer night in a bar long after it closed its doors for the evening. He stayed and played till six in the morning and still, the 20-odd people who had listened all night were in no hurry to leave.'

According to Newman, Alex was too proud to ask his brother for more help. 'He didn't want James to think he was begging. Look, James is a great guy, we all know that. It must have been difficult for him because he had to worry about his own career first. He might have done the right thing by not interfering too much. Maybe he didn't want his sister and brothers to be able to exploit his name. If he didn't support them as much as they would have liked by introducing them to the right people, he definitely encouraged them by showing up at their concerts and by making suggestions about their music. Taylor wanted to give his siblings their own space to develop creatively and the opportunity to make it themselves.'

Walter Yetnikoff was persuaded to sign Kate Taylor after he listened to her sing. He thought her voice was one of the purest he had ever heard.

'Kate Taylor is a true professional,' Martin Smith said. 'It's not her fault that she was the sister of one of the most notorious musicians of a whole era. If I was working at a label as an A&R person I would have signed her without hesitation. The more Taylor's people wheedled for Columbia to sign her, the more it made sense. She was not signed because of whom she was related to. It certainly helped, but she could carry a tune as well as anybody.'

21

MORE FAMILY FEUDS

Taylor spent the rest of 1977 relaxing at home with Carly and the kids, although he managed to write several songs for the Broadway musical *Working*. He was talked into the work by manager Peter Asher, who expected Broadway to be a good new direction for his client. He was wrong.

'It was one of the biggest flops ever on Broadway,' said a woman who worked on the show's production crew. 'Taylor got involved because it was being released on Columbia, which is the label he records on. They thought it would start something new for him, but instead I think it wound up hurting him because he associated himself with a project that received terrible reviews. One song that he wrote, 'Un Mejor Dia Vendra', was a beautiful tune but it really didn't go anywhere. The bad reviews the show was receiving spread like a pox on anything associated with it. Taylor came to one of the first shows and we all got to meet him. He seemed to be very nice and positive about the whole thing. I felt bad for him because his music might have been put to better use in another production.'

But Taylor accepted the fact that this project would not even become a small success.

After the show closed Taylor conceded to several close friends, 'If I had to do it all over again, I'd probably do it differently. I think I'll stick to do what I do best for the next little while, writing my own music and performing live.' And he kept his word.

During the summer, Taylor worked with Simon on her upcoming *Boys in the Trees* album. In September 'Devoted to You', the duet the couple recorded, was released. But it seemed the song and every public appearance the pair made was a desperate effort to show the world that their marriage was still strong. Carly Simon would stay close to her husband whenever they went out, always conscious that a photographer should snap only 'happy family' shots of them.

'If there weren't so many rumours about how bad things were between them, I don't think they would have done the song,' said author Esmond Choueke. 'Carly was a master at putting a new spin on things. "Devoted to You" was meant to try to get the press off their backs. Carly was tired of having so many photographers chase them wherever they went. She didn't want the kids to grow up around all this. The song turned out to be a bit too cheesy and I don't think it convinced anybody. Even their close friends were still suspicious. A well-known entertainer who knew them both very well told me shortly after that it was difficult to be around them because they were always arguing. She said that she gave the marriage another year or two, max.'

Don Grolnick, Taylor's good friend, was equally concerned. He told a journalist, 'Sometimes I wonder if they would be better off apart. It's not good for two people to stay together if they're not happy. They're both amazing people but they drive each other a bit crazy. I just hope one of them doesn't snap. They both have strong personalities and I wouldn't want to see one try to beat the other into the ground. I've often told James that if he feels like snapping that he should just leave. I'd hate to see him wind up doing something he might regret for the rest of his life.'

Their relationship was stressed to the point where they no longer slept in the same bed. Taylor knew that when his wife stomped off to bed with an angry snort, he was free to sleep anywhere in the house – but not with her.

'Carly had a tough personality and found it hard to tolerate a lot of the things James did,' said one of their children's former baby-sitters. 'They were great to work for and they always treated me with respect. But I could overhear some of their arguments. Many times they fought over stupid things, like one time Carly got mad because she accused James of not noticing her new hairstyle. She had gotten it cut shorter and had highlights. She said he was too wrapped up in himself to acknowledge anything else around him. I thought she was being a bit too hard on him,' recalled the sitter. 'I remember I thought that then. Now I'm older. I'm married, and I know how selfish men can be sometimes. Now I think maybe she had a point.'

Simon seemed to overlook the many efforts Taylor made to spend more time with the family. It wasn't long – autumn 1977 – before he started trying to drown his sorrows with booze. After Simon gave an interview to a New York radio station, Taylor drank tequila and rum all night. He was disturbed by all the attention his wife was getting. He was happy that she had reduced her schedule to spend more time with the children, but it seemed that whenever she started to get even the slightest attention, his insecurities would take over. Once she showed him an article about her in a magazine. He began to read it, then angrily tossed it across the room and walked out without saying a word.

Simon was disappointed. Again, she threatened to leave him if he didn't shape up. She later reflected on her husband's attitude to writer Alison Steele: 'I think it would be easier for James if he could be married to someone who wasn't into having a career, who would stay in the Vineyard all year and bake wonderful pies – although I bake a pretty damn good apple pie . . . You either have to disappoint the record company or your manager or your children or your husband. There's always guilt. I'm half-Jewish, and that half Jewish part of me is just pulled into action daily by always feeling as if I'm not doing my job in one part of these areas as well as I should be doing it.'

Simon's marriage to a very difficult man was constantly scrutinised by the entertainment press. To make matters worse, she was torn by the concerns of modern working mothers – how to give her time to everyone at once.

Carly had decided against a big tour to support her new album, because she hesitated to leave Taylor alone with the kids. In fact, on the few occasions when she had to leave, she became anxious and nervous. Simon always took small framed pictures of the children with her when she travelled. When she got to her hotel room, she would line them up on the night table so she could see their faces when she went to bed and when she woke up in the morning.

Taylor 'can go off for a month and maybe miss the kids a couple of days,' Simon told *People* magazine. 'I am so neurotically bound to them that I would have to call three times a day to find out if they went to their lessons and took their vitamins and to tell them I loved them. When he goes on tour the first few days I feel like I can't live without him . . . by the time he comes back – while I'm glad to see him – my gut reaction is, "Hey, buster, you're in my house. Hang up your coat and show a little respect!"'

Taylor loved his children, but he was less given to expressing it with worried concern.

'Carly was a bit overprotective of her children,' said Jennifer McConnachy, a former neighbour of Simon in New York. 'I'd see her and her husband walking them in a stroller and Carly always seemed to be the one in charge. Her husband seemed much more laid-back. If they'd go to the park, Carly didn't leave them alone with her husband for a second. She seemed to be uneasy, almost paranoid that someone was going to steal her kids. I think she took it a bit to the extreme.'

Everyone who had access to their home had to reassure Simon that they were loyal, honest and trustworthy. Employees who didn't pass Carly's stringent security clearances never made it past the front foyer. Simon screened their nannies harder than the best agencies did.

22

SALLY AND BEN COPE WITH FAMOUS PARENTS

When it came to their children, Taylor and Simon were obsessed with secrecy. For many years they rarely discussed the lives of Sally and Ben. Carly referred to her children in several interviews, but gave almost no details about their daily activities or progress. This was frustrating for interviewers, who knew her as a doting mother involved in almost every aspect of her children's development.

'They tried to shield them from the media,' said photographer Robert Whiting. 'The last thing they wanted was for their kids to be on TV and the cover of magazines. Carly told James from day one that the kids would get an education first and when they were old enough, they would be free to make their own decision to choose what they wanted to do, be it music, art or becoming a lawyer. Carly and James were determined not to push their kids into something they might not have wanted to do.'

The Taylors had seen too many children of celebrities reveal the pain and anxiety their parents had caused them by putting them on stage.

Sally Taylor remembers her parents trying to protect her and her brother Ben from the Hollywood paparazzi. 'They were great parents who wanted us to lead normal lives,' she said. 'A lot of kids who have famous parents feel pressured to follow in their footsteps. Our parents always let us choose our own path. They were there whenever we needed them. They never told me to pick up a guitar or to learn how to sing. I pursued that on my own. Deep down, I know that whatever I decided to do, they would fully support me. We've been through so much together. There were a lot of highs and a lot of lows. But they've always been there for us to fall back on.'

Taylor and Simon's parenting alternated between moments of extreme love and adhering to the strict rules of the household. They showered Sally and Ben with gifts, clothes and trips but tried to keep them sequestered from the rest of the world.

'My parents were protective, a bit overprotective,' Sally says. 'They were wary of a lot of people and tried to keep us away from them. But they were very open and liberal. When people were around whom they trusted, it was easier. There were a lot of fun times. I think things just got a bit heavy when one of them would go off on tour and the other would be left at home to care for us. It wasn't easy because they had to play two roles – one as the mother, the other as the father. My mother's a very strong woman and she always said that she'd do anything to make sure that we had a normal childhood. She wanted us to go to school and be like all the other kids. That's why she tried to keep the media away from us. She didn't want us to go to school and to be looked at as celebrities by the other kids.'

Like Sally and Ben Taylor, many children of famous entertainers find it difficult to cope with their parents' fame. Lucie Arnaz, the daughter of Lucille Ball and Desi Arnaz, once said that growing up with one famous parent is hard enough, but with two life often becomes unbearable. 'Any child who grows up with a famous parent will have more pressure on them than any other kid. In my case I grew up with two famous parents. It wasn't easy because they weren't always around to watch me and my brother grow up. It's the little things that count in a child's life. Sometimes I'd have to spend special times alone because my parents were too busy working. Back then I grew up in the spotlight because the times I was able to spend with my parents, many of them were surrounded by cameras and reporters. It wasn't easy.'

Jacob Dylan, lead singer of the Wallflowers and son of Bob, said that he often felt he was being forced to grow up in the shadow of his legendary father. 'For many years I didn't see him too much. He often felt like a stranger because he would be out on the road for so long. When I started getting into music he didn't try to pressure me. He let me find my own way, which in many ways was good. When my music started getting recognition it was a bit tough at first, because a lot of people were comparing me to my father. It wasn't my fault that my father was so well known. Even if I didn't have a famous father, I'm sure I would have still done music. Sure, his name helps, but I still have to go on stage and perform on my own merits.'

Perhaps the final word goes to John Lennon's son, Julian. 'It was very difficult growing up. Being the son of a famous singer often worked against me. When I started getting into music, most people thought I was just trying to exploit my father's name. He was never there for me. I'd go years without seeing him, and when we did meet, it was as if I was with a total stranger. I think that he cared about me but I always thought he should have been there for me more.'

Canadian scholar Richard Davis conducted an intense study on celebrity offspring called *Behind Celebrity*. His investigation was sparked by a meeting he once had in London with Charles Finch, the son of actor Peter Finch. Charles is well respected in showbiz circles as an entertainment agent for the William Morris Agency. Davis was fascinated by the way Finch managed to stay in the same business as his father yet carve his own niche.

'Not many people associate him with his father,' Davis said. 'He's one of the few examples of a celebrity's kid who managed to escape his father's shadow. Most of the kids I based my report on had enormous difficulty coping with it all. Many of them became addicted to drugs or committed suicide.'

Davis was curious as to how often the lives of celebrities' children were ruined by the very fame that made the parents stars. In his report he referred several times to Sally and Ben Taylor's experiences. 'It couldn't have been easy for them because both of their parents were famous rock stars with very flamboyant personalities. They're both great kids but it's easy to tell that they're having trouble finding their own identity as musicians. The pressure on them is enormous . . . No matter what they put out, comparisons will always be drawn.'

Davis's subjects included Liza Minnelli, Chastity Bono and Jade Jagger. The results of his research are alarming.

'A lot of these kids take drugs because they have so much trouble coping. Liza Minnelli, for example, is one of the all-time great entertainers, but she can't go anywhere without her mother's name, Judy Garland, being brought up. One of the reasons for her many relapses with drugs and alcohol is because of all the pressure of her mother's fame. She once said that if she started over today, she might consider using another name to try to avoid the comparisons to her mother.'

In his study *Celebrity*, British psychologist Anthony Garner reached a similar conclusion. 'Gradually, the lives they lead enter into a world of sorrow and despair. Not many people who are born into famous families enjoy the experience . . . It's always the same story. They have trouble trying to get a life . . . And those who are lucky enough to break through, in many instances their parents start to resent them for stealing the spotlight.' Joan Crawford's crushing of her daughter's first attempt at acting has now become a legend as it was described first in the book then in the movie *Mommie Dearest*. Other publicized battles between famous parents and their children are even more unsettling.

Sally Taylor admitted that it took her many years to record her first album because she was afraid that the media would say she wasn't as talented as her parents. Finally, in 1998, she released *Tomboy Pride*, an eleven-song collection recorded in the picturesque hills of Lyons, Colorado. 'I went off and recorded in a friend's studio without telling my family. I never really thought I would be able to do my own album. But when I decided to do it I wanted to do it without anybody's help. I told my parents what I was up to midway through the project. They both gave me full support. My dad played on a track and he seemed so proud of what I did. I know that a lot of people will always make comparisons. That's why I'm happy that I did it at an age when I wasn't young enough to let it get to me. Now I have the attitude that if people compare me to my parents, I treat it as a compliment.

'If he didn't like my music my father wouldn't criticise it, but he also wouldn't say it's good. He's the type of person who is very easy to read – if he doesn't like something, it's easy to tell. I'm sure there's a lot of things on the album that he thinks could have been better but his attitude is that of a real artist. He respects other people's expression and tries not to impose his own. Without his support it would have been very difficult for me. Could you imagine if either of my parents had said it sucked? I would probably have had a hard time feeling comfortable doing a live tour. They're not like that with me, my brother, or anybody else. They like to encourage people to express themselves.'

In their studies, both Davis and Garner claimed that it is better for the children of showbiz celebrities to pursue careers in other fields. Davis said that people like Sally and Ben Taylor would have had less pressure if they'd pursued law or teaching. He concluded that any career unrelated to music or entertainment would give them a much better shot at leading normal lives.

Sally Taylor agrees with their conclusions. However, she pointed out that because her parents raised her in two places, a New York suburb and Martha's Vineyard, she was able to lead a more normal life than most other celebrities' children. 'They made sure that my brother and I went to good schools and participated in activities with kids who were from normal families. The last thing they pushed us to do was music. If we did it, it would have to be done on our initiative. I'm lucky that I didn't have to grow up in Hollywood, like a lot of the kids who have famous parents. I think it's more difficult for them to cope. In my case, things were more normal. We have a very tight-knit-family and I'd get to do things like spend time with my grandparents and go to family gatherings. If I look back, I can honestly think of a lot of rough times we had, but it's the good times that really stick out most.'

Friends of both Sally and Ben say that neither of them tried to use their parents' fame for their own gain. 'Both of them are so down-to-earth,' said one friend. 'You'd never know that they came from such a famous family. They're such good-hearted and caring people. When I first met Sally in Boulder, Colorado, a couple of years ago, we became good friends. I didn't find out who her parents were for several weeks. When I did, I couldn't believe it. I asked myself, "How could someone from such a famous family treat everybody else on the same level and have no ego?" If it was me, or anybody else, it would be hard to act the same way as Sally. She's quite a remarkable and unique individual.'

James Taylor is the first to admit that it wasn't easy for Sally and Ben. If he could turn back the clock, he says that he would have tried to devote more time to them. 'I missed out a bit on their childhood,' he told the London *Times*, '. . . but I do think I was less available to my kids because of my addiction. On the other hand, the drugs actually saved my life in the early days . . . fatherhood was one of the things that pulled me toward life, as opposed to wanting to lock myself in a refrigerator.'

For a time, Ben found it difficult to grow up as the son of famous parents. Along the way, however, he's said that he was able to gradually accept who he was. He told journalist Nigel Williamson, 'I think the child of any parent will come up with a list of pros and cons . . . for a while I had a problem with people introducing me as the son of James Taylor and Carly Simon. But the way I look at it now is that a large part of what I am comes from who my parents are. And people introduce me like that because it does say something about me. It doesn't mean I'm any better than anybody else, or deserve to be treated differently, but I'm honoured to be identified with them. I idolize both of them musically. They're great people and they never embarrass me.'

Ben and Sally both agree that many people they know who are the sons and daughters of famous people went through much more emotional turmoil. For them, however, the temptation to rebel wasn't as strong. 'I never really went through a rebellious phase,' Ben told Nigel Williamson. 'I never had any resentment against my parents, because they never pressure me, and they never told me not to do anything. They told me their ideas, what they'd found from certain experiences, and discussed them. When I went out as a teenager and experimented with things, I was confident I could let my parents know about it . . . drugs and alcohol weren't as intriguing to me, because they were straightforward about them. They said, "If you're going to experiment, that's what you're going to do, but this is what can happen."'

Sally Taylor has inherited her father's temperament. This, she admitted, sometimes means she can be rebellious. 'I have some of my father's traits,' Sally said. 'When things get tough, sometimes I get going. I like to be out on the road a lot to explore what's out there. My parents were very open about drugs and that's why I think we didn't get into them as much as a lot of the other kids. If they had tried to hide things from us, maybe things would have turned out differently. The thing that helped keep our heads on straight was the fact that our parents always were there for us and they didn't put any pressure on us to go into show business, like a lot of famous parents do to their kids. I know when I have a child I'll do the exact same thing. Every child in this world should be encouraged to do what's really in their heart. You only live once.'

When Ben and Sally were little, Simon and Taylor had a full-time nanny look after them when they were on the road touring. 'One of them was usually there to look after us,' Sally said. 'But when both of them were away, it was difficult. We really missed them and sometimes we needed them when they weren't there. If a major crisis happened, we had to turn to our nanny. It would have been a big deal if our parents spent weeks or months away at a time. But it didn't happen that way. When they were both gone, you could be sure that at night our phone was ringing off the hook. They would check in several times a night. They made sure everything was going well and that we got into bed on time. We always felt as though our parents were with us, even if we were really thousands of miles apart.'

Despite the fact that Sally and Ben do not regret having two famous parents, many believe it will be difficult for them to ever escape singing in their parents' shadows. Indeed, ever since the release of Sally's debut album and Ben's record deal with Sony in 1998, they've both been frequently compared to their parents. 'I've heard them both sing, and let me tell you that it's not difficult to tell which family they're from,' said freelance music journalist Kim Elman. 'That whole family sounds alike, from James to his brother Livingston to Carly to the kids. I heard Sally's album and I couldn't believe how much she sounded like her mother. If I was in her shoes, I would have debuted with a techno-dance album or alternative grunge – anything to escape the comparisons. I feel bad for both her and her brother, because it will be hard for them to get a good following. I went to one of Sally's concerts in Colorado, and a lot of the people there were James Taylor fans. They came out of curiosity or respect for her father. I asked one guy how he heard about it, and he said he read it on a Carly Simon newsgroup on the Net.'

The comparisons, however, are not enough to dissuade the Taylor kids from pursuing their dreams. 'This is the music I was brought up listening to and I really enjoy and respect it,' Sally said. 'I'm not the type of person who does something just for the sake of being different. I do what really means a lot to me. And if people want to draw comparisons or label me as a copycat of my parents, so be it. I'm just trying to be me.'

James's longtime backup singer Kate Markowitz sympathises with Sally and Ben. The stunning Markowitz is regarded as one of the best backup singers in the business. She said that the public image of Taylor and Simon could minimise their kids' achievements. 'It's tough shoes to fill. They've both got to be willing to pay their dues. I've seen them grow up and I sympathise with them. The pressure will be harder on them than the regular person starting out. But they handle it well. They've sat in with their dad for a tune or two at many of his concerts over the years, and they both seem to love being onstage. They handle that well. There's always a lot of love in the room when James is with his kids. He's so proud of them . . . Sure, it's a lot of pressure being the children of James Taylor and Carly Simon. But Sally and Ben are incredible people. It would be easy for them to try to use their parents' good names to further their own careers, but they're both determined to make it on their own. And I'm confident they will. I admire them for the way they've approached things.'

23

CARLY TURNS TO TRAVOLTA

By 1979 Taylor and Simon had been interviewed, reviewed or photographed by every newspaper and magazine. Any titbit about the couple's private lives sold copies. They were the media's most popular music dish to be served up to the reading public. In turn, the readers bought enough music to keep them high on the charts. When Taylor released his second album for Columbia on 26 April, record stores across the country sold out and took orders for the next batch. *Flag* was the envy of the music industry, even though it didn't receive reviews as good as the previous *JT*.

'When Taylor released his first album on Columbia it was hot, everybody wanted a copy,' said Bryan Nifkin, a former manager of the Discus Record chain store. 'So when *Flag* was released, everybody expected it would be better. During the first few weeks, it was impossible to meet the demand. Every day we had to reorder more copies. And in those days it wasn't easy for the labels to print new copies like they do today. You had to wait weeks or sometimes even months to get new stock. We had a lot of unhappy customers.' One helpless clerk at a New York City store was forced to call the police because of *Flag*. He had been working alone that day as more and more customers bought the album until stock ran out. Then the eager fans started lining up to put their name down for the reorder. The young man had to call for help as the customers waited and the store filled with too many people.

Although *Flag* sold well, it was clearly not one of Taylor's finest works. His original tunes lacked the edge that his fans had grown accustomed to hearing. And this time the covers that usually were able to spawn initial interest in his work were atrocious. He almost killed the Beatles' 'Day Tripper' and sounded like a white man trying to sound black on the Drifters' 'Up on the Roof'. His regular cast of musicians – Danny Kortchmar, Les Sklar, Russ Kunkel, Don Grolnick and producer Peter Asher – again made the grave mistake of trying to move away from the simple, easygoing Taylor style. Fans complained that *Flag* offended their delicate Taylor sensibilities. With this album their enthusiasm for his records started to wane. Some critics speculated he just didn't know what to come up with anymore. Others pointed to bad management and bad artistic decisions. For whatever reason, it was the beginning of the end of Taylor's heyday. With *Flag* he turned a corner in his career.

'One of his worst albums, probably his worst ever,' says Taylor fanatic Debrah Teitleman. 'I remember lining up at a local record store the day it came out. A lot of people wanted to get this album because it got a lot of advance publicity. What a disappointment. I was also a big fan of the Beatles and I wasn't at all pleased with his version of "Day Tripper". He sounded as if he hadn't slept the previous six nights before he recorded it. And the band seemed to play out of synch. Maybe he was under pressure from his marital strife, because he sure didn't deliver anywhere near his capabilities. After this album his career never seemed to be the same. I bought his next couple of albums, and they were also a bit of a letdown. After that I stopped buying his stuff, although years later I bought one of his albums in a one-dollar bin at a used-record store. But I still go to his concerts.'

The negative reviews for *Flag* didn't deter other Taylor fans from buying tickets to his live performances. When he launched a tour to support *Flag* on 3 July 1978, his management had to add several shows because of the high demand. Taylor crammed in 25 shows during his six-week tour across the country. The two performances at the Blossom Music Center in Ohio were taped for a cable television special. Arguably, Taylor was the biggest solo artist in music. He didn't need an album to ensure that he would fill big venues when he performed live.

'He had become the Grateful Dead of solo artists,' said pop critic Neil Adams. 'Only the Dead could fill places the way he did without having to have a smash record. I've seen many of his concerts, and let me tell you that each one of them is special, the way the Dead concerts are. They all seem fresh and are very spiritual. When you go to a Dylan concert, you never know what to expect. Many years Dylan was just awful and was milking the public based on his previous exploits. But not

Taylor. He did have some bad album releases but when it comes to performing live, he's the master. He exudes a certain kind of energy and mood that is almost euphoric.'

In September of that year, Taylor continued his feverish pace, performing as part of the antinuclear concert series, *Muse/No Nukes*. For Taylor, it was the start of many benefit concerts to come; he still performs at several each year. With his time and talent he has fought against racism, the destruction of the rain forest, and poverty. The *No Nukes* concert was recorded and a three-record album was released in December 1979. Taylor played on six tracks and recorded a seventh, 'Stand and Fight', for the *No Nukes* feature film, which played in major theatres across North America in the summer of 1980. The proactive approach that his mother ingrained in him when he was young was starting to happen. Taylor has become one of music's staunchest human-rights activists.

'James Taylor has always been one of the biggest proponents of human rights causes,' says Eliza Burton, a London peace activist who has participated in many benefit concerts, including Wembley's famed Nelson Mandela concert. 'Taylor and his music stand for peace and harmony. Unlike a lot of other musicians, who get out there for the extra publicity to help boost their record sales, Taylor does it because he is a real humanitarian. Some musicians exploit other people's misery in their lyrics so they can sell more records. Not Taylor. He goes about things in his own quiet way and has an impact. He comes from a very liberal background, a background that taught him not to tolerate social injustice.'

In the summer of 1980, three-year-old Ben fell gravely ill. He had a recurring high fever for weeks. His once-chubby cheeks grew thin and sallow. Always dutiful, Carly Simon shuttled her son from one exclusive specialist to the next. None of the best doctors was able to diagnose the problem. Ben's condition deteriorated to such a point that his chances of survival were poor. Simon was furious that Taylor was off on tour while their son lay helplessly in bed. She worried constantly about Ben while she hunted for any information that could save the boy. Taylor was on the road and far away from the torment of their sick child.

'We were both traumatised,' Carly told *People* magazine. 'I tend to get hysterical, while James is clinical and often tried to escape.' Taylor tried to encourage Simon and support her; he felt that nothing could be gained from panicking. But she wanted him near to face this tragedy.

She read medical books. She hounded doctors and medical staff for answers. Finally, her motherly persistence paid off.

A specialist recommended by a friend of Carly finally came up with the right diagnosis. One of Ben's kidneys was malfunctioning and had to be removed. The operation scheduled at Babies Hospital in New York City. Carly Simon shifted into supermother gear. She rallied support from friends and both their families. She gathered cards, wishes and prayers for Ben's sickroom. 'She was like a mother bear protecting her cub,' recalled a staffer who worked in the hospital at the time of Ben's surgery. 'She was really nice to the staff. She wanted to surround her little boy with a happy, positive environment for the surgery.'

Meanwhile, Taylor was away performing a benefit concert for presidential candidate John Anderson. Ben's surgery was successful, but Simon could not forget how her husband had failed her. A couple of nights later, after a fight with Simon, Taylor showed up at the rock bar Trax in Manhattan and told his friends, 'Jezebel kicked me out, so I'm up for grabs.'

'James was upset by his son's illness but he didn't know how to deal with it properly,' recalled a close friend. 'So he tried to keep busy by performing and going out. It was the only way he knew how to escape what was going on. But you could tell that he was hurting inside. Ben's illness almost put him over the edge. He seemed disoriented.'

Ben was lucky to survive. He needed two six-inch incisions to remove the kidney and reconstruct his urethra. Carly, who has always supported sick kids, visited many of the hospital's terminally ill patients. 'I sang them everything from "Three Blind Mice" to "Farmer in the Dell",' Carly recalled to *People*. 'Ben had so many toys that I started playing Robin Hood and stealing the stuffed animals from him to give to others . . . There's nothing like the pain, too, of being a mother. When your child is sick or unhappy and you can do little about it.'

For Simon, the past few years had been the hardest. She had all but abandoned her music career. There were only fleeting glimpses of her, an odd record release here or there. But Taylor got to enjoy the best of both worlds. When he was not off touring, he spent his time building a new house. With an architect friend, he had helped design the modern mansion they planned to complete on more than sixty-five acres on Martha's Vineyard. (Taylor had been a good carpenter since his father taught him to fix things when he was a young boy.) Their new home would include a complete recording studio for both himself and Carly, a 45-foot observation tower for spectacular views of the Vineyard, and a large, open, fully equipped play area for Sally and Ben. But for Simon, a piece of the puzzle still seemed to be missing.

'If I'm not in bed by eleven-thirty I won't be too zippy the next day,' she told Jim Jerome. 'I really miss having a nightlife, hanging out in bars or talking and walking in the country waiting for the sunrise.'

Rumours of their marriage dissolving began to surface again. The situation was getting too complicated for Simon's family as well. 'Carly needed James to help her out with the kids, and he wasn't around,' said one of Simon's sisters. 'It was a terrible situation for her. Ben was sick and she was running around with him to every hospital in New York until she found someone who could help him. Meanwhile, she had to pick up Sally from school every day and help her with her homework. The kids needed a father, but during this time James wasn't around too often. Carly was becoming frantic. She had sacrificed her career for years to look after the kids. Now it seemed she was being rewarded by being taken extra advantage of.'

According to music critic Martin Smith, Simon often felt that Taylor was doing to her and the children what he did with the women he dated before he got married. He rarely let them know his true feelings. 'He loved fatherhood but didn't always live up to his responsibilities. Poor Carly. She was left to hold up the fort while he was off having fun playing music. I think she got sucked in too fast to sacrificing her career. It was a move that she would regret for many years.'

In May 1980, Simon was spotted by photographers several times in the arms of *Saturday Night Fever* heartthrob John Travolta. Rumours circulated that they were having an affair while Taylor was on tour with his band. According to a close friend of Simon, Carly fell deeply in love with Travolta and wanted to ditch Taylor. Travolta, however, treated Simon the way he did many of his ex-flames – if things got too hot, he put out the fire.

'Travolta was the biggest swinger in Hollywood and he was far from ready to settle down,' the friend said. 'Carly lost complete sense of herself. Travolta charmed the pants off of her while her husband was away. Then, before she knew it, he dumped her. It was very hard on her.'

When Taylor found out about his wife's affair with the king of disco, he was furious. He spent several nights drowning his sorrows at various watering holes while he was still on tour. He finally called Simon and told her the marriage was over. He told her that things could never again be the same. He said that he wasn't sure if he still loved her. But Simon didn't care. She was too busy extolling the virtues of Travolta to the press.

'John has an almost magical way of knowing when I am in need,' Simon told a reporter. 'When James couldn't be there, John came to me during that week before Ben was to go in the hospital. He is sensitive, loving and very immediately there.'

Travolta took her to some of New York's top discos, including the famed Studio 54. She was the envy of every woman in the club, getting the opportunity to dance with the world's most famous disco dancer.

'It really stroked Carly's ego because she knew how much every woman would have liked to dance with John Travolta,' said Elaine Tate, a former Studio 54 barmaid. 'When she danced with him, she seemed to be in heaven. They danced very close and had big smiles on their faces. At one point were rubbing their bodies against each other. People in the club stared at them the whole night. They were quite the couple. I didn't realise how beautiful Carly Simon was until I saw her up close. Years later when I saw Travolta dance with Princess Di at the White House, I remembered back to that night I saw him dance with Carly Simon. Princess Di had the same twinkle in her eye that Carly had. I think any woman in the world who ever got the chance to dance with him must have had the same feeling.

'It was a bit weird because I knew that Carly was married to James Taylor, and there she was boogying the night away with Travolta. This dance was not something that can breakup a marriage, but it sure didn't bring Carly and James any closer together, either.'

Some people thought that Simon was using Travolta to get publicity. 'Carly wanted to revive her career,' said entertainment author Esmond Choueke. 'Travolta was Hollywood's leading man, and wherever he went he had a whole line of cameras following him. There's no proof that Travolta and Carly were anything more than friends. The people who speculated they were lovers were only saying that because the couple had been spotted dancing together in several clubs in New York.'

Simon added insult to injury by writing 'Three of Us in the Dark' – a song that explored the idea of a *ménage à trois*. 'James was left shaken by her acute behaviour, and from that point things were never the same between them,' said rock photographer and historian Carl Widger. 'I know people who say that he told them he was disgusted when Carly started making the rounds with Travolta. He couldn't believe she'd fall for a sex-symbol type who was so much younger than her. He thought that she had grown out of her fascination with bedding Hollywood's leading men. I think in some ways he was relieved because it finally gave him the excuse he was waiting for to leave. James was just waiting to put an end to their years together. Their life was filled with anger and torment. A lot of his friends say that he looked more relaxed after it all unfolded.'

While she caroused with Travolta, Simon never stopped caring for their son. Ben recuperated from his operation. Simon and Travolta got more serious. Simon acquired a new wardrobe. She seemed to bloom, becoming even more beautiful in party gowns by big-name designers. She and Travolta were spotted feeding each other raviolis in a small, exclusive trattoria. Meanwhile, Taylor performed concerts at a feverish pace: in August 1980, he did 23 shows in a four-week period.

'It's what he needed,' said author Esmond Choueke. 'If he didn't keep busy, he might have been tempted to resort to his old heroin habits. By now he had kicked his drug habit. But another old habit kept calling, and so he did drink – though he managed to reduce his drinking to a manageable degree. He rarely got hammered the way he used to. Playing music was the best remedy for him during the time his relationship with Simon was coming to an end. You can tell from his music that he was maturing as an artist. He was able to sing with more feeling than ever before.'

Simon accused Taylor of being an absentee father like his own father. She told him that he was never around during the times the family needed him most. Taylor admitted his wife had a good point. He told Timothy White, 'I missed my father when he made a two-year trip to Antarctica when I was young . . . I missed him whenever he went to work. I'm a travelling father now, and when I leave, my son cries . . . but I think it's important for children to get the feeling that you enjoy yourself and that life is enjoyable. I see some people – including myself – frequently saying, with a moan, "I'm sorry, Daddy has to go to work now." And my son is crying and my daughter is removing herself from me, and I'm saying, "I don't want to go" . . . Being a celebrity is not so great a gig, and it's not as good as being a good musician or having a particular skill. Celebrity always misses the point, and you end up disappointing the people who thought you were what you never said you were . . . People approach your children not only for who they are but for reasons beyond their knowledge or control . . . To be a celebrity raising children is tough.'

Aside from Travolta, rumours were circulating that Simon was seeing several other famous men. A report linking her to Woody Allen surfaced. She was quoted by *People* magazine as saying, 'I'd give Woody just the tiniest little toot of cocaine to give him that extra confidence to be a great conversationalist.' Her fixation with Allen was real, but there's no proof they were ever involved romantically. Then Simon was reported to be having a tryst with Pablo Picasso. She said of the artist, 'He'd get along well with James, but I'd give him a little Valium to calm his ego.' Whatever truth was in these rumours, it became patently obvious to Taylor that plenty of other men were interested in his wife.

'Carly was furious with Taylor for being away from the family. And she was hurt that Travolta stopped giving her the time of day,' said *Globe* tabloid reporter Burt McFarlane. 'Even the tabloids caught on to her game to try to make Taylor jealous. We didn't let her use us. We knew the marriage was on its last legs and that's what we concentrated on. The whole thing about Woody Allen, Picasso, and several other men was false. She was trying to set us up. Carly always liked to play little games with the media. At the beginning, it worked but people started to catch on. We wouldn't let her trick us anymore.'

Taylor and Simon discussed divorce in October 1980. They finally realised that their differences were irreconcilable. But there was one provision: they decided not to bring up the subject of divorce again until Ben had completely recovered. They continued living together, but the relationship was strictly platonic. Still the two shared a passion for protests. Their mutual social conscience had in fact drawn them together in the early years. Fittingly, then, one of their last acts as a couple was participating in a campaign to block McDonald's from opening a franchise on Martha's Vineyard. Both Taylor and Simon feared the fast-food corporation would begin commercialising the island they loved. They sought advice from their good friend the left-wing Senator Tom Hayden (then married to another of the couple's good friends, Jane Fonda). He advised them to start circulating petitions of protest.

The Taylors paid for printing the petitions and flyers. With morning dew still on the grass, they would bundle up and set out to spread the word. They knocked on doors and talked to residents as neighbours. 'The fact that they're both celebrities helped,' said one longtime resident. 'But they really did the door-to-door legwork themselves.

Someone in the protest group had put up a sign. It was Ronald McDonald's face in a circle with a diagonal line across it. It was really funny and it expressed how we felt at the time.'

'If not for the Taylors hard work, McDonald's would have been open smack in middle of the island,' said Tina Redding, a regular vacationer on Martha's Vineyard. 'They rallied everybody together and told McDonald's to stick it. It worked.' By the end of the protest campaign, McDonald's was convinced that everybody on Martha's Vineyard would boycott the restaurant if it opened. The company abandoned its plans.

Simon and Taylor celebrated their victory by throwing a huge party for hundreds of people on the island. Interestingly, while Simon was spearheading the campaign to stop McDonald's, she had aspirations for a business of her own on the Vineyard. Before the end of 1980, Simon announced that she was opening the island's first disco, the Hot Tin Roof.

'At least she got something out of her time with Travolta,' joked one of the club's patrons on opening night. 'Carly's club will be a place where locals can party their asses off from dusk till dawn.'

Many of the celebrities who lived on the Vineyard attended the opening. Comedian John Belushi got very drunk at the bar. He was later spotted in the bathroom doing several lines of cocaine with a young female friend. Indeed, the opening had Animal House written all over it.

'It was a wild party,' Belushi said. 'We all went to show our support and to try to start some sort of party scene. Before Carly opened the club most of the partying on the island was restricted to small pubs or private parties. This was the start of a new nightlife scene. It was great news to everybody. We no longer had to drive miles to have a good night out. The only thing we worried about was staying sober enough to get home in one piece without stumbling into the ocean.'

Simon smiled with the satisfaction of a job well done. 'We were ecstatic because we managed to get rid of McDonald's,' Simon said. 'It was the last thing we needed on the island . . . When I opened the disco I wanted to create a place with atmosphere and fun. People here needed somewhere they could go and just let it all out and have fun. I really got a kick out of it.'

It wasn't unusual for patrons at the disco to be greeted by Taylor or Simon serving up drinks at the bar. They were more than pleased to mingle with regular people.

'They were so friendly, it was almost as if they had invited you into their living room,' Belushi said. 'Carly would be at the bar pouring drinks for the locals. They loved her. She was always polite and smiling. People were amazed that they were being served by a big star. But I think that's what Carly always wanted, just to be a regular person and not to get special treatment.'

While Simon's pet project thrived, Taylor had news of his own. The work he had done on Sesame Street's *In Harmony* earlier in the year wound up winning a Grammy for best children's recording. 'He always sang us to sleep when we were kids,' Sally Taylor recalled. 'Dad had a big repertoire of children's tunes. That Grammy meant a lot to him because he was able to bring happiness to the lives of so many kids.'

On 25 April 1981, Taylor embarked on a 47-date tour spread out over three months. He was touring to promote his third release on Columbia, *Dad Loves His Work*. Many believed the title of the new album was a message to Carly.

'The album wasn't too strong, but its message was very clear,' longtime Taylor fan Ellis Dixon said. 'Taylor was telling Carly that what she said all the time about him being away from the family was not true. JT was telling the world that he had to be away because he loved his work and needed to support his family. And some of the songs clearly gave the message that their marriage was over, especially "Hard Times" and "That Lonesome Road". When I first heard it, I told my girlfriend that within a year Taylor and Simon would be finished. I know the way JT uses his music to give subtle messages. He's very honest to his fans. He doesn't try to hide things from them. In this case the message was very clear.'

In September 1981, Taylor took another shot at acting, this time playing a truck driver in the PBS version of *Working*. With this project, he felt more comfortable and received accolades for his performance. 'Not bad for a guy who clearly had a lot on his plate then,' said Taylor's good friend Don Grolnick.

But at home, Taylor and Simon had retreated into a white-knuckled silence that was far deadlier than fights. They were both sick of each other and they knew their relationship could not be saved. They held on through the fall and through their worst Christmas ever. By spring of 1982, they no longer needed to talk to know how much they each wanted out. That summer, Taylor would frequently see Simon, her face covered in tears. She would just look at him and walk out of the room. She did not think she would fail at marriage.

In August Taylor and Simon finally announced they were getting divorced. It was time for both of them to move on. Over the past year Taylor and Simon had become strictly living companions; the physical attraction they once shared no longer existed.

Both spent the next couple of years trying to start their lives over. Taylor was forced by the divorce to do what he should have done for the marriage; cut down on his touring. He spent most of his time juggling schedules with Simon to spend time with Sally and Ben. He spent the rest of his time exercising. 'There was a lot of bitterness on both of their parts, but they tried to stay civil to each other for the sake of the kids,' said archivist Steve Bellows. 'Taylor never forgave her for roaming around publicly with Travolta while he was on tour. Carly was bitter because she had to put up with his drug habits for so long. It was a huge embarrassment for Taylor to have his wife roam around with other men. He was furious at the shame she had caused him. It took many years before both of them got over their anger.'

Amid all the turmoil in his personal life, Taylor managed to fly to Brazil to perform the most memorable concert of his career. On 12 January 1985, Taylor performed at the *Rock in Rio* concert. Years later, in a 1998 chat on America Online, Taylor recalled the experience as the highlight performance of his career. 'I'd never been in Brazil before. It was remarkable. It was a whole other experience.'

The Rio concert was indeed a much-needed breath of fresh air for Taylor. He fell in love with the Brazilian people and tried to assimilate into their culture. Wherever he went, he carried a Berlitz English-Portuguese dictionary. He promised himself that he would not speak a word of English.

'He is so sincere and respectful,' said Rui Pasqual, a São Paulo journalist who conducted a lengthy radio interview with Taylor. 'You could tell how good he felt about being in Brazil. He was polite and tried to speak Portuguese to whomever approached him. I've never seen that before in an American artist who visits here. They usually only speak English and tend to be a bit cocky. Some of them think that because they're stars, it's a reason for them to feel superior than everybody else. But not Taylor. Over the years I've interviewed hundreds of big-name foreign artists, but Taylor's one of the two classiest and most approachable. The other is Sting.'

The Rio concert was the start of a long-term love between Taylor and the people of Brazil. He became outspoken about protecting the rainforest, and several Brazilian artists covered some of his more popular songs in Portuguese. 'He's treated like a god here,' said Maria Moreina, a guitarist from Rio. 'I play "Fire and Rain" at all my concerts and the people people go crazy. We love his music here. He likes to keep his music pure and meaningful, sort of the same way some of our respected artists do here like Caetano Velosa and Milton Nascimento. And we appreciate the stance he's taken to support our country. We look at him as being a goodwill ambassador for our country.'

Then, after Taylor returned from Brazil, in the strange world of Taylor and Simon a stranger thing happened in February 1985. Simon became involved with Taylor's longtime drummer and good friend Russ Kunkel. Their attraction for each other probably began at a mutual friend's party. Carly was gorgeous in a long, slinky, black dress. Kunkel found her irresistible. 'Carly knew how to dance with a man and drive him wild at the same time,' said a friend of Simon. 'Nothing obvious, nothing wanton, but she had this bizarre power. She could move during a dance so that a guy was helpless with wanting her.' They had known each other for 14 years but were never anything more than good friends. For Taylor it was the most awkward situation of his life.

'He was upset and hurt,' author Esmond Choueke said. 'Carly had embarrassed him enough in the past when she was caught roaming around with younger men when he was away. But even though they were divorced by now, this hurt him a lot. He thought that Kunkel had befriended him.'

Simon said that for her, it 'seemed like the most natural thing in the world.' But she admitted that she didn't know how her ex-husband would react. 'They're very close. I haven't talked to James about it, but Russell's going on tour with him in September.' Asked how she had become involved with Kunkel, Simon replied, 'Well, we'd both taken a lot of drugs – no, just kidding. I asked him to come and play on a song of mine on the record, which was "Make Me Feel Something". And he just listened to the words of the song!'

At first, Taylor considered throwing Kunkel out of his band. But he realised that it would be unfair to punish him. He figured that Carly was using Kunkel to get back at him.

Simon and Kunkel announced plans to get married that summer on Martha's Vineyard. Kunkel also produced and played drums on Simon's new album, *Spoiled Girl*.

'Carly was determined to get back at James. She was very bitter,' said one of Simon's close friends. 'I think in many ways she used Russ to get her revenge. She knew how badly this would affect James.'

Taylor, 37, tried to overcome his jealousy. He found a new love himself, actress Kathryn Walker. Walker was the veteran 42-year-old actress familiar to TV soap opera fans as Barbara Randolph II on *Another World*. She landed many leading and secondary film roles, including a principal role in the 1981 feature film *Neighbours*. Without a doubt she was the most stable and mature woman Taylor had ever been with.

'She was very together and she didn't have any hang-ups,' said TV critic Daphne Potter. 'Kathryn was the perfect woman for Taylor. She was stable and she wasn't the rocker and wild partier like Simon and the other women who had been in his life.'

It took Walker several weeks to assimilate it all. She told friends that she couldn't believe that she was dating the man whose music she revered. One night Taylor took his new love out for a special romantic evening. Late in the night, he quietly pulled a beautiful diamond ring from his jacket and proposed to her. She was ecstatic. On 14 December 1985, she became the second Mrs James Taylor when they were married in Manhattan's historic St John the Divine Cathedral.

Taylor was no longer lonely. With Walker he finally found the happiness that he escaped him for so many years when he was with Simon. His friends thought that he had found the perfect woman.

'They were right for one another,' Don Grolnick said. 'Whenever they were together you'd notice they both had a twinkle in their eye. It was so nice to see James so happy. It had been a long time since I'd seen him look and feel so comfortable and relaxed.'

The newlyweds would surprise each other with gifts and food treats. 'I can be quiet with her,' Taylor told a friend. 'Even the silences are happy.'

Taylor was riding an emotional high. Aside from his new marriage, he had another reason to celebrate: seven weeks before he married Walker, he released his first album in more than four years. *That's Why I'm Here* became Taylor's first album to have three Top Ten adult-contemporary hits – with the title track, 'Only One', and a cover version of Buddy Holly's popular 'Everyday'. Although the album didn't manage to go gold and was his lowest-charting effort since *Sweet Baby James*, Taylor came across to his fans with a new image. He appeared on the album's cover with a balding head, abandoning his notorious hippie-look. He seemed to have aged ten years since his last album.

'That album was important because it dictated the direction of his career,' said longtime Taylor fan Dean Somerville. 'Nobody knew what to expect, because it was his first album since he split up with Carly. But from the look of the cover and the sound of his music, it was evident that he had grown up and was at peace with himself. This album really put him in the adult-contemporary category. I guess he figured that his fans had grown up and that the best way to keep them was by delivering something a bit more mature, sophisticated, and easy listening. And it worked. Since that album he has kept this image going and is still able to pack concert halls all over the world. Just because he's changed his look and sound I don't think that he's a sellout, like some of his die-hard fans contest. I think he was just smart enough to realise how important it is to grow up with your audience. Look at some artists, like the Rolling Stones, who still try to do the same style they did 25 years ago. It doesn't work. They get laughed at because they look like old geezers on stage. Not Taylor. He knows how to adapt to the times.'

As Taylor's tour progressed, the media were still hot on his trail, hoping to find out more about his failed marriage to Simon. Taylor was furious when he discovered that several of his close friends had been offered tens of thousands of dollars by several of the tabloids, including the *National Enquirer*. Simon reportedly declined over a hundred thousand dollars to talk about her ex-husband. Taylor was also unhappy with the tabloid photographers and reporters who were relentlessly stalking the people close to him.

'It really made him visibly upset,' said a writer for the *National Enquirer*. 'But the complete truth had not yet come out and the public deserved to know what really happened. It was all so strange. Simon became involved with Taylor's drummer [Russ Kunkel], and then Taylor got remarried. There was a lot of animosity between them and nobody was willing to talk. Not even for the big bucks that were being waved in their faces . . . The rumour going around was that a clause in their divorce settlement forbade them from commenting in public about what happened.'

'They went through a very bad divorce,' one of Taylor's close friends recalled. 'They both hired top lawyers and the divorce settlement was filled with many clauses. They reached an understanding that neither of them would voice resentment toward the other publicly. They mutually decided that the best way to resolve things was not to dredge up the past but to go forward with their lives.'

The *Enquirer* tried to track down relatives and close friends. 'Usually we have no problem getting a story like this,' said tabloid reporter Burt McFarlane. 'But we kept reaching dead ends with the people close to Taylor and Simon. Nobody wanted to talk. One of Simon's sisters assured me that I was wasting my time trying to get the story. She said that nobody would talk about the divorce for the sake of their children. They didn't want Sally and Ben to be caused any further embarrassment.'

In his first year of marriage to Walker, Taylor reviewed his priorities in life. He was characteristically charitable with money, but he made a commitment to do more. He hit up friends and family to donate money to some of the causes he supported and instructed his manager Peter Asher to book him more benefit concerts. He had admired Bob Geldof's work with the *Live Aid* project and was determined to follow in Geldof's footsteps, but in a quieter way.

'James Taylor is a real role-model musician because of the way he works hard to support people who are less fortunate than him,' said Steven Adelman, who did volunteer work for Live Aid. 'He almost never says no, no matter how busy his schedule is. And he doesn't help only important causes in his own country. Just look at some of the things he's done in Brazil during the last 20 years. Not many musicians afford as much time as he does to the important issues that our society faces. His music is only a small part of the generous person inside him.'

21

TAYLOR'S SMILING FACE

Taylor's marriage rekindled his artistic motivation. For the first time in years, he worked hard at writing new songs. His detractors questioned his songwriting talent – four years had gone by since his last album – but nobody questioned his ability to perform live. He was still at the top of his class. In the '80s, many of Taylor's contemporaries, including Paul Simon, Joni Mitchell, Bob Dylan and Jackson Browne disappeared for years at a time. Their careers would be put in limbo as the result of the success of new-breed electronic artists like the Eurythmics and Bryan Ferry. Taylor was one of only a few acoustic acts able to ride the switchback of success and keep a high profile.

'I went from the very interior kind of process of making music and finding a personal outlet to thinking of how to best prepare for a huge audience,' Taylor said. 'That process can be very disruptive, especially to musicians and songwriters who in many cases are ill adapted to that kind of public life. In a way, that is why we've seen so many burnouts. You can count the people who went down. I'm not saying it was only because they were popular, successful and commercial. But being marketable and incorporated into a larger capitalistic system certainly couldn't have helped them.

And Taylor was grateful that he was getting a chance to almost start over again. He seized this opportunity to redirect his life midstream with a still-vibrant career and a new love at his side.

'It is very hard to make that shift,' Taylor said. 'That is another one of the miracles about the Beatles. In spite of the fact that everything they did was accompanied by wave after wave of public and press onslaught, they continued to come up with more and more meaningful stuff. That's amazing to me . . . By the time you're 40 and 50, your life is largely what it is going to be, and I think that's a crushing blow to a lot of people once they find that out. Your job is what it is, your kids are who they are, your home is where you made it, you have a mortgage, and you became what you were going to be. Physically you may be losing your hair, slowing down a little bit, and in need of some major dentistry, but basically a lot of the mystery doors have been opened and the contents are clearly there. Unfortunately, a lot of people look at that and fold up.'

Taylor could appreciate that most people never get a shot at the fortunate position he was in. He set out to make the most of it.

Aside from a more sophisticated and 'respectable' look, the most instantly noticeable thing about Taylor's new image was the way he sang. There were few traces of the angst and protest that had underlain his music for so many years. Barely a month after he married Kathryn Walker, he toured Australia. His fans started to notice a new James Taylor.

'I almost didn't believe it was him until I heard him start to sing,' said Lance Wilson, who saw Taylor perform in Melbourne in late January 1986. 'He looked so different from the guy whose music I grew up admiring. There was more expression in him, more life . . . he looked like he had been totally revitalised. His voice was always calm, but [now] it was even calmer. More mature. This James Taylor had become a polished pro. He mixed his new stuff with all his old hits. He showed more energy than anybody had ever seen him show. I'm sure that anybody who saw that performance would agree that Taylor had turned a new page in his life. He talked to the audience between songs and he cracked a few jokes. He showed us a side to him that we had never seen before. He no longer had long hair and he now looked more like an insurance salesman than a pop star, but he sounded better than ever. It was one of the best and most memorable concerts I've ever attended.'

Before he married Walker, Taylor said that he wasn't motivated to write music because of all the tension between him and Simon. He developed a severe case of writer's block. 'I've never really had this kind of silence before,' he told journalist Dan Forte. 'This is as bad as it's gotten . . . What I'm counting on now is, I've gotten myself a place to write, and I'm to the point of desperation where I'm actually giving myself about four hours a day to just sit there and either come up with something or go crazy with boredom. I'm hoping that in the next couple of months I can finish the stuff that I really want to touch up. I can't think of any other way to deal with it, aside from just waiting it out . . . If I haven't gotten my material in the shape I want it in, if it doesn't suit me yet, then I'll postpone again. I'm not going to put anything out until I really feel good about it.'

Around this time, Taylor became more co-operative with the media. When he gave an interview, he was more open than ever before and didn't try to camouflage his dark past. 'I want to write great songs,' he told *Rolling Stone*. 'But I don't want to suffer, you know. I'm not going to wear a couple of shoe sizes too small just because I might write a better song.' He told *Newsweek*'s Harry F. Waters that he didn't regret living the way he did because it made him grow up. 'I spent a lot of time with a feeling of negative faith. An assumption that the world had a nasty surprise just around each corner. But I'm comfortable now. I don't have any investment any longer in things turning out badly.'

Danny Kortchmar, the guitarist who played with Taylor for many years, had once told his friend that he would be better off if he focused more on his music than what the media was saying about his private life. Now Kortchmar's advice was paying off. 'There's still a lot of music left in him,' Kortchmar said. 'He has to put everything behind him and concentrate on what he does best. If he does, he'll be in a class by himself.'

Taylor was a master at predicting how things would shape up. When he divorced Carly Simon, he told friends that it was meant to be and that he was sure that there was another woman out there waiting for him. Shortly after that, he met Kathryn Walker. He was also good at predicting how things would shape up in the music industry. Although he was not noted for his technical ability in the studio, Taylor was one of the first rock musicians to foresee how common the concept of the home studio would become. In May 1984, long before the days of Cakewalk and Cubase digital computer software-operated home studios, Taylor predicted in a *Guitar Player* magazine interview that home studios would become popular over the next few years.

'I did get one of those Teac Porta-studios, the four-track cassette, but I didn't use it that much. I bought an Otari half-inch eight-track, and I've used that on the road a few times to try to record shows. But to record live with a band, I think you need 16 tracks to get the separation you need. I hear that there are a couple of digital programs coming out that can be used with an IBM personal computer, so it should be an exciting time coming up for recording live and in small home studios.

I'm really looking forward to that. And I'm really excited about the technology of trying to interface guitar with synthesizers.'

Many industry people were impressed by Taylor's knowledge. 'Not many folk musicians recognise digital audio today, let alone back then,' said Milo Janofsky, who owns and operates a recording studio in New York. 'Taylor has lasted all these years because he adapts to the times. He recognises the importance of technology and how it shapes the future of the recording arts. Too many musicians limit themselves. They get afraid once they hear the word digital. They're just shooting themselves in the foot. The advancement of digital audio has made it easier and cheaper to record an album. I'm still a fan of analogue recording, and I'm sure judging by Taylor's music that he is too, but there's no use in not incorporating the two. Digital audio makes the sound so much fuller. It opens up a lot of possibilities in the production process. You'd think that someone like James Taylor would have been the last person in 1984 to recognise digital audio because his sound is completely analogue. He clearly showed how open he is to advancing.'

Although his new image seemed very mature, Taylor was determined not to appear too grown up. During a five-week tour of Europe in March 1986, Taylor, 38, demonstrated his desire to stay young by getting into exercise. Taylor had read several books about living healthily. He was convinced that it would not only enable him to enjoy life more, but also add years to his life. He also faced the chilling fact that if he didn't clean up his act, he would be a perfect candidate for cancer or cardiovascular diseases. All those years of drug abuse would eventually catch up with him. He consulted a nutritionist and resolved to gradually incorporate healthier foods into his diet. He devised a daily routine to include exercise and relaxation.

Whatever city the tour rolled into, Taylor would get up at 7 a.m. and go for a six-mile run. Then he would cool down with some calisthenics before going to the restaurant in his hotel for a healthy breakfast. 'He really got into exercise and healthy living in the '80s,' said Taylor's road manager Brian Reed. 'He was determined to live more healthy. He became a fanatic for staying in shape and eating healthy food. He really enjoys outdoor sports. On the road he'd always be out and about cycling or roller blading. It would make him feel very relaxed before a show.'

When he wasn't exercising, Taylor was writing songs in his hotel room. By now he had finally managed to kick his heroin habit. 'Getting into exercise was a way for me to release a lot of energy,' Taylor said. 'It also made me feel good about myself and helped me understand and get to know my body better. It made me realise how important it is to be in tune with your body if you want to go out every night and move around onstage. It's a very demanding job that requires a lot of energy. It's impossible to maintain that pace if you keep abusing your body the way I did for so many years.'

The only demon that Taylor still struggled with was booze. It was too tempting for him to drink some of the world's finest beers and spirits when he was on the road. 'He finally kicked heroin but after concerts, especially in Europe, you would see him drinking with his band mates in the local pub,' said author Esmond Choueke. 'There were some reports of heavy drinking, but clearly, Taylor was intent on cleaning up his act. He looked healthier than ever before. And he seemed more spirited onstage. The real James Taylor finally stood up.'

The first couple of years of the Taylor-Walker marriage were paradisical. Taylor trusted his new wife more than any woman he had ever been with. Because of their busy schedules, several weeks would often pass without them seeing one another. When they reunited, they would take trips to exotic places and spend long, languid days making love in their hotel room. They still felt like newlyweds.

'We shared a very similar appreciation for life,' Kathryn Walker recalled. 'The first few years of our marriage were beautiful. We were meant to be together. We had had a lot of similar experiences in the past. Something special brought us together. I was able to bring out a lot in him that he didn't even know was in him, and he did the same for me. We were both appreciative of some of the simpler things in life, like just waking up healthy every day and appreciating what we had. I look back at those years with a lot of beautiful memories.'

Between his regular gigs, Taylor started working on another album in 1987. When it was released the following year, *Never Die Young* did only marginally well. Many of his followers reasoned that it had no hit single because Taylor didn't cover any popular tune from the fifties or '60s on it.

'On his previous albums he always made the charts with one of the cover songs like 'Everyday' that he interpreted in his own unique way,' said Taylor fan Erin Johnson. 'He didn't do that on *Never Die Young* and it hurt him. He delivered a good album but it was obvious that he didn't have a song that would deserve a lot of airplay.'

Taylor's musical buddy Don Grolnick produced *Never Die Young*. Taylor wrote or co-wrote every song. The title song and 'Baby Boom Baby' both did well on the adult-contemporary charts but were unable to crack the pop charts. Taylor didn't care. He didn't want to sacrifice his artistic integrity anymore just for the sake of winding up in the Top Ten. He still believes *Never Die Young* was one of his best albums. Taylor's new ease with himself – his certainty about his artistic and personal integrity – were now his protection from criticism.

'It was getting together with Don Grolnick in October 1986 to assess and sift through the material that made it come alive,' Taylor recalled to Timothy White. 'I didn't trust the worth of what I had until Don had gone over it with me, and he'd been a big help that way for years, which is why it was natural for him to produce the *Never Die Young* album. As for the song "Never Die Young", I'd thought about calling it "Rosy Children", but it went past that phrase to say a lot more about getting old and rising above that state of being.'

A lot of industry insiders believe *Never Die Young* would have been more successful if Sony had done more marketing. Sony skimped on spending money for promotion because they were confident that Taylor's reputation preceded him.

'That's a big problem that a lot of big labels make,' said former music executive Robert Katz. 'They think that just because a certain artist has done well on previous albums, it guarantees that the new album will do just as well. They get too overconfident and try to divert a lot of their promotional dollars into new and upcoming artists. Just look what's happened to people like Sting, Phil Collins and even Tina Turner to a lesser degree. They've almost disappeared because their management refuses to spend the kind of money on marketing that they once did. The fans aren't stupid. They don't go out and buy Sting's albums because of the success he had with the Police. They buy his music only if it still has something to say to them.'

But according to Katz, Taylor's album was not prey to the same shortsighted business decisions. He claims Taylor's new midlife style was the reason Sony faltered on promoting it.

'In Taylor's case, the big problem was that it took a while for his management to find the right way to market his new image. He went from looking like somebody right out of the '60s to a real estate agent. The change was very radical. Sony did not know how to put the right spin on it. And it interfered with his artistic growth. They were promoting his old hits much more than his new stuff. People came out to see him more for what he had done in the past, not the present. That must have been extremely distressing for him.'

As Taylor had feared, his royalty statements were nowhere near where they used to be. 'It was frustrating for him,' said his backup singer Kate Markowitz. 'He went through some dry periods. But he persevered. A lot of artists call it quits if things aren't working out the way they did at the height of their careers. But not James. He's always said that the only thing he wants to do is make music. I remember him talking about it one night on the bus when we were in middle of a tour. Somebody asked him what he would do if he didn't do music and he didn't know what to answer. He said that he really had never remotely considered doing anything else than making music.'

As the Generation X '90s approached, Taylor decided it was time to make several changes in the lineup of his band. He used four backup singers because they had become a focal point of his show. Joining Taylor veterans David Lasley and Arnold McCuller were Valerie Carter and Kate Markowitz. All four of them were well respected in music circles, having worked with other big-name artists, including Jackson Browne and Linda Ronstadt.

'Any one of them could have gone on to have very successful solo career of their own,' said pop critic Neil Adams. 'When Taylor hired them, it was the start of him carefully polishing his act. He was trying to prolong his career by filling in some gaps. At this point his show became a real event. There were so many different new elements. The musicians and singers were all heavy duty. Not many live acts were as tight and professional as Taylor's band. His records might not have been selling like they once did but his live act was an easy sell. Promoters from all over the world knew that there was no risk in booking him. They were guaranteed a full house.'

Taylor's new accompanists motivated him to increase the quality of his own musical technique. At the recommendation of his friend the singer Paul Simon, he hooked up with a New York guitar teacher who showed him how to play more complicated chords and guitar voicings. He had long felt insecure about his guitar playing. After seeing some of his jazz guitar heroes like George Benson and John McLaughlin play live, Taylor felt embarrassed about his own playing.

'When fans came up to him after concerts and told him how much they liked his playing, he always had a weird feeling,' said Don

Grolnick. 'JT didn't know how good he actually was. He had an amazing feel for the guitar, especially the way he played folk music. But he felt intimidated by some of the guitar players he would meet on the road at festivals and events. I think it bothered him a bit that he wasn't as good as them. So being the guy he is, when he was in his early 40s he decided to spend a lot of time improving his skills. That's the beautiful kind of person he is. He always strives to improve.'

25

TAYLOR GIVES BACK

As James Taylor approached his 40th birthday, there were pros and cons for him to consider regarding his career. He still had the engaging, cosy sound that had been with him since his early days, and his live shows continued to draw sellout crowds. But he felt that it was important for him to give something back to the artistic community. He often said that he was lucky to get the big break that usually eludes most people in the music business. He had several beautiful homes; he was loved and admired by millions. He felt that giving back was the responsibility that comes with the gifts of fortune.

'I'm lucky to have had a lot of success,' Taylor said. 'There are so many talented musicians out there. A lot of them are struggling because they haven't gotten their big break. The key is to persevere and to continue doing what you love to do. I've met brilliant artists all over the world when I've toured. The world is rich with artistic talent and creativity. I think it's important for artists who have had success to reach out and help others. As artists, we're part of a big family.'

In May 1989, Taylor made good on his promise. His manager, Peter Asher, was well aware that Taylor wanted to give something back to the arts community. Asher arranged for Taylor to go to the National Academy of Songwriters on Hollywood Boulevard in Los Angeles to give free professional advice to a dozen struggling songwriters. Everybody who attended was overwhelmed by his courtesy, charm and openness with regard to life and the music business. He set them straight on some of the harsh realities of the music business.

'It's a great business to be in and I wouldn't dream of doing anything else, but you've got to be in it for the long haul and not just the short term to try to make a quick buck,' Taylor told them. 'If you persevere, you will succeed. Work on your songs. Master them. And be real.

Don't try to copy other people's styles. Find your own voice. There's a lot of competition in this business but if you're original and true to what you're doing, you'll find your own niche. It's good to listen to people's advice how to adjust your style and your playing but you've got to be able to draw the line. The great musicians like Dylan and Ray Charles have done so well because they don't try to be anybody else but themselves.'

Taylor told the songwriters that one of things that pleases him most is when he gets complimented on his songwriting or guitar playing by a fellow musician. 'That's the ultimate compliment,' Taylor said. 'To be recognised by one of your peers.'

Taylor spent several hours that day listening to the demos some of the young musicians had brought with them. He critiqued each songwriter's demo, pointing out several ways they could improve.

'It was an amazing experience,' said Mark Fleming, a New York stock exchange analyst who used to be a songwriter. 'I met him going up the elevator. I couldn't believe it was him. He seemed to be very different from the James Taylor of the '70s. He was bald, dressed in jeans, and very amenable. He had no trapping of rock stardom whatsoever. He clearly had no ego. Inside, I played him about forty seconds of a song I wrote called 'Boyfriend Wannabe' before he turned it off the tape recorder. I thought I had a hit song but he made me realise it needed a lot of work. After he heard all the demos he sat down at the piano that was in the room and showed us some melodies. Everybody was all ears. He was such a pro. I had never before considered some of the realities he told us about songwriting. I came out of there feeling how real and sincere he is. I was in the music business for many years before I moved to New York and switched careers. I met a lot of well-known musicians over the years. Nobody was as classy and nice as James Taylor.'

The greatest impact of Taylor's mentoring that day was the way he encouraged the young musicians to persevere, even if they do not remain in the music business. 'He gave us a reality check,' Fleming said. 'He told us that in a few years some of us will go on to other things in life and be successful at them. But he said that music will never leave us and that we should always keep playing because it's one of the most beautiful things to do in life. To this day I remind myself of his strong words. I make a good living with the full-time job I have in a different field, but I find the time to escape from it all by playing music. Taylor was right. Music is like therapy. It's one of the most important things in life. The world needs music and as an artist, I need to keep playing, even if I have to do something else to make a living.'

A year later, in 1990, Joey Simmons – a musician based in Portland, Oregon got a chance to meet Taylor after a concert. He recalled with affection on the advice Taylor gave him: 'I was very depressed at that time because I had tried to get a record deal for so long without any success. I had spent over two thousand dollars making demos and sending them off to record companies and all that I got back was a pile of rejection letters. Taylor made me feel better. He made me feel equal to him. He didn't put himself on a pedestal and he showed me a lot of respect as a fellow artist. He suggested several ways that would increase my chances of getting somebody interested. He also made me aware of doing something independently and told me how I could start my own label to sell my music. All the free advice and time he gave me made up for all the money I spent trying to get a deal. It changed my perspective. Today, I play in a blues band that has released two independent CDs and has toured across North America. I credit Taylor for a lot of my success because he helped me when I was at one of the lowest points of my career. If I hadn't talked to him that day, I'm not sure if I would have continued doing music. I would probably now be working as a salesclerk at some place like Borders or Wal-Mart.'

Taylor resolved to be a good role-model musician. He spent time talking to his fans when they recognised him on the street. He did everything he thought you should to be a humble artist.

'He's always treated his fans like close friends,' said entertainment author Esmond Choueke. 'It's incredible the way he spends so much time talking to them and finding out about their lives. Very few people in show business do that. They usually have big egos and look down on their fans. Not Taylor. He thrives on spending time with his fans. He truly respects the people who are responsible for making his career so successful. Earlier in his career, he was more reserved. After he broke up with Carly Simon and remarried, he was a different person. In public he appeared much more relaxed and appreciative of life. A lot of entertainers could have taken a lesson or two from him about staying humble and loyal to their fans.'

According to one fan who has met Taylor several times backstage after concerts, the singer rarely leaves a concert venue without answering all the questions of the fans who manage to slip backstage. 'I don't know where he gets the energy,' said Richard Stoker of Albany, New York. 'He has just finished singing out his heart for almost three hours, sweat is pouring down his forehead, and he must feel like falling flat on his face. When he comes backstage he's surrounded by many people, and he talks to everybody. He even remembers your name if you bump into him again. It's no wonder why he has lasted so long. The music business today has been infiltrated by so many rats like Marilyn Manson and Courtney Love. These are musicians that do much more bad than good for society with the music they put out. Taylor is different. He remains one of the few bright spot in an industry that will promote hate and violence to our youth in order to sell records. If there were more James Taylors in the music business, our youth might not feel so at ease with violence. They might be less obsessed with shooting and killing if it were not a part of the culture of youth through the music. James Taylor only spreads positive messages that move you to tears and give you goosebumps. His music still is able to make people take a step back from their daily routines and rethink their priorities in life. He speaks honestly and without false modesty.'

26

UNDERSTANDING NIRVANA

In the early '90s Taylor worried that his career might be over. The record industry changed suddenly with the dawning of Generation X. Many independent labels sprang up, severely denting the sales of artists on major labels. Grunge, the heavy rock laden with power guitar chords and screaming vocals, became the most popular music. Stalwart artists like Sting, Phil Collins and Tina Turner weren't able to sell records anywhere near the numbers they had sold in the '80s; they were forced to take a backseat to angst-ridden bands like Nirvana, Soundgarden and Stone Temple Pilots. Nineties youth wanted nothing to do with the commercial sounding artists of the '80s. They preferred hammering each other in a moshpit to the new breed of heavy guitar bands.

Taylor's first release in the '90s, *New Moon Shine*, belonged to the contemporary-adult category. Produced by Don Grolnick, the twelve-song album had two big hits: 'Everybody Loves to Cha Cha Cha' and 'Copperline'. *New Moon Shine* didn't receive good reviews, however; music critics said that Taylor's sound was becoming too commercial.

'When I heard this album, I thought he was just trying to make a load of money,' critic Ellen Grant said. 'It didn't have any edge. It sounded very close to elevator music. I was disappointed. I expected something more advanced and progressive. I wanted Taylor to try something with more edge. He started getting in the habit of putting out schlock, and I think it turned off a lot of potential fans. He still had his loyal following that stayed with him since the early '70s, but if he'd tried something more innovative, he would have been able to gain a lot of new fans. I think he played it too safe. As an artist it's important to take chances.'

Privately, Taylor admitted that *New Moon Shine* was not one of his best albums. The bad press he received made him wonder if there was still a place among America's youth for his music. He told a musician in his band that it was important for him to understand the new grunge sound in order to keep up with the times. Taylor bought several CDs by some of the hottest grunge bands. After listening to Nirvana's *Nevermind*, though, Taylor became more optimistic about his own career. He realised that to understand grunge was as important to today's society as it was to understand folk when he was young.

'It inspired him,' Sally Taylor said. 'My father has always liked to keep up with the times. He listens to all kinds of music. He learns a lot that way. I think he was able to relate to some of the grunge because it reminded him of some of the troubles he experienced early in his career.' Taylor did not want to perpetrate the same kind of blind judgement of new styles that had plagued the early artists of folk and rock.

Taylor remained at the forefront of human-rights and environmental issues. His 1992 summer tour supported the Natural Resources Defense Council, which Taylor referred to as 'a sort of law firm for the environment'. Taylor still packed major arenas. Year after year his summer tour was one of the hottest concert tickets. After a concert at the Pacific Amphitheatre in California, critic Janice Page said, 'He's still full of surprises . . . considering that the standard rap against this singer long has been that his songs sound hypnotically similar, this crowd's pleas for more, after 23 songs and three encores, must have been music to his ears.' In 1993 Sony released a two-CD James Taylor live album. Produced by Don Grolnick and George Massenburg, *Live* went platinum.

'It reinvented his career,' said Ellen Grant. 'Like so many times in the past, just when everybody thought that James Taylor might be finished, he was able to bounce back with something big. *Live* covered his whole career. It included everything from "That Lonesome Road" to "Fire and Rain". It was a good decision to release something more raw than the last couple of albums he released, which were too overproduced. Once again, Taylor was back.'

On Taylor's 45th birthday – 12 March 1993 – a family tragedy resulted in the singer going through one of the saddest times of his life. Taylor's oldest brother, Alex, died of a massive heart attack. Alex, 46, had made numerous attempts to kick his heroin and alcohol habits, but unlike James's his attempts were unsuccessful. On that March day the many years of substance abuse finally caught up to him. James Taylor later described his brother's death in a curt sentence: 'Alex's death was caused by the old family demon.' Alex's body was cremated in a special ceremony in Florida. Taylor said nothing about his brother's death for several years before finally paying tribute to Alex on a couple of songs, 'Alice' and 'Enough to Be'.

'The ashes that went up a smokestack in Florida seemed to turn into an amazing storm that followed us home from that ceremony, tearing up the East Coast from Carolina to Massachusetts,' Taylor told Timothy White about 'Enough to Be on Your Way'. 'The idea is of somebody who can't get home, who can't find home late in their lives. As you get older – and I'm pushing 50 – you grasp that the loneliness of the human condition stems from a wholeness from which we seem separated. Consensus, just the sense of connection with other people, feels so great, and it motivates an awful lot of what we do. The more successful or thwarted you are as an isolated individual, the more you need reconnection.'

Taylor took off several months to try to come to terms with his brother's death. He did some soul searching while travelling around Europe on a much needed vacation. While walking aimlessly around the streets of Paris one day in January 1994, he got the idea for 'Alice', the song that dealt with the circumstances surrounding Alex's death. Originally, Taylor started the song for a woman named Alice whom he'd last seen in Sante Fe before Alex died. But after his brother's death, Taylor reworked the song around Alex. 'I was there by myself for a long time, walking around by myself in the streets,' Taylor said in a *Rolling Stone* interview. 'And the song came out at me from alleyways and in cafes.'

Alex's death made Taylor realise how important it was to educate society's youth about the perils of drug abuse. He wanted to reach out to the new Generation X: discontented, blasé post–Baby Boom youth who were receiving considerable media attention. This was the generation of Microsoft and its founding genius, Bill Gates, and the world's hottest music group, grunge icons Nirvana. In February 1994, Taylor made his first big overture to Generation X by appearing on the popular TV show *The Simpsons*. It paid off. Taylor talked about his drug and alcohol addictions to youth groups, at schools and at his concerts. He made youngsters think twice about abusing drugs. Alex Taylor's death inspired James to take a more affirmative stance against drug and alcohol abuse. And in the process, a lot of new, young music fans started to become interested in Taylor's music. A whole generation had heard his songs, even liked them, but most Generation X music lovers had never really known him.

'I had never even heard of him before,' said Mitchell Wheaton, a computer software programmer in San Diego. 'I was really into bands like Smashing Pumpkins and the Beastie Boys. When I saw his character on *The Simpsons* I was curious to find out more about him. The next day I went to a secondhand record store and bought one of his earlier albums. I spent that whole night listening to it. It might have been recorded over twenty-years ago but the message in his lyrics and music reached out to my generation. I was 22 at the time and feeling more confused than ever. His music set me straight on a lot of things. He didn't have the angst of Kurt Cobain or Billy Corgan but he was clearly a voice for America's youth, just like Kurt and Billy. Since then, I've seen at least a half dozen of his concerts and have bought several of his albums.'

Entertainment author Esmond Choueke said that it was brilliant marketing for Taylor to appear on *The Simpsons*, adding that most of Taylor's artistic contempories were struggling because they couldn't find a way to communicate with the new generation. 'It was such a brilliant PR move,' Choueke noted. 'It exposed millions of new people to his music and probably helped prolong his career for at least another ten years.'

Taylor kept up his efforts to relate to Generation X. The body of Nirvana singer Kurt Cobain was found by Seattle electrician Gary Smith the morning of 8 April 1994. When Taylor first heard the news of Cobain's death on the radio he was able to relate elements of his own life to the late grunge star.

Taylor was a Cobain fan. He loathed some of the new screaming bands, but he thought Kurt was a very talented songwriter. He loved playing some of Kurt's songs at home, including 'Smells Like Teen Spirit' and 'Come as You Are'. The fact that Kurt's fans accused Cobain's camp of emotional negligence struck a chord with Taylor. It wasn't long ago that many people looked up to Taylor the way they now viewed Kurt – as the voice of a generation. Like Kurt, Taylor often felt he was being used by his handlers to sell lots of records. He often said that if the executives who run the record industry were more concerned with the lives of the artists they managed, many lives could have turned out differently.

'I can't help but think about that with him [Kurt Cobain] and identifying with it a little bit,' Taylor told Orange County journalist Mark Brown. 'No matter what happened, he was forced into a position he hated being in.'

Mark Brown found Taylor shaken by Cobain's death. The roads to rock stardom for both musicians had had striking similarities. 'When you think of it, the parallels between Cobain's and Taylor's early successes are remarkable. Taylor was only 22, Cobain just 25, when they both made deeply personal music that redefined rock. Both rocketed to sudden fame and found solace in drugs. Both poured personal pain and confession into their songs, with Taylor's 'Fire and Rain' and 'Long Ago and Far Away' being every bit as bleak as Cobain's 'Dumb' or 'Rape Me'. And there came a point where Taylor himself was in danger of being a casualty of what he calls the "toxic effect of the marketplace."'

Taylor had a long discussion with his son, Ben, about Kurt's death. He told Ben, who also dreamed of being a rock star, that he should beware of some of the industry's pitfalls. 'Many people in this business will only be your friend because they want to get something out of you,' Taylor said. 'You've got to stay clear of those vultures. If you can't spot those people who are out to use you, you might go through a very rough time. A lot of great musicians unfortunately have.'

It took Taylor a long time to come to terms with Cobain's death. In June 1994 he told Mark Brown, 'It's sort of a loss of innocence. It's easy to sort of get lost. I feel tempted to talk about Kurt Cobain a little bit. I really dug his music. It seemed like that transition really hurt for him – becoming known, preempted, co-opted, public, all that stuff.'

Taylor's willingness to talk about Cobain's death made noise in entertainment circles. Some people thought he was trying to exploit Cobain's death to bring attention to his own career. 'Anybody who said that is talking complete nonsense,' said Cobain's best friend, Dylan Carlson. 'Taylor's concern was genuine. His life was similar to Kurt's. They both had heroin addictions and were chronically depressed. Why would Taylor do something like that? His career was still going strong when Kurt died. Taylor was showing concern for a fellow musician. How would he benefit from speaking out about Kurt's death? They're two completely different styles of rock.'

Carlson continued, 'A lot of people did try to benefit from Kurt's death. Several bands ripped off his style of music and hired blond singers as the frontman. Taylor was one of the few people who spoke out that was genuinely concerned. He had kids who were part of Generation X.

His own experience years ago with drugs was similar. He understood what drove Kurt to do hard drugs. People can draw their own opinions but I think it was brave of Taylor to come forward. A lot of musicians from his generation weren't open to Kurt's music because they thought it was too angry. Taylor's an open person. He doesn't prejudge things without giving them a fair chance.'

Taylor said that Cobain's death made him realise how lucky he was to be alive. Like Kurt, many times he considered suicide because he found the crushing grind of the music industry unbearable. 'There's a stage of your life where it's an urgent process to try and invent who you are and assemble your persona – a sort of finding yourself phase,' Taylor told Mark Brown. 'Later you just want to lose yourself. You want to have some relief from the delusionary system you've surrounded yourself with.'

There was no one in the music industry in the '90s whom Taylor admired more than Kurt Cobain. He respected the cynical, angst-ridden singer as an artist, and looked up to him for not being afraid to speak his mind. Kurt's honesty helped Taylor deal with his own lingering bouts of depression. He told Mark Brown, 'I tend to be more conflicted and depressed, to tell you the truth. It's a miracle to me some mornings that I can get my socks on.'

Crushed by Cobain's death, Sandra Owen, who used to see several of America's top grunge bands perform at Seattle's Crocodile Club, decided to give up her alternative lifestyle. Owen, who dyed her hair purple and had a pierced belly and nipple, went back to college and started listening to old '60s and '70s music by several artists, including Joni Mitchell, Donovan and James Taylor. Owen said she turned to the folk-style music because she found those smooth songs more soothing to the psyche than the grunge sounds.

'Kurt's death changed my life completely,' Owen said. 'I needed to find something more calm. The only bands I had listened to were heavy grunge bands. A friend of mine, Carolyn, exposed me to some of the music of the '60s which I found to be just as rebellious as grunge but in a much more lucid manner. She lent me Taylor's *Sweet Baby James* album. I must have played it for over six hours the first night I had it. So many of the things Taylor said really hit home. Since then I've become a big fan of his. I still love Kurt more than anybody but in my mid-20s I've been fortunate enough to find another hero in Taylor. He's been through so much and manages to convey it without shoving it down your throat, like a lot of the musicians do today. There's nothing pretentious about him. He plays from the heart.'

Taylor's longtime backup singer, Kate Markowitz, said it is startling to realise what Taylor has endured. 'Not many people on this earth have been through what he has. It's amazing that he's the type of person he is. No bitterness. His attitude is so positive. Many times during tours when things get a bit rough, James cracks a joke and everybody feels better. He's just that type of person. A person who treats everybody equally and with respect. He might be a world-famous musician but first and foremost he's a great person.'

Taylor has descended into a personal hell, fought drugs, depression, and despair, and always emerged a better person. In all areas of his life, he attempts to see not what he can get but what he can offer.

27

JT TV

In May 1994, Taylor threw himself into a killing round of touring and promotional appearances. His attitude toward work pleased everybody at his Sony Music label. While most of his contemporaries had already retired, Taylor showed no signs of slowing down. On 16 May 1994, Jay Leno invited Taylor to be a guest on a special *Tonight Show* taping in New York. Taylor brought down the house when he sang 'Sweet Baby James'. Leno was overwhelmed by Taylor's performance and asked him to sing another tune; Taylor chose 'Almost Like Being in Love,' the romantic ballad from the musical *Brigadoon*. Taylor had been a regular guest on the *Tonight Show* since one night in 1985, when he sang 'Everyday' for host Gary Shandling (subbing for Johnny Carson). On 2 February 1988, Taylor was interviewed by Carson and sang 'Never Die Young' and 'Sweet Potato Pie'.

'James has appeared on the *Tonight Show* many times and has always turned in a wonderful performance,' Leno said. 'He's become a regular on the show. The people love him. They love the way he's so down to earth. He's a popular guest. He's also an easy person to interview. He gives straight answers. He doesn't try to dance around any questions that he might not like.'

Taylor was also a regular guest on NBC's popular *Saturday Night Live*. He first appeared on the hit comedy show in October 1976 when he sang 'Sweet Baby James' and 'Shower the People'. Guest host Lily Tomlin commented that Taylor was one of the greatest songwriters to emerge in the last 50 years. Taylor also appeared on *Saturday Night Live*'s hundredth episode in 1980, singing a medley duet with Paul Simon of 'Sunny Skies', 'Take Me to the Mardi Gras', and 'Cathy's Clown'. The most memorable appearance for him on the show was 13 November 1993, when he played himself in a spoof of the Frank Sinatra duets album. He also sang three songs – Chuck Berry's 'Memphis', 'Slap Leather', and 'Secret o' Life'. Guest Host Rosie O'Donnell complimented him after the show. 'He's the ultimate pro,' O'Donnell said. 'His voice still sounds as good as it did twenty years ago. And he was great in the Sinatra skit. I've listened to him since I was a kid and it was a great pleasure for me to work with him tonight.'

Taylor was a hit with the show's hip audience. Letters from all over North America poured in, requesting that the producers book Taylor for more appearances. John Gorman from Brookline, Massachusetts, has watched *Saturday Night Live* since its first show on 11 October 1975. He's sat in the studio audience at NBC's legendary Studio 8H in New York City's Rockefeller Center three times, in two of which Taylor appeared. 'One time I waited in line more than five hours for tickets because I knew Taylor was going to be a guest,' Gorman said. 'I had to be there. He had been my favourite since "Fire and Rain" in the early '70s. The most memorable time I saw him appear was in 1988. Robin Williams was the guest host. He was so funny. He was on fire. It was vintage Williams. When Taylor came on, he seemed very relaxed and upbeat. Apparently, during the commercial break he had broken out laughing backstage because of one of Williams's jokes. When he came on the stage to get ready during the commercial break he was still laughing. It was quite a sight. I had never really seen him laugh before. He always seems so serious.'

In September 1995 Taylor appeared in the TBS *Colorado River Adventure* TV special. He took his 18-year-old son, Ben, along with 13 others for a three-week adventure ride in handmade dories down the Colorado River, through the Grand Canyon and ending in the deep water of Lake Mead. The idea of this special was to show to the public why the Colorado River was in danger. Master dory boatsman Martin Litton and Taylor talked about how the daily rising and lowering of water levels threatened to erode the banks of the river. The producers of the TV special, William Anderson and Alice Arlen, were impressed with Taylor's concern. Anderson said that Taylor was awed by the area's natural resources and was determined to do everything he could to help preserve it. 'Taylor is really into protecting the environment,' Anderson said. 'He appreciates and respects our natural resources.'

Taylor's management and his record label were thrilled by his commitment. 'In this business talent is just a small part of it,' Taylor's road manager Brian Reed said. 'The artist has got to dedicate himself to working hard on so many other things like promotion. JT has lasted all these years because he never shies away from a challenge. He doesn't complain if he's asked to a special appearance. He treats it as being part of the job. He's dedicated in every way to help make the whole thing a success. He's one of the few people I've worked with who almost never complains. That's the way he is. A real team player.'

Taylor was recognised for his lifetime commitment to the arts on 7 May 1995, when he received an honourary doctorate of music degree at the Berklee College of Music commencement ceremony at Boston's Hynes Convention Center. For Taylor, it was the biggest honour ever received; Berklee is recognised as one of the top music schools in America. James said that he never thought that he would ever receive such an award. 'It's a very big honour,' he said. 'There are so many other musicians who deserve it more than me. I'm very grateful to receive it.'

Taylor was ecstatic that Natalie Cole was also being honoured. He was a big fan of both her and her legendary father, Nat King Cole. 'My mother used to play his records at home,' Taylor said. 'He was an amazing talent as both a singer and pianist. His music will live on forever.'

Taylor and Cole joined an elite class of past honourary doctorate recipients like Duke Ellington, Dizzy Gillespie, Paul Simon, Quincy Jones and B. B. King. Berklee professor Herb Pomeroy, a teacher at the school for 40 years who was retiring, was also honoured that day. Pomeroy was a jazz legend, performing with such greats as Charlie Parker, Stan Kenton and Frank Sinatra. Taylor was chosen to be the commencement speaker at the ceremony, addressing more than five hundred Berklee graduates and three thousand guests.

In his speech, Taylor stressed the importance of supporting the performing arts. He warned the students that society no longer supports the arts the way it once did; its priorities have got to change or the arts will be endangered. He continued, 'I want to talk about music as spiritual food. I applaud and admire your decision to make music the focus and the centre of your lives, because in spite of the increasing presence of corporate priorities in music today, it is not a safe career choice to become a musician. There are risks involved, and I thing it's important to remember why we take those risks. My wife Kathryn refers to this period of time that we're in now as "high late capitalism", and I agree with her that it's characterised by a general, ongoing attempt to put a dollar value on pretty much everything. In fact, as a culture we seem to feel uneasy and sceptical about anything that doesn't have a number attached to it that represents money in the bank.

'I would just like to make one simple and obvious point that was clear to me when I started out, but that has become more obscure as I've repeatedly taken myself to market. And that's simply that it's a gift. It's a blessing, and we really are the lucky ones to have music in our lives and at the centre of things. Because as you know, music is the true soul food, and not that other stuff. You can criticise it, you can put a spin on it, you can analyse it and interpret it in terms of its cultural significance. But basically, that doesn't affect music. Music is beyond the fashion of consensus reality, and basically, it either connects with us, or it doesn't.'

Parts of Taylor's speech were interrupted with thunderous applause, especially when he advised the students not to make the same mistake he did and fall into drugs. 'So render unto Caesar that which is Caesar's, but keep the moneychangers out of the temple, and keep music to yourself,' Taylor said. 'I would advise you to keep your overhead down, avoid a major drug habit, play every day and take it in front of other people. They need to hear it and you need to hear it. And persevere. The Japanese say, "Fall down seven times, and stand up eight times." So remember why you chose this risky enterprise. Well, Class of '95, carry on.'

The audience gave Taylor a standing ovation. Many people were in tears. 'One of the most inspirational speeches I've ever heard,' commented one graduating student. 'This man is unbelievable. To get up there and tell us about the way it really is and what we should expect is so brave of him. He didn't give us any false illusions about the music industry. I'll remember his speech until the day I die. I'll always look back on it when things get a bit tough later on down the road.'

Taylor's growing concern with the state of the music industry was an important part of his commencement speech. At a reception after the ceremony, a graduating student asked Taylor what he would do if he were graduating and starting his career. 'It would be much more difficult than it was when I started out in the '60s,' Taylor replied. 'Back then things were wide open. Playing music and having fun were the top priorities. Then came the business part. Today it's reversed. But it's important to persevere and live out your dreams. No matter how difficult it is, I would never try to deter anybody from pursuing a music career. It's one of the most enjoyable things to do in life.'

While Taylor had managed to improve his public image, he was now drawing criticism for not releasing any new material in over three years. As usual, his concerts were selling out, but music critics were tired of hearing him perform the same repertoire of old hits.

Los Angeles Times critic Mike Boehm blasted Taylor after a June 1994 concert before a capacity crowd of fifteen thousand at the Irvine Meadows. 'What's frozen, and has been since early in his career, is Taylor's artistic development,' Boehm wrote. 'Ideally, a performer's path can take new directions even as he or she moves through middle age. Taylor doesn't seem interested in such shifts . . . As soon as Taylor finished "You've Got a Friend", significant numbers in the house turned into walking men and women, even though there was still a good deal of music yet to come. The last half hour of the concert was marked by an exodus to the parking lot reminiscent of Dodger Stadium after the seventh inning. Not even "Fire and Rain" could halt the defections. Maybe the fans wouldn't be so eager to get a head start if they knew Taylor had some fresh twists and surprises in mind.'

Taylor read Boehm's comments the day after the show. He called Peter Asher and told him that it was time to work on something completely new. 'I love performing the old songs but I need to work on something different,' he told Asher. 'I need to create.'

Taylor's wife Kathryn Walker came up with a brilliant and important idea. A longtime lover of classical music, Walker suggested that he perform his repertoire with a symphony. This got Taylor thinking. He had appreciated classical music since his mother had played it on the family phonograph. It would get a lot of publicity and he would be able to a play with a big orchestra, something he had dreamed of doing since he was a kid. Taylor remembered listening to some of his idols performing with strings, including Charlie Parker and the Beatles. Taylor himself – who needed to improve his music sight reading to do this tour – had once performed in the late '80s with John Williams and the Boston Pops. It was a memorable performance for him. 'I was very nervous,' he said. 'Being onstage with the Boston Pops was something else. It was like being in heaven.'

Taylor phoned Peter Asher and asked him to make some inquiries. Asher was at first sceptical, worrying about the exorbitant amount of money an event like this would cost. But as usual, he never tried to dissuade Taylor from pursuing his dreams. He picked up the phone and started making calls.

Through a connection with his wife's family and the family of Warren Kessler, the San Diego Symphony's former board president and chairman, Taylor hooked up with symphonies across America and embarked on a 22-city tour in the fall of 1995. Kathryn Walker's sister, Sally, and Kessler's sister, Karen, had been roommates at Wells College in Aurora, New York between 1957 and 1961. Their families became close friends. Kathryn Walker connected with Warren Kessler in 1992 in Santa Fe, New Mexico and exchanged phone numbers. She now called him and explained to him Taylor's desire to perform with a symphony. Without hesitation, Kessler invited Taylor to perform with his symphony at San Diego's Copley Symphony Hall. Taylor waived his performance fee to help out the symphony, which was having financial troubles. The concerts quickly sold out and raised over two hundred thousand dollars. They were the only benefit shows that Taylor did on his orchestral tour.

Once again, Taylor managed to turn the critics around. He received some of his most favourable reviews in years. Critics praised him for extending his repertoire with several popular classics like George Gershwin's 'Fascinating Rhythm' and Jerome Kern's 'The Way You Look Tonight.'

Los Angeles Times critic Mike Boehm, who had lambasted Taylor a year before for not trying anything new, was impressed. In his review Boehm said, 'His last appearance in Orange County, in 1994 at Irvine Meadows, made it clear that the routine was played out. Many fans streamed for the exits long before the end of the marathon performance . . . [In this appearance, however,] the orchestral backing lent sweep and scope to other Taylor nuggets, including 'The Frozen Man', 'Millworker', and a splendid 'Carolina in My Mind'. There wasn't a hint of syrup or bombast, and Taylor's warm, wistful voice remained at the emotional and musical core of every song. The widened aural scope was not achieved at the expense of the personal, intimate feeling that is the essence of Taylor's singing and his best songwriting . . . In an intimate hall, with the warm, rich sound of a well-tempered orchestra surrounding him, it was obvious that Taylor's best performing home is not lined with bare concrete. The only thing shed during this fine evening was the tedium of the same old thing.'

The Pacific Symphony's conductor, Edward Cumming, patted Taylor on the back several times during the concert. Cumming said that he couldn't believe how easily Taylor was able to adapt to playing with a different orchestra in each city. 'That's not easy to do,' Cumming said. 'Not too many people can do that. But if anybody can, it's James Taylor. He's very talented and determined.' Cumming cracked up the crowd when he introduced Taylor by saying, 'For the first time, I'm working with somebody who's taller and skinnier than myself.' Taylor also made the crowd laugh several times by joking about still being referred to as Sweet Baby James after so many years. Before he introduced a new song, he joked that 'it sounds like all the old songs. It's technically new.' With a good idea and a new way to present his songs, Taylor was riding high again.

Taylor described that fall tour as being a real eye opener. 'It closes things down and makes them narrower, in terms of what you can do with improvisation,' he said. 'On the other hand, it expands it into this amazingly rich harmonic thing. But it's somewhat daunting if you're a pop musician, to be in the company of people in an orchestra, who have studied so seriously. To a certain extent I feel like a bull in a china shop.'

Taylor's orchestral tour gained him many new fans but alienated some of his old ones. 'It was the first time I didn't go see him when he came to town,' said Amy Wallace of Los Angeles. 'I refused to go because I couldn't bear hearing him sing one his classic tunes in a classical way. I don't think he was doing it to make money because he was very rich. Maybe he got bored and needed a change. I respected his decision but I decided to wait to see him in concert until he had his regular band with him. I wanted to remember his music in its natural state. Not embellished with strings and a brass section. No matter how good it sounded, it could never sound the same.'

But no matter what he tried, Taylor was still king to his legion of fans. 'It might not be as raw as before, but I like it,' said a female fan. 'The voice is the same. No matter what setting he plays in, his voice still rings out. As long as he doesn't try to change it I'll go see him even if he's performing in a country hillbilly band.'

28

TAYLOR AND SIMON REUNITE

Back from a several-month hiatus from performing, Taylor flung himself into the preparations for the Rainforest Action Network. The benefit concert was set to take place at Carnegie Hall on 12 April 1995. For Taylor, it would be a chance to perform with some of his favourite artists and to lend support to a cause that he had been supporting for many years. Taylor's close friend and band mate Don Grolnick was hired as the show's musical director. Grolnick got the rest of Taylor's regular band to lend accompaniment to the other artists. The big-name bill for the show included Paul Simon, Sting, Elton John, Billy Joel, Bruce Springsteen, Jessye Norman and Jon Bon Jovi.

'As artists it's important for us to come together and help worthy causes,' Taylor said. 'I feel very privileged to be able to perform with such wonderful talent to help the Rainforest Action Network. It's important that we keep doing concerts like this. The impact gets bigger and great strides are being made to change things and to save this planet.'

The concert enabled Taylor to perform a duet with Springsteen on 'The River' and one with Sting on Antonio Carlos Jobim's 'Obsession'. He also lent backup vocals to Sting's 'Fields of Gold'. But the highlight of the show came when Taylor joined Sting and Elton John for an emotional version of 'It's a Wonderful Day'. The trios' harmony on the classic pop standard got a standing ovation.

'It was an incredible feeling when we sang together,' Sting said backstage after the show. 'It was fitting to sing that song because it's positive. That's why we came here today. To give hope to everybody and to raise awareness . . . I commend James Taylor and his band for working so hard to make this show successful. They were great. Taylor's one of my all-time favourites. He's such a class act.'

Elton John also sang praises. 'There are some artists in this business who care and there are others who don't,' he said. 'James Taylor is one who cares. He's always there when you need him to lend support for a worthwhile cause. It's important to have artists like us get out there and raise money and awareness. We're in a position to do that. It's the public that supports us and it's important to give something back. The more we keep working together, the more impact we will have.'

Back from his tour with the symphony orchestras, in August 1995 Taylor flung himself into the preparations for another benefit, this time on Martha's Vineyard. The special concert made pop-music history because it reunited him with his ex-wife, Carly Simon. The concert, billed as *Livestock '95*, benefited the Martha's Vineyard Agricultural Society. The organisers of the event thought it would be fitting if the Vineyard's two most famous citizens reunited onstage. They thought it would attract more attention even than Sonny and Cher had when they reunited a few years back on David Letterman's late-night television show. At first, both Taylor's and Simon's camps were against the idea, unsure if they could put aside their past woes and put on a brave face. In the end, however, Taylor and Simon were convinced that if they joined forces it would start the event on the right foot.

'The concert was for a good cause and by getting Taylor and Simon to reunite showed everybody that people could put behind their differences, no matter how severe they are, and open the lines of communication,' said Pete Deluca, a Boston musician who attended the concert. 'It was very emotional to see them together again. Chills ran up my spine. After all they had been through, they showed everybody how important it is to still be friends. It was one of the most emotional experiences I've ever had.'

By getting Taylor and Simon to perform together, the concert's organisers got more publicity than they imagined. *Livestock '95* made international headlines. Television crews from all over the world came to get the first footage in more than twelve years of Taylor and Simon appearing together. Backstage, people marvelled at how relaxed the former lovers looked.

'Taylor appeared more relaxed than Simon,' said a member of the concert's security team. 'He was in high spirits, cracking jokes and keeping everything loose. Simon appeared more nervous than he did. I saw her go up to him before they went on and she gave him a big hug. It was very emotional. I thought they were both going to cry. It was a hug that had the words, "Let's put the past behind us" written all over it.'

Onstage, Taylor and Simon held forth in the grandest manner. The crowd went wild during their performance. The applause was so loud that it drowned out the music.

'Everybody came to see them together again,' said Pete's brother Johnathan Deluca, who also attended the concert. 'It's not often that you get to see two music legends reunite. Especially after they went through a bitter divorce. I think that nothing could have moved me more than seeing them together again, not even if it was the Beatles up there. Taylor and Simon had been through so many hard times. I don't think there was a dry eye in the crowd when they got up there. We in the audience were all touched by the emotional weight of this reunion.'

Backstage after the concert both Taylor's and Simon's spirits were high. Carly admitted that she'd had butterflies in her stomach for several weeks leading up to the show. 'I've always been nervous before performing,' Simon said. 'But this time I was more nervous than ever. A lot was going through my mind. I'm just glad that we were able to do our part and help out for such a good cause. It's always good to do something good for Martha's Vineyard. It's a place that's been very dear to myself and my entire family for so many years. The best times I've had in my life have been right here.'

The historic reunion concert led to speculation that Taylor and Simon would collaborate on a new album. Both camps quickly quashed the rumours. 'The concert on Martha's Vineyard was for a special event,' a member of Taylor's group said. 'There are currently no plans for any further work together. It's a nice idea but both James and Carly are involved in other projects. They don't have much spare time these days and the only firm plans they have together in the future is to continue raising their two children, Sally and Ben.'

29

1996: A TRAGIC YEAR

Perhaps the most difficult time in Taylor's life since his drug withdrawal was still ahead. In 1996 his career had lost none of its steam, but his personal life was plagued by one crisis after another. Taylor was under a lot of strain. His marriage to Kathryn Walker was faltering and two of the people closest to him were terminally ill. By the end of the year, his life would be completely turned around.

On the marital front, James and Kathryn's relationship had fallen apart. They were both working too hard and found little time to spend with each other. The idyllic early times in their marriage, when they shared breakfast in bed and took long walks on the beach, were long in the past. Those honeymoon days had given way to hectic careers and constant travel. On those rare occasions when they were together now, they felt like complete strangers. Neither of them felt like making love or doing the romantic things they once did together. They had been turning their relationship on and off for the past couple of years. They often spent months apart while Walker was working in a remote location shooting a new film or Taylor was on tour. Both of them were reluctant to alter the rigid schedules of their showbiz careers to suit the other.

Toward the end of 1995 Taylor and Walker realised that their marriage was doomed. Walker sued for divorce on the grounds of 'irreconcilable differences'. In May 1996 the divorce became official. The fine details were settled before Taylor and Walker stepped into the courtroom. Their lawyers had worked out a settlement that reportedly had Taylor pay Walker a generous five-figure settlement. The couple have never spoken at length about the breakup of their marriage. A clause in their divorce settlement forbids them from talking about the details.

'That was the one thing Taylor was adamant about,' said a close friend of Taylor's. 'He was willing to pay Walker what she wanted but he needed to make sure that she wouldn't turn around and sell her story to the press. He didn't want his family, especially his children, to be caused further embarrassment. He was smart to do that. I don't think Walker realised how valuable her story was. She could have probably made more money than she got from the settlement if she went to one of the big tabloids with her story. But for some reason she preferred to want to put it behind her and get on with her life.'

Some people suggested that Kathryn Walker didn't want to go public with her story because she feared the backlash of the power of Taylor and his record label, Sony Music. Walker wanted to keep acting. If she were to drag Taylor through the mud, she would have automatically cut off many important connections. 'Taylor is a powerful player in show business,' said entertainment author Esmond Choueke. 'He knows everybody. And his record label, Sony, is one of the most influential entertainment companies. If Walker had nothing to gain by talking negatively about Taylor. She was smart. So many times in this business an ex-spouse goes to the media and blasts the former partner. In many cases these people never work again. They become automatically characterised as troublemakers.'

Although we may never know the whole story of their breakup – unless one of them decides to break the silence – both Taylor and Walker provided a few details to close friends. Walker once admitted to a close friend of Taylor's that she felt that from day one of the marriage, Taylor brought with him too much emotional baggage. She said that his troubled past concerned her, but that she had blinded herself to the potential consequences of it when she fell deeply in love with the rock star. Walker also told the friend that she wanted to have a family with Taylor but after a few years of marriage, she realised her dream would never become a reality. Taylor's long workdays and his harried touring schedule meant that he wouldn't be around to raise a family if they had children. Walker said that even if Taylor wanted to have children with her it would have been difficult for him even to impregnate her because he was in a perpetual state of near exhaustion.

'It was obvious that during the last few years of their marriage they were almost strictly friends,' said author Esmond Choueke. 'I think Walker was frustrated because Taylor was too tired to make love and give her the attention she wanted.'

After all the details were worked out, Taylor and Walker went ahead with their lives with few traces of bitterness. 'It was nothing like what he went through with Carly,' Choueke added. 'The Taylor-Simon relationship had become nasty by the time it was over. They were both very bitter for many years.' Today, Taylor and Walker rarely speak to each other, but when they do bump into each other at functions or awards ceremonies they chat with the cordiality of old friends. In fact, Walker remains a fan of her ex-husband's music. She often plays his albums in the background when she entertains dinner guests, and she still encourages her friends to buy them. In fact, when Taylor released a new album in May 1997 – a year after their divorce – Walker made it a priority to rush out and buy a copy. The only question about their marriage that still lingers in her mind is what would have happened if Taylor had been more open to starting a family together. She often wonders if they would be living happily ever after in a big house somewhere on Martha's Vineyard. And she has pictured in her mind how talented their child might have been because he would have been influenced by both of his parents' artistic gifts.

'Too bad things didn't work out,' said Taylor fan Eric Noseworthy. 'When JT had children with Carly Simon they both drew on their parents' musical talent. With Taylor's second wife's acting talent, a child would have been more cultured and would have been able to consider a career in both acting and music. It would have been interesting to see Taylor and Walker have children. When Taylor was raising his children with Carly, a lot of the time he was messed up on drugs. When he was with Walker, he was straight. I think he was more prepared to be a father with Walker than when he was with Carly.'

Taylor's divorce was the start of a series of tragic episodes in his personal life. That same year, 1996, Don Grolnick – Taylor's best friend, musical director, and band member – learned that he had lymphatic cancer. For Taylor it was a severe blow. Nobody during the last decade had been closer to him than Grolnick; he trusted Don like a brother. When Grolnick died at the age of 48 on 1 June 1996, Taylor wept like a baby.

'Don Grolnick was one of the finest musicians and arrangers in the business,' Taylor backup singer Kate Markowitz said. 'He was both a great person and musician. JT and him were like family. It was a very sad day when he passed away. We will never be able to replace Don. But I'm sure he's proud of JT for continuing on. Don always liked people who were musicians and treated them with so much respect. His loss created not only a void in JT and the rest of the band's lives but also the entire music business. He was just that type of person. A person who has an impact on the lives of everybody he comes into contact with.'

Grolnick, who had produced three of Taylor's albums, had become one of the most respected people in the music business in his short career. Everyone who worked with him described him as honest, sincere, and talented. 'If there's one thing that I remember about Don, it's that you'd never know how talented he was when you first met him,' said Patricia Burton, a Chicago-based vocalist who worked with Grolnick. 'He's as humble as they come. And he has a sense of humour. A good sense of humour. He can break the tension in a room by cracking a joke or by acting funny. But once he got behind the controls in the studio, you knew that you were working with the best. He knew what he was doing inside and out. I might have worked with him for only a couple of hours but I learned more from him that day than almost anybody I've ever worked with.'

But Taylor had another great loss to come in his life. By the time his pain over the death of Grolnick subsided, his father, 75, had contracted several ailments. Isaac was told by his doctors that he didn't have much time to live. After his divorce from Trudy, he had happily remarried a much younger woman named Sue, but grown severely depressed after Sue died of cancer a year earlier. In the hospital now, it was clear that Isaac's will to live wasn't strong anymore. It was harder and harder for him to get around. His bones ached and his body wouldn't do what he wanted it to do. 'My grandfather was a great man,' said Isaac's granddaughter, Sally Taylor. 'It was very hard when he died. He was so good to his grandchildren. But in the end his health gave out.' As a tribute to her late grandfather, Sally Taylor wrote a song on her first album that she dedicated to him. 'It was something I wanted to do because he was such a special person,' Sally recalled before a concert in Los Angeles in March 1999.

Isaac's death on 1 November 1996, reunited the Taylor family again. 'Unfortunately, that year the family kept being brought together because of death,' a family member said. 'In recent years, the family had started to grow apart. Everybody was busy leading their own lives. But Isaac's death really brought everybody together again.'

Isaac's death also brought together more than five hundred people at a special memorial service in Boston on 30 November 1996. Moments before the elegant service, James Taylor gathered his brothers and sister in a quiet corner. They huddled and cried as James shared some private thoughts. Then he threw back his shoulders just as the service was about to start and said to his family, 'Come on, guys, we have to do this now, we have to be brave and do this right for Dad.' Then they all walked out to begin the ceremony.

James and his siblings got up and told stories about their late father. It brought tears to the eyes of most of the people packed in the Church of the New Covenant in Boston's Back Bay. Taylor tried to realise something positive out of his father's death. 'The "New Jerusalem" passage had a lot of layers of meaning for father,' Taylor later told *Billboard* editor Timothy White. 'The biblical aspect of a new beginning is there, and settlers coming to this country who were looking for the same sort of new start, but also my dad had a sailboat that he dearly loved, and he named it *New Jerusalem*.'

Taylor had selected the passage himself. From the depths of his own pain at the loss, he was hoping to make sense of his father's life. He wept for the last time over the disagreements and bitter words that had once passed between them. 'When all is said and done,' he told a friend, 'nothing is left but the positive we've done . . . The discord and the things we fight about, they just are meaningless in the end.'

30

HOURGLASS

After his father's death, James Taylor became determined to finally finish his first studio album in almost five years, the longest time he had gone in his career between albums. Taylor hired his good friend Frank Filipetti to produce *Hourglass*. Filipetti and Taylor had remained close friends ever since they first collaborated on Taylor's 1985 album *That's Why I'm Here*. Filipetti made his name in the music industry by producing big-name artists like Taylor, Patricia Kaas and Taylor's ex-wife Carly Simon.

Taylor dedicated *Hourglass* to his favourite producer, the late Don Grolnick. Taylor respected nobody whom he ever worked with more than Grolnick. 'Don and I had been working together since the early '70s,' Taylor told *Billboard* magazine. 'He had produced my last four albums and was my main musical collaborator. He was the leader of my band without any question, to say nothing of being my best friend, so it was very questionable what it was going to be like to try to work without him.' Now he was going to have to go on without his father in his family life and without Don Grolnick in his professional life.

Filipetti encouraged Taylor to deal with the tragic losses of the previous year in the album's music. It was an eclectic mix ranging from folk to soft jazz and was recorded on a budget of four hundred thousand dollars. Taylor rented a house on Martha's Vineyard and converted it into a studio. Filipetti hired several music superstars to fill in the gaps, including Branford Marsalis, Sting, Michael Brecker, Shawn Colvin, Stevie Wonder, the classical cellist Yo-Yo Ma, Mark O'Connor and Edgar Meyer. When word got out about the all-star roster with Taylor on *Hourglass*, it became one of the most anticipated albums of the year. Interview requests poured in from all over the world; the Sony hype machine sprang into action. 'You're talking about country, rock, pop, jazz and R&B artists that are all part of the jambalaya that is James Taylor,' Columbia Records senior vice-president Will Botwin said. 'It's not like he's targeting people to get on the record for a purpose other than they fit musically. His whole process – the evolution of how he makes records and how they sound, from a production standpoint – is very natural.'

A month before *Hourglass* was released, Taylor got big publicity for appearing on VH1's *Storytellers* series about the lives of well-known musicians. A video clip of Taylor's live performance of a song from the new album, 'Little More Time With You', went into heavy rotation on VH1. 'It was great timing because the new album was only a month away from hitting record stores,' Filipetti said. 'Essentially we got a free video out of the deal. The reaction to the video was so good. It was then that we realised that the *Hourglass* album was destined to be a big success.'

But even with all the advance publicity, nobody in Taylor's camp, including the singer himself, had any idea what to expect. Taylor wondered if his fan base was still strong enough to show respectable sales figures. When *Hourglass* was released on 20 May 1997, not even the ever-optimistic Filipetti expected the overwhelming positive reviews. Critics were impressed with Taylor's reverent authenticity spiced with more originality than he had displayed since the early '70s. *Hourglass* shimmered with subtly effective studio embellishments that attractively framed Taylor's versatile vocals. The songs revealed a wide-ranging musical intelligence matched by brilliant lyrics about the events in his life during the past few years. To top it off, the sales figures were much higher than any of Sony's executives expected.

Taylor thought some reviewers would criticise him for using too many styles of music on *Hourglass*, something known as a death wish in the music industry. 'The biggest mistake artists can make is to incorporate a bunch of styles into their music,' said Richard Walker, a former Sony marketing executive. 'It doesn't make sense. It becomes hard to label artists if they're jumping from rock to reggae to the waltz. The first thing that people look for in artists is their style. That's how they develop a following.'

In Taylor's case, the scenario was much different. Music critics welcomed *Hourglass* as a refreshing change because it came from the heart. Too much of the music released in the '90s sounded formulated. *Hourglass* became one of the most favourably reviewed albums of 1997.

'*Hourglass* is not a morbid work,' a *Rolling Stone* review said. 'Rather, it emphasizes the beauty of the world and the importance of enjoying our fragile passage through it. As he closes in on 50, it seems that James Taylor has reached a new creative peak.'

Stephen Holden wrote in the *New York Times*: 'Taylor appears to have found a tentative peace and accepted the inevitable changes life brings. The songs evoke a Zen-like embrace of life's simple pleasures.'

Neil Strauss, also writing in the *New York Times*, was equally impressed: '*Hourglass* is vintage James Taylor from the very first word, I (signalling the confessional singer-songwriter style he pioneered) to the second word, remember (a confession of someone attached to his past), to the third and fourth words, Richard Nixon (the calling cards of a true-blue Baby Boomer).'

Time magazine: 'At 49, James Taylor has lost his hair and gained a great American face. It is a face out of Steinbeck: long and spare, radiating intelligence and surprising strength for a man known for his soft lyric . . . *Hourglass* is vintage Taylor, blending ironic detachment with personal reflection. In 'Enough to Be on Your Way', the finest song on the album, he probes in part the death of his brother. During recent rehearsals with his band in Los Angeles, there was a long silence in the room every time he finished playing it.'

A review in the popular British music magazine *Mojo* helped boost Taylor's record sales across the UK: '*Hourglass* just happens to be among the very best records that James Taylor has ever made.'

'This album seemed to have the kiss of heaven right from the start,' said a Sony Music executive. 'Great reviews one after another: some people mused it was mystical, almost as if Taylor's father and Don Grolnick were up there guiding the album to reward Taylor for his courage in the past year. I don't think it was divine intervention, but I do know it's rare for an album with such a range of styles to be received so well.'

Taylor's fans were thrilled with their hero's new work. *Hourglass* debuted on the *Billboard* charts at number nine and sold close to 80 thousand copies in its first week of release. 'I think it was Grolnick making it happen,' says longtime Taylor fan Walter Haimovitch. 'This new style was iffy from the get-go, and when it did so well, I knew it was Don reaching out from wherever he is to say goodbye and good luck to James.'

Taylor's management was besieged with requests from concert

promoters all over the world to add new dates to the North American tour that they had already planned for the summer. 'It was like a zoo,' a Sony executive said. 'Nobody expected the album to do as well as it did. Taylor had not released anything in years, so it was difficult to predict what would happen. So many of the old artists from the '60s and '70s who tried to release new material in the '90s were unsuccessful. Their fans just seemed to have disappeared. The week *Hourglass* was released our phone lines lit up. Everybody was interested in getting Taylor for a promotional appearance on television or to perform. I was shocked. I remember seeing Taylor that week and even he seemed to be surprised. He couldn't believe what was happening.'

Whether it was helped from the beyond or not, *Hourglass* was an overwhelming success. It was yet another incident of great joy coming on the heels of great sorrow in Taylor's life.

The people most pleased by Taylor's success were his legions of loyal fans. 'I bought eight copies of *Hourglass* when it came out,' said Donna Heller of North Carolina. 'I bought one for myself and the rest were gifts for relatives and close friends. Everybody whom I gave one to thought it was such a good gift. It was appropriate to buy that many copies because James Taylor has given so much to music and to society over the years. I wanted to do my part by buying several copies of his album as a way of saying thank you to him for all the wonderful moments he's provided his fans with over the years. When I read in the newspapers about how well *Hourglass* was doing, I was happy. It deserved every good review it got. It is such a wonderful album. Every song is special. There's not one that is there just to fill up space on the CD. It is obvious that Taylor worked very hard on *Hourglass*. It's one of my favourite albums of his.'

One of the recurring themes on *Hourglass* was Taylor's attempt to try to shed light on life's spiritual side without believing in God. Unlike many artists and famous people who become reborn after experiencing tragedy and hardships, Taylor was adamant that he would adhere to his nonreligious upbringing. In 'Gaia' Taylor calls himself a 'poor, wretched unbeliever'. In 'Up From Your Life', Taylor sings, 'For an unbeliever like you, there's not much they can do.'

'Well, I find myself with a strong spiritual need, in the past five years, particularly,' Taylor told *Rolling Stone*. 'And, certainly, it's acknowledged as an important part of recovery from addiction. Yet it's hard for me to find an actual handle for it. I'm not saying that it's not helpful to think of having a real handle on the universe, your own personal point of attachment. But . . . I think it's crazy. But it's an intensity that keeps us sane. You might call a lot of these songs spirituals for agnostics . . . Twelve-step programs say an interesting thing: either you have a God, or you are God and you don't want the job.'

Taylor's summer tour attracted sold-out audiences. The band was tighter than ever and Taylor was in fine form. Between tour dates, Taylor spent his time working out in the gym, in-line skating and eating strictly healthy foods. 'He really got into a lot of sports and outdoor activity,' said Taylor's backup singer Kate Markowitz. 'He's become a bit of a health nut. Today he stays in tremendous shape and spends a lot of time communicating with nature. When he does something he does it to the extreme. He's not the type of person who will go into a gym for an hour a day thinking that that's his answer to staying healthy. He might do the gym but he'll also spend the rest of his day doing activity and eating well to get maximum results. Just look at him. He's over 50 and he looks better than ever.'

The reviews Taylor received during his summer tour in 1997 meant a lot to him, because he had put in a lot of hard work to prepare for the concerts. He rehearsed with his band for two solid months before the tour kicked off in early June. 'It's hard to believe any of the eight thousand folks at the Mark of the Quad-Cities on Tuesday night went away disappointed,' wrote Mark Ridolfi of the *Quad-city Times* in Illinois after Taylor performed there 7 July. 'As much as any other top performer, he cleverly melds old with new. His two-hour set held enough Top Forty gold to satisfy. But by putting them to ambitious new arrangements, he keeps playing them in big arenas instead of recycling them at fairgrounds oldies shows. . . . He's still writing as strongly as ever and is giving the songs more sophisticated instrumentation and dynamic vocal arrangements.'

Perhaps the only disappointment for Taylor that summer was his performance at New York's Madison Square Garden on 10 September. The concert was special to Taylor because he knew that the impact of the New York media's reviews could boost the sales of *Hourglass*. For weeks, Taylor told band mates drummer Carlos Vega, bassist Jimmy Johnson and keyboardist Clifford Carter how much the New York show meant to him. 'I want to put on the best show there that I've ever done in New York,' Taylor said. 'Never has the band been in better shape, so I want to show it off to the people of New York. I've had some good shows there in the past but I think this one will be the best one by far.'

When it came time to perform in New York, though, Taylor's game plan fell apart. On stage he appeared more nervous than usual and he failed to move the New York crowd the way he'd moved audiences everywhere else. *New York Times* pop critic Neil Strauss was far from impressed. 'James Taylor fell victim to his own predictability,' Strauss wrote. 'Introducing his song 'Frozen Man', he announced, 'I got this idea from – but before he could complete his monologue, an audience member yelled, "*National Geographic*"! Taylor persevered with his introduction, growing more and more flustered as laughter exploded sporadically throughout the theatre from fans who had heard it all before. The more Taylor tried to improvise his story to make it seem new to his audience, the less coherent he became . . . The world needs Taylor the way it needs cocktail stirrers and paper doilies, as a sign that everything's normal and taken care of.'

Backstage after the show, Taylor seemed distraught. 'Things didn't go as well as they could have,' Taylor said. 'But that's the way it goes. Some nights things aren't as magical as others. That's the music business. But you can't let it get you down. You have to forget it and start concentrating on tomorrow night's show. It's the only way you'll last in this business.'

31

ANOTHER LOSS, ANOTHER FRIEND

After his celebrated *Hourglass* tour, several new chapters unfolded for James Taylor. A new woman, Boston Symphony Orchestra marketing director, Kim Smedvig, entered his life. Taylor was spotted in Paris arm in arm with Smedvig looking happier than ever. Taylor said in a 1997 *Time* magazine interview that Smedvig was the perfect woman for him. She rekindled his drive to do things and inspired him to build a new house, learn cello and take French lessons. 'I'm an entertainer, so I'm very sensitive to what other people's judgement of me is,' Taylor said. 'When I engage someone else, I care very much what their opinion of me is, perhaps more than I might at this age.'

In February 1998, Taylor's *Hourglass* album was honoured with an unexpected Grammy as best pop album. It was James's first Grammy since the early '70s and the third of his career. Taylor didn't even make plans to attend the awards ceremony, because he didn't think he would win. Instead, he continued his European tour and took several days off to go skiing in Geielo, a small town in Norway. 'You could've knocked me over with a feather,' he said. 'I had put it out of my mind . . . I had pretty much dismissed any possibility of winning the award. I considered the nomination more than I could hope for. I got the call at 5 a.m. It was about 11 p.m. in the US at the Grammys. Someone hysterical on the other line telling me I'd won. I dismiss those as being BS. But it's amazing how fast you change your mind when you actually win one. It's been a long time.'

When Taylor returned from Europe he was shocked by the death of another one of his band mates and close friends, drummer Carlos Vega. On 7 April 1998, Vega, 41, died at his Los Angeles home of an apparently self-inflicted gunshot wound on the eve of a scheduled appearance with Taylor on the *Oprah Winfrey Show*.' Vega, who had also worked with such music legends as Linda Ronstadt, Joni Mitchell and Vince Gill, was the person in his band to whom Taylor was closest and trusted most after the death of Don Grolnick. Taylor found it more difficult to deal with Vega's death than any of the others in the past few years because it was totally unexpected. It had been only a few days since Vega returned from a European tour with Taylor. According to several people in Taylor's camp, Vega showed no signs of being suicidal. In fact, at the time of his death he had been preparing to return to touring with Taylor. Taylor was visibly shaken by Vega's death, and cried for hours. He later said in a written statement, 'It has been a great privilege and delight working with Carlos for the past 13 years and wonderful to have collaborated with so talented a player. I miss him terribly as a friend and an artist.'

Former Taylor band member Michael Landau, a close friend of Vega since they went to the same high school in the '70s, thought Vega was the ultimate pro. 'Nobody I worked with played as good as Carlos,' Landau said. 'Carlos was also one of the nicest people you would ever want to meet.' Producer George Massenburg, who once worked with Taylor, said Vega's death devastated him. 'My life and all of my expectations will change for this,' he said. 'How will we ever feel comfortable with being happy in the studio again?'

In 1997 Peter Asher was offered an executive position with Sony Music. The new job forced Asher to sever ties with Taylor – working for the same label as an artist he represented posed a conflict of interest. Taylor signed with a new management company, Borman Entertainment; it was headed by Gary Borman, who also represented pop group Garbage and singer Faith Hill. Shortly after he signed with Borman, Taylor received another personal blow when his longtime assistant Cathy Kerr decided to leave him to work for singer Randy Newman. Rumours were rampant that Kerr had fallen out with Borman over the direction of Taylor's career. Kerr wanted to have more control and opted to work for Newman with a guarantee that she would call the shots in his career.

'Taylor became good friends with Borman and was impressed with his ideas,' said Taylor's backup singer Kate Markowitz. 'I think it was a good change for him because he had been with the same manager for so many years. Borman had built up a lot of contacts and had many new ideas how to shape his career. For Cathy, she had an opportunity come up with Randy Newman that was too attractive to pass up. In the end I think it worked out well for everybody.'

Since Borman took over, Taylor has managed to stay in the spotlight. He continues to perform to sold-out arenas and stadiums all over the world; his public profile has never been higher. On 24 January 1999, Taylor was featured on CBS's popular *Sunday Morning* with host Charles Osgood. During the segment Osgood asked Taylor about what advice he gave to his children, Sally and Ben, who had recently embarked on careers in the music business.

Taylor replied, 'I have occasion to say to people sometimes, you know, that they should try to watch out for three things: avoid a major addiction, don't get so deeply into debt that that controls your life and – don't start a family before you're ready to settle down. You know, just basically sort of keep things simple. But, you know, you can't say these things. You have to – you have to show them by example, and – let it go.'

James Taylor is today living and learning in a more stable lifestyle. He is working on a new album due to be released soon.

No doubt the future holds many more great joys and sorrows in the magnificent voyage that is James Taylor's life. Because he is James Taylor, he generously shares the wisdom he has gained so far: 'I've been lucky being able to do what I want to do,' Taylor says. 'Very little commercial pressure on me to dress up in the latest fashions. I've been allowed to steam along on my own course.'

EPILOGUE

Freddy Stark sat in the fourth row of a James Taylor concert in Toronto during the summer of 2003. Stark, drinking a glass of cold beer, is a wealthy clothing retail entrepreneur. On this night, he was wearing the ill-fitting rough clothes of a Russian peasant and kept a cap pulled down over his forehead.

'It does not matter how you dress here,' Stark said. 'That's what JT concerts are about. Everyone here is welcome. More than 30 years after he launched his career, JT sounds better than ever. In 150 years, very few pop artists will be remembered. Only a handful, The Beatles, Elvis, Madonna and JT will have their music played. The rest will be long forgotten.'

Since the initial release of this book more than three years ago, there have been many changes in James Taylor's life. In August 2002, after a busy five year break from recording, during which Taylor got married and fathered twin boys, Taylor released a new album, *October Road*. Taylor reunited with his old producer friend Russ Titelman, who last worked with him on 1976's *In the Pocket*. Taylor invited several of his notorious musician friends to lend a hand, including Ry Cooder, Michael Brecker and violinist Stuart Duncan.

Again, album sales and critical reviews were impressive. With the 12 songs on *October Road*, Taylor managed to provide a fresh, engaging folky-jazz sound that appealed to fans old and new.

'I had never even heard of James Taylor before *October Road*,' said Darla Sherman, a topless lounge dancer in Miami who now uses JT's love ballad 'Caroline I See' as part of her routine. 'A customer gave me *October Road* as a gift. After hearing it, I went out and bought four more of his albums. Now, I can't get enough of his music.'

A successful tour in the summer of 2001 reminded music fans that few in the business are more phenomenon, successful and richer than Taylor. The tightness of his band combined with Taylor's great energy onstage proved that Taylor is still a musician way ahead of his time. During the tour, party invitations kept pouring in, but Taylor declined most of them because he needed to preserve his energy for the stage. After a concert at the Hollywood Bowl, longtime Taylor fan Johnathan Mendelson remarked how fresh Taylor's music remains after all those years.

'I've been to over 20 concerts this year and no one inspires me the way JT does,' Mendelson said. 'The man is ageless. He has a uniqueness, a vision and energy that I have never seen before. His voice sounds better than ever. Every time I see him perform he sounds better than before. Never have I seen a singer who is such a perfectionist. Even though he has been around for over 30 years, after what I saw tonight, I wouldn't be surprised if his best albums have not been recorded yet.'

There is clearly more to Taylor than being a musician. Aside from being brilliant, affable and charming, Taylor is a devoted family man. The news that Taylor became a dad again in winter 2001, made headlines throughout the world. Taylor and his third wife, Kim Smedvig, became surrogate parents to twins, Henry and Logan. Smedvig wanted to have children more than anything. After several pregnancy attempts failed, the couple received their biggest wish ever when a friend volunteered to carry their child. Shortly after, the couple received the incredible news that their friend was carrying twins. As soon as the two gorgeous babies arrived, Taylor told friends that he felt better than ever. He played guitar and sang for Henry and Logan, pushed the stroller and changed diapers for the first time in more than two decades.

Taylor's incredible news received mixed reaction from both friends and family. Many of his close friends rallied to his side, sent baby gifts and congratulations. Some wondered if Taylor, now in his fifties, was too old to look after twins. 'It's weird because I know a lot of people are grandparents at his age,' said one friend. 'But I'm sure that JT will find the time and energy to be a great dad again, just like he was to Ben and Sally.' Taylor's daughter Sally, a successful independent recording artist, told David Browne of *Entertainment Weekly* that she had mixed feelings. 'I was shocked and fearful and happy and freaked out,' Sally said. 'Fearful that it would take him away from us, my brother and I.'

Many friends and fans wondered if Taylor's new life might slow down his career. 'I think he'd look back from the corner of his eye and chuckle,' said longtime fan Trina Davidson. 'This is not the first time people have speculated that JT's career would slow down. The fact is that as long as JT's breathing, I'm sure he'll always be active in the music industry. Whether it's singing his own tunes or recording with people like Mark Knopfler and Michael Brecker, JT always seems to be working on a new musical project.'

Amid all the news in Taylor's life, few would have thought that his vocal performance on 'Don't Let Me Be Lonely Tonight' would receive much publicity. Taylor sang the mellow ballad on jazz legend Michael Brecker's critically acclaimed album, *Nearness of You: The Ballad Book*. Some critics knocked the production, claiming Taylor's vox was too below the final mix. 'Taylor's yearning tenor is warm and expressive,' music critic Ken Micallef said. 'But the band treats him with kid gloves, as if playing too closely might break the singer in half.'

But his fans showed their usual immense enthusiasm and support. Brecker said the success of his album was largely due to Taylor's incredible professionalism and contribution. One of Taylor's most valuable abilities is his timing when releasing new material. This is the nature of the mystery that makes him so mesmerizing to the rest of the music world. This is an ability that few can duplicate: the simple proposition that what you create is not as important as when you release it. Taylor often operates outside the gravitational pull of the market. He entertains no illusions.

When the hottest pop stars gathered at the 44th annual Grammy Awards, Taylor was not considered a favourite to walk off with the award for best male pop vocal performance. Taylor himself didn't bother to show up. Not many people expected him to beat the likes of Elton John, Michael Jackson and Brian McKnight.

'Once again JT proved you should never count him out,' said New York music critic Jason Kusiak. 'Tonight he proved that he belongs with the world's elite. Who would have ever thought that JT would win over Michael Jackson. But the fact is that he deserved it. He's finally getting the recognition he deserves.'

JAMES TAYLOR DISCOGRAPHY

James Taylor
Apple Records, 1968
Produce: Peter Asher

Sweet Baby James
Warner Bros, 1970
Producer: Peter Asher

Mud Slide Slim and the Blue Horizon
Warner Bros, 1971
Producer: Peter Asher

One Man Dog
Warner Bros, 1972
Producer: Peter Asher

Walking Man
Warner Bros, 1974
Producer: David Spinozza

Gorilla
Warner Bros, 1975
Producers: Lenny Waronker and Russ Titelman

In the Pocket
Warner Bros, 1976
Producers: Lenny Waronker and Russ Titelman

Greatest Hits
Warner Bros, 1976
Producers: Various

JT
Columbia Records, 1977
Producer: Peter Asher

Flag
Columbia Records, 1979
Producer: Peter Asher

Dad Loves His Work
Columbia Records, 1981
Producer: Peter Asher

That's Why I'm Here
Columbia Records, 1985
Producers: James Taylor and Frank Filipetti

Never Die Young
Columbia Records, 1988
Producer: Don Grolnick

New Moon Shine
Columbia Records, 1991
Producer: Don Grolnick

Live
Columbia Records, 1993
Producers: Don Grolnick and George Massenburg

Hourglass
Columbia Records, 1997
Producers: Frank Filipetti and James Taylor

October Road
Columbia Records, 2002
Producer: Russ Titelman

The Best of James Taylor
Warner Bros, 2003
Producers: Various

INDEX

Abramowitz, Jonathan, 106
Acid use, 90–9
Adams, Neil, 200, 216–17, 236
Adelman, Steven, 229
Alcohol use, 32, 87–93, 122, 234, 244
Alexander, Dean, 26–7
'Alice', 244
Allen, Peter, 95
'All I Want', 218
'All the Things You Are', 139
'Almost Like Being in Love', 249
Amar, Mitchell, 156
Anderson, John, 218
Anderson, William, 250
'Angel of the Morning', 61
Apple Records, 75–86, 98
Arlen, Alice, 259
Armstrong, Louis, 178
Asher, Peter, 17, 75–83, 88, 89, 92, 98–104, 111, 114, 123, 126, 132, 134, 135, 136, 138, 140–42, 166, 170–71, 184, 192–97, 208, 229, 238, 253–54, 277
'Autumn Leaves', 139

'Baby Boom Baby', 235
'Baby, Let Me Follow You Down', 152
Baez, Joan, 100, 169
Bahnsen, Greg, 139
Bailey, Oswald, 110
Barney, Phyllis, 96–7
Barry, Dave, 55
Baxter, Peter, 60
Beatles, the, 72, 75–81, 86, 109, 157, 172, 178, 230, 253, 258
Beatty, Warren, 129, 162, 180
Bellows, Steve, 170–72, 176, 179–180, 183–84, 190, 225
Belushi, John, 223–24
Benefit concerts, 30, 217, 218, 229, 254, 256–57
Benson, George, 237
Benson, George, 237
Berger, Julie, 60
Berklee College of Music (Boston), 251–53
Berry, Chuck, 37, 45
Billboard 1998 Century Award, 15–21
Blackwell, Mary, 78
Blossom Music Center (Ohio), 216
Blue (Mitchell), 127–28
Blumenthal, Cal, 181

Boehm, Mike, 253, 254–5
Bond, Lahri, 137
Borman, Gary, 17, 271–2
Bort Carlton Handbags (Boston), 56
Botwin, Will, 265
Boudreau, Lou, 22
Boys in the Trees (Simon), 203
Brackman, Jacob, 153
Bradley, Ed, 54–5
Brandt, Jerry, 157–8
Brazil, 225–26
Brecker, Michael, 264
'Brighten Your Night With My Day', 62, 83
Brooks, Garth, 15, 16
Browne, Jackson, 98, 102, 135, 230, 236
Brown, Mark, 246, 247
Burton, Eliza, 217
Burton, Patricia, 262

Cambridge School (Massachusetts), 51–2
'Captain Jim's Drunken Dream', 191
Carlson, Dylan, 246–47
Carmichael, Hoagy, 20
Carnegie Hall (New York), 184–5, 256–7
'Carolina in My Mind', 82, 83, 95
Carter, Clifford, 268
Carter, Valerie, 236
Chandler, Chas, 72
Charles, Ray, 34, 46–7, 239
Charter Behavioural Health Systems, 54–4
Choueke, Esmond, 55, 112, 113, 162, 167, 183, 204, 220, 221, 226, 234, 240, 245, 260, 261
Christensen, Elizabeth, 164
'Circle 'Round the Sun', 85
Clapton, Eric, 72
Classical music, 33, 75, 243–45
Cline, Patsy, 34
Cobain, Kurt, 245–48
Cocker, Joe, 115
Cohen, William, 148
Cole, Natalie, 251
Collins, Phil, 235
Colorado River Adventure (TV special), 250
Coltrane, John, 115
Columbia Records, 189–95, 197, 198, 200, 203, 215
Colvin, Shawn, 15, 16–7, 264
Cooke, Sam, 34
Coolidge, Rita, 178
'Copperline', 242
Corgan, Billy, 245
'Country Road', 110
Crawford, Joan, 210
Croce, Jim, 102
Crosby, David, 125, 184
Crowe, Colin, 72–3
Cumming, Edward, 254–55

'Daddy's All Gone', 191
'Daddy's Baby', 173
Dad Loves His Work, 224
Davis, Richard, 199–200, 209–10
'Day Tripper', 215–16
Delbanco, Nicholas, 155
Deluca, Johnathan, 258
Deluca, Pete, 257
Depression, 45–6, 47–51, 62, 108, 131
'Devoted to You', 203, 204
Digital audio, 232–33

Dixon, Bradlee, 59
Dixon, Ellis, 244
Dog Eat Dog (Mitchell), 132–33
'Don't Be Sad 'Cause Your Sun Is Down', 191
'Don't Let Me Be Lonely Tonight', 166
'Don't Talk Now', 85
Dorfman, Myra, 130
Drug use, 38–9, 61–5, 67, 86, 88, 92–3, 107, 111, 118, 121, 122, 124, 143–44, 145, 165–66, 175–76, 178, 186, 244–45, 252
See also Heroin; Marijuana
Dunn, Richard, 160, 161
Dylan, Bob, 18, 57, 74, 75, 78, 84, 93, 95, 96, 98, 109, 112, 157, 196, 208–09, 216–17, 230, 239
Dylan, Jacob, 208–09

Eastman, Max, 153
Education, 28, 36, 40–1
'Elektra', 158
Elektra Records, 158, 180
Elephants Memory, 152
Elman, Kim, 213
'Enough to Be on Your Way', 244
Epstein, Brian, 86, 140
'Everybody Loves to Cha Cha Cha', 242
'Everyday', 227, 249
Exercising, 225, 233–34

Fabulous Corsairs, 44–6
'Fading Away', 173
'Family Man', 191
'Fascinating Rhythm', 230
Ferry, Bryan, 230
'Fields of Gold', 256
Filipetti, Frank, 264–65
Finch, Charles, 209
Finch, Peter, 209
Finkleberg, Shelly, 191
'Fire and Rain', 14, 104–08, 121, 140, 170, 226, 243, 246, 250
Flag, 215–16
Fleming, Mark, 239–40
Flying Machine, 58–62, 67, 136–37
Folk music, 32–3, 35, 45, 56, 67, 95–7, 99, 105, 113, 237
Forte, Dan, 232–33
For the Roses (Mitchell), 128, 129
Foster, Stephen, 20
Franklin, Aretha, 144
Friedman, Roger, 169, 175

Gadfly Records, 136
'Gaia', 267
Garcia, Jerry, 97, 133
Garfunkel, Art, 191
Garner, Anthony, 209–10
Garrett, Jeremy, 26
Gaye, Marvin, 115
Geffen, David, 180–81
Gershwin, George, 254
Gibbs-Brown, June, 55
Gill, Paula, 188
Gill, Vince, 271
Goffin, Gerry, 144
Goldman, Brian, 100–01
Gorilla, 177–78, 187, 189
Gorman, John, 250
Gowers, Bruce, 18
Grammy Awards, 140, 197–98, 244, 270
Grant, Ellen, 242, 243
Grateful Dead, 96, 216

Greene, Ernie, 130–31
Grolnick, Don, 15, 171, 172–5, 182, 183, 204, 216, 224, 227, 235, 236, 237–38, 242, 243, 256, 261–62, 264, 266, 271
Grossman, Albert, 157
Grunge, 242, 243, 247–48
Guthrie, Woody, 28, 34, 41, 95

Haimovitch, Walter, 266–67
Hairston, Effie, 41
Haley, Bill, 45
'Handyman', 20, 197
'Happy Birthday Sweet Darling', 200
'Hard Times', 224
Harrison, George, 80
Harvard University concert (1970), 112
Hawkins, Jack, 73
Hayden, Tom, 222
Heller, Donna, 267
Hellman, Lillian, 153
Hellman, Monte, 137
Henderson, Adrien, 200
Hendrix, Jimi, 72, 93, 100, 112, 125, 178
Henley, Don, 132
Herbst, Peter, 117, 200
Heroin, 23, 60, 62–3, 64, 67, 89–93, 107–08, 122, 143, 144–45, 166, 234, 246
Hewson, Richard, 76, 82, 140
'Hey Jude', 74, 78
Hilburn, Chad, 102–03
Holden, Stephen, 19, 265
Holzman, Jac, 157–58
Home studios, 232–33
Hotcakes (Simon), 169
Hot Tin Roof (Martha's Vineyard), 223–24
Hourglass, 264–69
'How Sweet It Is to Be Loved by You', 166, 177, 190
Hughes, Warren, 17, 108

In Harmony, 224
In Perfect Harmony, 126
In the Pocket, 189–91
'It's a Wonderful Day', 256

Jacobs, Paul, 104
Jagger, Bianca, 160–61, 177
Jagger, Jade, 203
Jagger, Mick, 72, 75, 78, 86, 160–62, 177, 178, 180
James Taylor, 82, 84
James Taylor and the Original Flying Machine, 136
James Taylor BBS Bulletin Board, 106
James Taylor Online Web site, 105–06
Janofsky, Milo, 233
Jerome, Jim, 219
Joel, Billy, 256
John, Elton, 102, 256, 257
Johnson, Erin, 15, 234
Johnson, Jimmy, 268
Jo Mama, 134
Joplin, Janis, 93
JT, 197–98, 199, 200, 215
'Junkie's Lament, A', 191

Kaas, Patricia, 264
Katz, Robert, 73, 194–96, 198, 235–36
Kelly, Robert, 108–09

Kennedy, Bobby, 89
Kenton, Stan, 251
Kern, Jerome, 254
Kerouac, Jack, 22
Kerr, Cathy, 271–72
Kessler, Warren, 254
King Bees, 58, 76
King, Carole, 101, 128, 134, 184
King, Martin Luther, Jr, 30, 89
Klein, Allen, 85–6
'Knockin' Round the Zoo', 60–1, 82, 132
Kortchmar, Danny ('Kootch'), 35–7, 38, 58–60, 87, 89, 92, 93, 101, 106, 113, 131, 139, 143, 216, 232
Kristofferson, Kris, 158, 159, 167, 180
Kunkel, Russ, 216, 226–27

Landau, Jon, 147
Landau, Michael, 271
Lasley, David, 132, 236
Las Vegas, Nevada, *Billboard* Award show (1998), 14–20
Lennon, John, 72, 75, 78, 81, 84, 93, 157, 171, 209
Lennon, Julian, 209
Leno, Jay, 249
'Lesson in Survival', 128
'Let It All Fall Down', 171, 173
'Let Me Ride', 140
Levy, Morris, 148
Lightfoot, Gordon, 125
'Little More Time With You', 265
'Little Red Wagon Painted Blue', 26
Litton, Martin, 250
Liv, 147
Live, 243
Live Aid, 229
Livestock '95, 257–58
London, 68–70, 71–88, 126
Loneliness, 27, 28, 38, 45–6, 47–8, 109, 139
'Long Ago and Far Away', 140, 246
Los Angeles, 98–102, 177

McCartney, Paul, 72, 76, 77, 78, 81, 86, 172, 178, 196
McConnachy, Jennifer, 206
McCuller, Arnold, 236
McFarlane, Burt, 222, 229
McLaughlin, John, 38, 237
McLean Hospital (Massachusetts), 46–53, 59–60, 147
Madison Square Garden (New York City), 268–71
Magnet, Ellen, 96
Maislin, Victor, 115
'Make Me Feel Something', 226
Manhattan Dirt Riders, 172
Marijuana, 38–9, 63, 64, 67, 143, 178
Markowitz, Kate, 213–14, 236, 248, 261–62, 268, 271
Martha's Vineyard, 31–2, 35, 36, 38, 40, 48, 68, 146–49, 155–56, 163, 182, 185–86
Martin, George, 171
Massenburg, George, 243, 271
'Mexico', 178
Meyer, Edgar, 264
Milton Academy (Massachusetts), 39–43, 46, 51
Minnelli, Liza, 22, 209
Missing Twenty Grand, 132

Mitchell, Joni, 95, 96, 98, 102, 124–33, 138, 152–53, 169, 180–81, 230, 271
'Mockingbird', 166, 169
Moore, Robert, 75
Moreina, Maria, 226
Mud Slide Slim and the Blue Horizon, 135–36, 138, 140, 143, 163, 165
Muse/No Nukes, 217

Nascimento, Milton, 226
Nash, Graham, 128
National Academy of Songwriters, 238
National Enquirer, 228–29
Natural Resources Defense Council, 243
Never Die Young, 234–35
'Never Die Young', 235, 249
Nevermind (Nirvana), 243
Newman, Phil, 201
Newman, Randy, 192, 271–72
New Moon Shine, 242–43
Nifkin, Bryan, 215
'Night Owl', 61, 82, 137
Night Owl Café (New York), 59–60, 62
Nirvana, 242–46
Nixon, Richard, 171
Norman, Jessye, 256
North Carolina, 24, 26, 37, 41, 55, 57–8, 63, 65–6, 68–9
No Secrets (Simon), 161, 169
Noseworthy, Eric, 261

Oates, Warren, 138
O'Brien, Joel, 58, 78, 149
'Obsession', 256
O'Connor, Mark, 264
Ode Years, The (King), 184
O'Donnell, Rosie, 250
O'Leary, Dennis, 55
One Man Dog, 166, 171
'Only One', 227
Orisek, Rudy, 95–6
Osgood, Charles, 272
Ostin, Mo, 166, 192–93, 194
Owen, Sandra, 247–48

Page, Janice, 242
Palmer, Edward, 83
Palmer, William, 106
Parker, Charlie, 115, 251, 253
Parker, Tom, 108, 109, 140, 141
Pasqual, Rui, 225–26
Perlmutt, Joseph and Helen, 28
Perry, Richard, 160, 178
Picasso, Pablo, 222
Platt, Bonnie, 152
Playing Possum (Simon), 177, 178, 179
Police, the, 18, 235
Pomeroy, Herb, 251
Potter, Daphne, 227
Presley, Elvis, 95, 108–09, 112
Presley, Lisa Marie, 108–09

Radio City Music Hall (New York), 152
Rainforest Action Network, 256–57
'Rainy Day Man', 61
Ray, Nancy, 29
Redding, Tina, 223
Redpath, Jean, 34
Reed, Brian, 17, 233, 251
Reeves, Martha, 178
Richards, Keith, 161

Ride in the Whirlwind (film), 137
Ridgely, Alice, 86–7
Ridolfi, Mark, 268
Rio de Janeiro concert (1985), 225–26
Risberg, Joel, 105–06
Robinson, Jackie, 153
Rock in Rio concert (1985), 225–26
Rolling Stones, 72, 86, 160, 161, 178, 227
'Roll River Roll', 36
Ronstadt, Linda, 102, 172, 236, 271
Roth, Sean, 117–18
Ruhlmann, William, 166, 198

Sainte-Marie, Buffy, 125
Saltzman, Brian, 47–8
Sanborn, David, 191
San Diego Symphony, 254–55
Sanford, Terry, 26
'Sarah Maria', 177
Saturday Night Live (TV show), 249–50
Schaffer, Arnie, 198
Seeger, Pete, 20, 74, 95, 124
Sesame Street, 224
Shandling, Gary, 249
Shapiro, Jane, 154
Sheldon, Stan, 40
Shirelles, the, 144
Shorter, Wayne, 132
'Shower the People', 190, 249
Simmons, Joey, 240
Simon, Andrea, 153–54
Simon, Carly, 19–20, 113, 151–69, 172–80, 189, 193, 197, 198–200, 203–06, 207, 212, 213–14, 219–29, 257–58, 261, 264
Simon, Joanne, 154
Simon, Lucy, 154, 156, 161, 185, 257
Simon, Paul, 95, 96, 194, 230, 236, 256
Simon, Peter, 151, 156
Simon, Richard, 144, 153, 155
Simon Sisters, 156
Simpsons, The (TV show), 244, 245
Sinatra, Frank, 109, 240, 241, 251
Sister Kate, 146
Sister Kate's Soul Stew Kitchen, 53
60 Minutes II (1999), 54–5
Sklar, Les, 139, 216
Smedvig, Kim, 270
Smith, Beth, 35
Smith, Gary, 245
Smith, Joe, 190
Smith, Martin, 84–5, 86, 89, 92–3, 103, 113, 125, 139–40, 157, 163, 169, 172, 177–78, 184–85, 189, 197, 201–02, 219
Somerville, Dean, 227
'Something Wrong', 95
Sony Music, 213, 235–36, 249, 260, 265–67, 271
Spector, Phil, 171
Spehr, Roberta, 128
Spinozza, David, 170, 171
Spoiled Girl (Simon), 226
Springer, Jerry, 17–18
Springsteen, Bruce, 256
'Stand and Fight', 217
Stanton, Paul, 20–1
Star Is Born, A (film), 167
Starr, Ringo, 178
Steele, Alison, 179, 203
Steiger, Rod, 131

Steinberg, Norm, 103–04
Stevens, Cat, 135, 158
Stevenson, Adlai, 30
Sting, 18–19, 226, 235, 256–57, 264
Stoker, Richard, 241
Stone Temple Pilots, 242
Storytellers (VH1 show), 265
Strauss, Neil, 266, 268
Streisand, Barbra, 167
Studio 54 (New York), 220
Suicide, 22–3, 39, 41–2, 45–6, 88, 104, 107, 247
'Suite for 20G', 104
Sunday Morning (TV show), 272
Sweet Baby James, 103–04, 108–11, 135–36, 173, 197, 227
'Sweet Baby James', 2, 104, 109
'Sweet Potato Pie', 249

'Taking It in', 95
Tanner, Harry, 106
Tapestry (King), 128
Tate, Elaine, 220
'Tax Free', 132
Taylor, Al, 145–6, 187, 190
Taylor, Alex (brother), 15, 23, 26, 28, 29, 32–3, 34, 36, 37, 44–5, 69, 92, 119, 146,147–52, 201–02, 243–44
Taylor, Benjamin (son), 20, 169, 197, 207–14, 217–22, 225, 229, 246, 250
Taylor, Chip, 61, 135–36
Taylor, Elizabeth, 177
Taylor, Gertrude ('Trudy') (mother), 22–3, 25–31, 33, 41, 43, 44, 50, 58, 66, 68, 70, 118, 119–20, 146, 262
Taylor, Hugh (brother), 26, 41, 47, 50, 147
Taylor, Isaac (father), 15, 22–8, 30, 32, 33, 35, 37, 44, 46, 50, 66–70, 91, 119–20, 143, 164, 262–63
Taylor, Kate (sister), 26, 30, 32, 33, 37, 40, 42, 46, 50, 52–3, 69, 138, 146, 147, 200–02
Taylor, Livingston (brother), 26, 29, 33, 37, 50, 53, 147, 151, 200, 213
Taylor, Sally (daughter), 20, 169–70, 173, 175–76, 182–85, 187, 189, 197, 207–14, 224, 225, 229, 243, 262, 272
Taylor, Theodosia (grandmother), 23
Teitleman, Debrah, 216
'That Lonesome Road', 224, 243
'That's the Way I've Always Heard It Should Be', 157
That's Why I'm Here, 227–28, 264
Thompson, Barbara, 146
'Three of Us in the Dark', 220
Time magazine story (1971), 114–18
Titelman, Russ, 177, 189, 195
Tobin, Steven, 105
Tomboy Pride (Sally Taylor), 210
Tonight Show (TV show), 240
Torney, John, 40
Townshend, Pete, 72
Travolta, John, 219–21, 223, 225
Trident Studios (London), 80
Troubadour Club (Los Angeles), 101–02, 124, 138, 158
Truman, Harry, 22
Turner, Tina, 235
Two-Lane Blacktop (film), 137

'Un Mejor Dia Vendra', 203
'Up From Your Life', 267
'Up on the Roof', 216

Van Morrison, 72, 96, 192
Vega, Carlos, 268, 270–71
Velosa, Caetano, 226
Vietnam War, 47, 49, 89
Von Schmidt, Eric, 157

Wadler, Joyce, 155
Walden, Phil, 147
Walker, Allen, 140
Walker, Joe, 64
Walker, Kathryn, 15, 227, 229, 232, 234, 251–52, 253–54, 259–61
Walker, Richard, 265
Walking Man, 170–72, 174
Wallace, Amy, 255
Walsh, Julian, 129
Warhol, Andy, 161
Warner Bros, 100–01, 114, 134–35, 166, 187, 190–96
Waronker, Lenny, 177, 189, 190
Waters, Harry F., 232
Waters, Muddy, 37, 41
'Way You Look Tonight, The', 254
Weiss, Nat, 186, 192–93, 198
Welles, Gwen, 178
Werbin, Stuart, 152, 156
Weston, Doug, 102, 158–59, 160, 168
Wheaton, Mitchell, 245
White Album (Beatles), 80
White, Barry, 115
Whitebook, Mark, 38
White, Timothy, 20, 23, 136, 140, 221–22, 226, 244, 263
Whiting, Robert, 207
Whitmore, Brian, 80–1
Widger, Carl, 220–21
Wiesner, Zach, 45, 58, 61–3
Wild Rebels (film), 137
'Wild Thing', 61
Wild Things Run Fast (Mitchell), 132
Williams, Hank, 34
Williams, John, 253
Williamson, Nigel, 211–12
Williams, Robin, 250
Wilson, Dennis, 137–38
Wilson, Lance, 231
With Friends and Neighbours, 146
Womack, Bobby, 190
'Woman Gotta Have It', 190
Wonder, Stevie, 199, 264
'Woodstock', 125
Woodstock (1969), 100, 125
Working (Broadway musical), 203
Working (PBS TV show), 224

Yetnikoff, Walter, 192–95, 198, 200, 202
Yorkville Village (Toronto), 225
You Can Close Your Eyes, 126
Young, Neil, 102, 125
'You're So Vain', 162–63
'Your Smiling Face', 198
'You Turn Me On', 129
'You've Got a Friend', 3, 108, 138–40, 145, 177, 184, 253